THE SMITHSONIAN

BOOK OF BOOKS

THE SMITHSONIAN BOOK OF

BOOKS

MICHAEL OLMERT

SMITHSONIAN BOOKS, WASHINGTON, D.C., MCMXCII

THE SMITHSONIAN INSTITUTION
Secretary: Robert McC. Adams
Assistant Secretary for External Affairs:
  Thomas E. Lovejoy
Director, Smithsonian Institution Press:
  Felix C. Lowe

SMITHSONIAN BOOKS
Editor-in-Chief: Patricia Gallagher
Senior Editor: Alexis Doster III
Editors: Amy Donovan, Joe Goodwin
Assistant Editors: Bryan D. Kennedy,
  Sonia Reece
Research: Jennifer McCartney
Senior Picture Editor: Frances C. Rowsell
Picture Editors: Carrie E. Bruns,
  Juliana Montfort, R. Jenny Takacs
Picture Research: V. Susan Guardado,
  Anne P. Naruta
Copy Editor: Elizabeth Dahlslien
Production Editor: Patricia Upchurch
Assistant Production Editor: Martha Sewall
Business Manager: Stephen J. Bergstrom
Marketing Director: Gail Grella
Marketing Manager: Ruth A. Chamblee
Marketing Assistant: Anne Carman

ISBN 0-89599-030-X

LIBRARY OF CONGRESS
CATALOGING-IN-PUBLICATION DATA
Olmert, Michael.
  *The Smithsonian book of books /
by Michael Olmert : introduction by
Christopher de Hamel.*
    p.   cm.
  Includes index.
  ISBN 0-89599-030-X
  *1. Books — History. 2. Book
industries and trade — History.
I. Title.*
  Z4.O54 1992
  002 — dc20   *91-39590*
                              CIP

*Manufactured in the United States
  of America*
First Edition
10 9 8 7 6 5 4 3 2 1

*Page 1: an illustration from Johann
Schönsperger's 1491 printing of Aesop's
Fables; left: a decorative border print
of Chaucer and Cupid by Eric Gill from
the 1927 publication of Troilus and
Criseyde by Golden Cockerel Press;
opposite: carpet page—intricate patterns
and colorful, interlaced birds—from the
Lindisfarne Gospels (c. 698) introduces
the Gospel of Saint John. Pages 6–7:
a variety of printers' marks of the 15th
and 16th centuries features those of
Johann Froben, Nicolaus Jenson,
Christophe Plantin, William Caxton,
Aldus Manutius, and Geoffroy Tory.*

CONTENTS

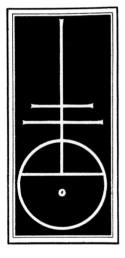

INTRODUCTION: PUTTING A PRICE ON IT

"BOOKS! BOOKS! BOOKS! We'll get fat on BOOKS?" asked the nagging wife of the medieval scribe in a cartoon that appeared in a 1983 edition of the London *Times* the day after Sotheby's sold the 12th-century *Gospels of Henry the Lion* for £8,140,000. Another cartoon in the *Daily Star* the same day showed the auctioneer selling the 800-year-old manuscript for this sum and a keen little man in a raincoat jumping up in the audience to ask, "Do you take book tokens?" In the corner a dog is muttering, "I think I'll wait till it comes out in paperback."

The fact is that ancient manuscripts are valuable and probably always were. The *Gospels of Henry the Lion* is encrusted with burnished gold initials and miniatures throughout and it looks expensive. It contains a dedication describing it (in Latin) as "this book shining with gold." Even in the cartoon just described it has flashes of light emanating from all around it. In 1861 it had been bought from Prague Cathedral by the King of Hanover for an enormous sum. For three and a half years after the Sotheby's auction—until the sale of van Gogh's *Sunflowers*, in fact—it held the world-record price for any work of art.

The veneration of books is of great antiquity, and probably in the Middle Ages, too, they often were valued far above paintings. Manuscripts were expensive and slow to make, and the materials used were costly. A book can have an almost magical or spiritual quality as the conveyor of a text. To a literate person, a manuscript was a precious link with the words of a long dead writer; but to someone who could not read, a book was invested with mystery and awe.

Some very early books were treasured because they were actual relics of saints. Three books still survive in the ancient town of Fulda in Germany that were believed on quite credible authority to have belonged to St. Boniface (680–755), the Anglo-Saxon missionary to Germany. Among them is the very book he is said to have been holding when he was martyred by the pagans and with which he tried to protect himself. Several of its pages show gashes from the murderer's sword.

Another extraordinary manuscript is the little *Gospel of St. John,* known as the "Stonyhurst Gospel" since it belongs now to the English Jesuit college of that name. It was found in 1104 inside the coffin of St. Cuthbert, bishop of the island of Lindisfarne, who had died more than 400 years before, in 687. This is a strange tale. When the Vikings sacked Lindisfarne in the eighth century, the monks there gathered up their most precious possessions, including the body of St. Cuthbert in its carved wooden coffin, and fled to the mainland. Joining a wandering caravan of monks that moved from place to place for centuries, they finally settled on the site of Durham Cathedral in 1104 and established a permanent shrine to their patron saint. When the monks opened the coffin and discovered the body of St. Cuthbert miraculously uncorrupted with a Gospel book under his head, the bishop, Flambard, exhibited the volume to the people during his sermon that day.

From the time of Charlemagne (742–814), scribes and artists spared no expense in creating lavish manuscripts that served as symbols of imperial wealth and power. This highly ornate, clasped cover was crafted around 1180 for the Gospels of Henry the Lion, *an elaborate work made for the duke of Saxony and Bavaria. On December 6, 1983, Sotheby's in London sold this manuscript at auction to the German government for a record £8,140,000 (about $15,000,000).*

9

From then on it is described as beginning to perform miracles. It lay on the high altar of Durham Cathedral until about 1540, when the cathedral priory was suppressed by Henry VIII. A hundred years later, the manuscript was in private hands in Oxford. In the late 18th century it was given to the Jesuits by a chaplain of the Earl of Lichfield, who had owned it. It now lies in a glass case on loan to the British Library, and its beautiful uncial script and original binding of the late seventh century are absolutely consistent with the period of St. Cuthbert himself.

Until the 12th century, most books in medieval Europe were made in or directly for monasteries or other church foundations. Books were an important part of the equipment of a monastery, and the monks would go to great effort to keep their reference and liturgical collections comprehensive. In a sense, a book that was a religious relic of a miracle-working saint had no market or resale value, any more than church furniture or vestments. An irreverent monk who impiously touched the Stonyhurst Gospel in the 12th century is recorded as having been divinely punished. The saint protected his own book, as it were. If manuscripts had ownership inscriptions of religious houses before about 1200 (and surprisingly few did), these were often in the form of "The book of St. Cuthbert" or "The Book of St. Mary of Rievaulx" or "The Book of St. Augustine," and so on, in Latin. In other words, the book was thought of as belonging to the patron saint of the monastery. It probably was supposed that no one would abuse a manuscript that was the property of a saint, even if the saint was safely buried.

From about 1150, however, all this began to change. Professional secular scribes and illuminators started to take over the book business. There is tantalizing evidence from the mid-12th century of traveling craftsmen who must have hired themselves out to those who wanted manuscripts made. The logical development is that by around 1200 there began to be settled professional workshops where manuscripts could be commissioned and bought. In Paris and probably in Bologna and other university towns there evolved tradesmen who acted as agents for the making of manuscripts and who dealt in secondhand copies. By 1250, probably very few books were made in monasteries. It would have been simpler and probably more accurate to have a copy professionally made and to pay for it.

The implications of this are enormous. Books were no longer the inalienable property of religious houses but were also bought by private individuals. Whole new classes of books came into being for a new public: textbooks for students, books of private devotions (such as Psalters and books of hours) for the fashionable pious laity, and literary texts for those who enjoyed tales of knights and battles and romance. It also meant that by the 13th century books had a commercial value—and a real value if re-sold. All the earliest regulations of the University of Paris concerning the book trade are about the secondhand market in manuscripts. The buying and selling of books goes back 750 years. Manuscripts were valuable enough to be used as collateral for loans of money, and notes recording pledges are not uncommon on the flyleaves of late-medieval

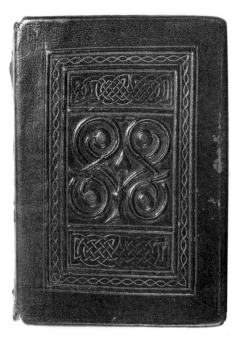

Still protected by its late-seventh-century decorated binding, the oldest one known from Europe, the Gospel of St. John, *above, also called the "Stonyhurst Gospel," appears none the worse for wear for having been carried around in Cuthbert's coffin for 400 years. It came to light—again—in 1104 when Cuthbert's remains and relics were installed in Durham Cathedral. Opposite, a group of monks opens Cuthbert's coffin and views his miraculously preserved body, as depicted in a 12th-century manuscript.*

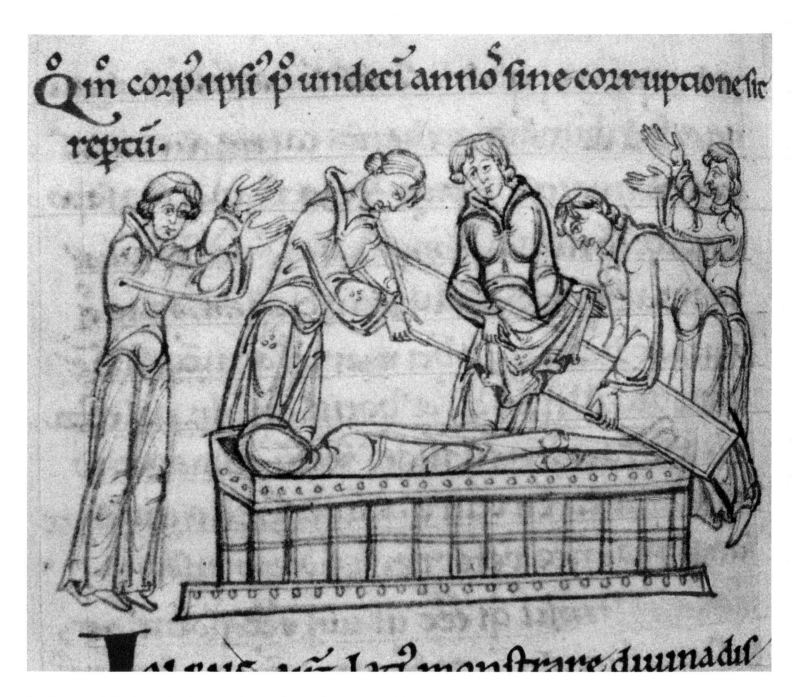

books, especially those that belonged to students whose personal finances were then—as now—notoriously unreliable. Even ecclesiastical institutions—the English cathedrals of Lincoln and Hereford are good examples—began to write prices on the flyleaves of their books. These cannot be sale prices, but must represent the value of some kind of security that a borrower would need to deposit if he wished to remove a book from the library. The price represented a (probably rather generous) estimate of a replacement value. A Gospel book at Hereford was assessed at 13 shillings, 3 pence, and a glossed Psalter at 20 shillings. One manuscript of St. Augustine at Lincoln was assessed at 20 shillings and a newer copy at 40 shillings. This is a vast change from the early days when

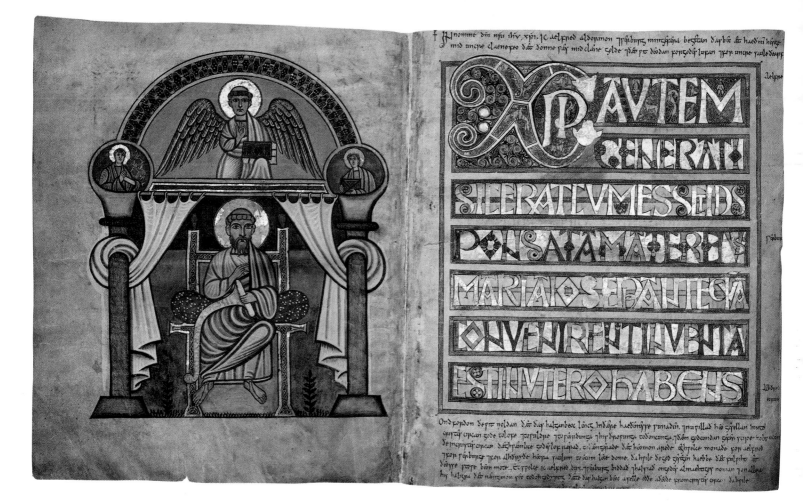

books were simply the sacred but valueless fittings of churches or the relics of saints.

An intriguing question is when did books become valuable enough to steal? The Vikings looted manuscripts in their raids on Anglo-Saxon England, presumably because of the gold on the bookbindings. One of them, the *Codex Aureus,* now in Stockholm, was stolen and ransomed back to its owners in the ninth century, but it could not have been sold elsewhere because there was no recognizable market in books then. Not until there was a commercial market for books could a thief hope to profit from stealing a volume. The old ownership inscriptions, as we have seen, dedicated a book to a patron saint, thus ensuring respect from members of the community. But with the evolution of a book market, we find evocative curses entered into manuscripts: he who steals this book shall be damned in eternal fire; may he who takes or sells this book be cursed forever; and so on. Such inscriptions are typical of the 12th century and later. The very necessity of such imprecations tells us that books were indeed liable to theft. Even now there is still something slightly creepy about selling a book with a 500-year-old curse against sale staring out from the flyleaf. It is pleasanter to read, for example, Jasper Fyoll's prattling note in his manuscript of about 1500, now in Cambridge. He writes that this book belongs to him, and "yf it fortune at any time to be recklesly forgoten or loste, he

A palmful of miniature books from the Smithsonian's Dibner Library features Witty, Humorous and Merry Thoughts *(top), a book-in-a-locket printed in Glasgow around 1895; Longfellow's* Evangeline *(left), published in London before 1917; and* Dew Drops *(right), a selection of verses from the Bible—one for each day of the year—published in New York in the 1850s. Opposite, a book lover pores over one of his treasured editions in this 1871 etching by George Cruikshank. A social satirist, Cruikshank illustrated more than 850 books, including many for children.*

Christopher de Hamel is Curator of Western and Oriental Illuminated Manuscripts and Miniatures at Sotheby's in London.

prayesth the fynder to bryng yt to hym again, and he shall have iiis.iiiid. for his labour & good thank of the owner and goddis blessyng."

Medieval books were valuable and were much collected. The great bibliophile bishop of Durham, Richard de Bury (1281–1345), refers to having patronized bookshops not only in his native country but also in France, Germany, and Italy. We know the names of booksellers in London, Oxford, Paris, Rouen, Erfurt, Bologna, Florence, and so on. We have thousands of surviving medieval manuscripts with inscriptions all across their flyleaves recording purchases, bequests, loans, gifts, pledges, prices, and all the human interest of book acquisition and ownership.

Illuminated manuscripts are probably the most luxurious and attractive of European books. They were expensive when they were new, valuable when they were secondhand, and collected when they were very old. They can still be bought, occasionally, and even today several hundred come onto the market every year. Whether sold for vast sums, like the *Gospels of Henry the Lion,* or for the modest sums of late-medieval textbooks, they surely represent one of the most consistently valued of all human commodities.

Printed books, of course, have been collected (in Europe, anyway) for only about 550 years, and they have a millennium or so to run before competing in longevity with manuscripts. Printing produces multiple copies simultaneously, and thus there can be a single moment when an entire print run is declared complete. Bibliophiles can revel in owning a first edition of a significant book, a concept of connoisseurship quite foreign to collectors of manuscripts, where the most one could hope to find would be the earliest extant transcription of a particular text, which might not represent the most accurate or most noble. The Bodleian Library of Oxford acquired a copy of Shakespeare's First Folio on publication in 1623; when the second edition was published in 1632, the library discarded its copy of the first because it had been superseded by a more up-to-date text. That shows a splendidly medieval and scholastic view of books, and causes modern book collectors to wince miserably. A passionate modern bibliophile would want the first *and* the second *and* the third folio editions of Shakespeare (or, if he were Henry Folger, every extant copy of each), and the same of Milton probably, and of Pope and Byron and Longfellow and Melville and Dickens and even Ian Fleming, and countless others.

There is an overwhelming fascination in the infinite choice of printed books. There are probably more books than any other human artifact on earth. Collectors can assemble shelves of bindings, private-press books, illustrated books designed by great artists, inscribed copies, books from a particular locality or publisher, books on specific subjects, books of special sizes (not at all as silly as it sounds), books in particular languages of typefaces, or just books for the love of books. All book collectors are to be saluted. But probably for my own choice, if one may return to the cartoon of the dog with which we started, I think I'll wait until it comes out in manuscript.

—*Christopher de Hamel*

PROLOGUE

NCIPIT: "HERE BEGINNETH." SO IT BEGINS. In an age before title pages, the medieval scribe signaled the start of a book with that single Latin word, a word freighted with both promise and magic. For a reader, that bold and confident INCIPIT meant the start of a journey that could run forward and backward in time, could crush the conventional notions of geography and cosmos, could instruct and delight, explain and justify. ❦ Books reveal the wisdom of the ages, and beyond. Muslims know the Koran to be no less than the exact word of God as revealed to the prophet Muhammad by the archangel Gabriel on a sublime Arabian mountaintop. It is only fitting that no effort be spared in embellishing those words with the finest calligraphy. ❦ In medieval Europe, books became portable art galleries, vying with the cathedrals for the minds and hearts of the devout. The power center of medieval monasticism was the scriptorium, where all sorts of manuscripts, devotional and secular, were copied and recopied, supplying a growing demand for ideas and art. ❦ Even after the invention of printing in the mid-15th century and the exponential increase in availability of texts, the book retained its almost magical hold on the imagination and intellect. The whole world could be compassed by a single leather-bound volume. The man or woman merely in possession of a book was regarded as profound and pious, inquisitive and supple of intellect. ❦ The four Evangelists—Matthew, Mark,

Preceding pages: Against a Venetian backdrop, the winged lion of St. Mark, painted in about 1500 by Vittore Carpaccio, rests his paw upon a book opened to the Latin words proclaiming, "Peace to you from Mark, my evangelist." Opposite, the Delphic Sibyl consults her prophetic scroll in a detail from Michelangelo's Sistine Chapel masterpiece. At left, a knotwork initial "I" from a ninth-century Celtic Gospel book by the monk Liutharius. Much of the illumination of manuscripts in the Middle Ages infused early Christian art with pagan mystery.

Luke, and John, symbols of the intellectual tradition that underpins Christianity, a religion based on a book—are nearly always depicted with their gospels. St. Jerome usually is shown with his cardinal's hat, his symbolic and docile lion, and the Latin Vulgate Bible he translated.

In the south of France, by the doorway to the chapel of Fontfroide Abbey, is a stone relief of St. Catherine of Alexandria. She not only holds a book but runs her palm along its spine, keeping her place with her index finger. This book is no public-relations ploy: both the artist and you the viewer have interrupted her reading. Catherine is the first widely acknowledged female intellectual, and the book is her badge.

Another work, a late-15th- or early-16th-century linden-wood statue in the Pierpont Morgan Library in New York, depicts the same theme of women and books. On the saint's hem is written "S. Elisabet," and, since the carving came from Germany, this is probably Elizabeth of Schönau, a visionary writer and intellectual who died in 1164. She, too, holds a book and keeps her place with her thumb.

Hers is a real book. Its binding has a center boss and corner protectors. Crane your neck around and you can see the wilt of its wooden pages, appearing limp under the weight of provocative ideas. It's a perfect Renaissance book: a small quarto—possibly from Venice—full of disturbing thoughts for an establishment set in its ways. The very fact that Elizabeth holds it at all, and could actually read it, might well have been considered subversive.

About 1543, Titian painted what is considered to be a portrait of Benedetto Varchi, a Florentine scholar working in Venice. To show he is a man of ideas, Varchi holds a small-format Venetian book, open, in his right hand. But Varchi is cautious about reputation and its cheap dependence on merely being portrayed with a book. So he modestly holds the book slightly back, as if to put a little distance between himself and the artistic convention. And with that gesture, Titian uses a book to make us admire Varchi. He's gentle, unassuming— a man of substance rather than surface.

Varchi is precisely the kind of man, and doubtless his little book is precisely the kind of book, that the Italian humanist poet Petrarch had in mind when he wrote that "books can warm the heart with friendly words and counsel, entering into a close relationship with us which is articulate and alive. Furthermore, none of them finds its way into the hearts of its readers unaccompanied, but each introduces its friends, so that one creates a desire for another."

In the deepest sense, a book is no mere collection of words, paper, ink. It is also, and foremost, the ideas that stand behind those symbols, those sounds, those pictures. And the sum of the ideas and pages is far greater than the parts. Books can move mountains—and have. People have died for their contents.

When Giovanni Bellini painted "The Assassination of St. Peter Martyr," about 1509, he placed in the work's foreground a book, a symbol of the Dominican reformer's love of learning. And not just any book, either, but a gilt-edged volume bound in red leather, with fine gold clasps and bosses and long bookmarks. And not just a single book, for Peter's companion, also facing his

In a detail from a series of frescoes depicting great men of antiquity, 15th-century artist Vincenzo Foppa portrayed the Roman statesman and orator Marcus Tullius Cicero as a schoolboy, above. Entranced by the small book he is reading, young Cicero embodies the essence of the Renaissance love of learning. Opposite, exquisite calligraphy adorns a page from an illuminated 14th-century Koran, the sacred book of Islam. Employed for centuries in the reproduction of God's word, calligraphy is the supreme art form of the Muslim world. Here the text is written in the calligraphic style known as Rayhani, and the frontispiece inscriptions above and below are in ornamental Eastern Kufic.

last few heartbeats on this earth, has dropped his calf volume, its tasseled bookmarks askew. The dropped—but not discarded—books represent the power of the ideas for which the two men gave up their lives when they were ambushed in April 1252.

For centuries, another kind of power connected with books—the prophetic practice of bibliomancy—was regarded as a dependable guide to the future. Simply open Homer, Virgil, or the Bible at random, believers held, and the first verse your eye comes to will illuminate the course of your life. During the English Civil War, a desperate Charles I opened *The Aeneid* and was crushed by this passage from book four: "May he be harried in war by audacious tribes, and exiled from his own land." Similarly, in *Far from the Madding Crowd,* Thomas Hardy, ever faithful to the folk beliefs of Wessex, has Bathsheba turn to the Bible to discover whether she should marry Mr. Boldwood. It was all a lottery, or "sort," which is why another name for this activity was the *Sortes Virgiliana*—the Virgilian lottery—or the *Sortes Sanctorum*—the holy lottery. Church fathers railed against the practice for centuries to no avail.

The magical properties of books are universal. The *I Ching,* or *Book of*

Faith and martyrdom were common themes of medieval art. Opposite, Burgundian nobles pay homage to the Madonna and Child in an illumination from the Hours of Mary of Burgundy, *a 15th-century book of hours, or prayer book, once owned by Charles the Bold, Duke of Burgundy. Books of hours generally consisted of a standard series of short hymns, Psalms, and prayers that were to be read by the laity at eight different hours of the day. Below, Giovanni Bellini's* Assassination of St. Peter Martyr, *c. 1509, depicts the slaying of St. Peter Martyr, whose vigorous defense of Christian orthodoxy led to his death in 1252 at the hands of the Cathars, a heretical Christian sect.*

Colorful depictions of the passage to the hereafter of the deceased scribe Ani and his wife decorate this section of the Papyrus of Ani, *one of the finest examples of the Egyptian Book of the Dead. Such texts were placed in tombs to serve as a guidebook to the gates of the afterlife. Opposite: the title page from* Areopagitica, *John Milton's eloquent defense of freedom of the press. First delivered as a speech before Parliament in 1643, the essay was published the following year.*

Changes, one of five ancient Chinese classics generally attributed to Confucius, was a system of divination by lots, using coins and a table of possible interpretations. It was found especially useful to an emerging bureaucracy concerned with governing a large nation. For the ancient Babylonians, *The Book of Destinies* recorded the fates of the living for the lord of the Underworld. The Egyptian Book of the Dead was a guide to special charms and behavior in the afterlife. And in the Old Testament, there is reference in both *Exodus* and *Psalms* to the Book of Life, a register of the righteous.

The power—and thus, implicitly, the threat—of books has always been recognized. There are countless instances of individual works on government or religion condemned to be burned. Surely Shih Huang Ti, emperor of China from 246 to 210 B.C., was not the first ruler to order the gathering and burning of official histories as well as almost all other books. Beginning in 1495 in Florence, the Dominican friar Savonarola's destruction of priceless material possessions and works of art, known as the "bonfires of the vanities," wiped out countless treasures, including works by Ovid, Dante, and Boccaccio. Even the rational, mod-

ern era did not end such conflagrations: almost five centuries after Savonarola, Nazis were conducting book-burning orgies in cities throughout Europe.

Yet in 1644 John Milton had leaped to the defense of books and bookmen with his magisterial essay against censorship, *Areopagitica,* also bequeathing to us in this work some of the most powerful prose the world has ever seen, all in praise of volumes, tomes, and tracts. "As good almost kill a man as kill a good book," he wrote; "who kills a man kills a reasonable creature, God's image; but he who destroys a good book, kills reason itself, kills the image of God, as it were in the eye. Many a man lives a burden to the earth; but a good book is the precious life-blood of a master spirit, embalmed and treasured up on purpose to a life beyond life."

Further proof of the power of books is that they allow us to converse directly with the mind of Socrates or Caesar or Jefferson or Lincoln. Or Hitler, for that matter. In a very real way, we can grasp any writer from the past by his or her lapels and demand "Why?" Answers will surely come from the books they left us. If that isn't magic, what is?

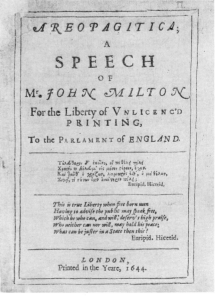

SCROLLS AND SCRIBES

ROM THE BEGINNING, BOOKS conferred mysterious powers on readers. Consider something as simple as silent reading; it implies a circumspect and civilized society. Plutarch tells us that both Alexander the Great and Julius Caesar read silently to themselves. Augustine recorded his pleasure at seeing Ambrose reading silently. What a storm of confusion such a sight must have created among the illiterate. ❧ A 1641 tale by English prelate and scientist John Wilkins captures the fear and dread that a text could conjure up in one who could not read. An Indian slave was once sent to deliver a basket of figs. He ate several of them along the way and when he arrived at his destination he was accused of stealing. His accuser: a letter that accompanied the delivery, stating the exact number of figs dispatched. ❧ Wilkins continues the story: "After this, being sent again with the like Carriage, and a Letter expressing the just Number of Figs, that were to be delivered, he did again, according to his former Practice, devour a great Part of them by the Way; but before he meddled with any (to prevent all following Accusations) he first took the Letter, and hid that under a great Stone, assuring himself, that if it did not see him eating the Figs, it could never tell of him; but being now more strongly accused than before, he confesses the Fault, admiring the Divinity of the Paper, and for the future does promise his best Fidelity in every Employment." ❧ A similar story of mystery and fear could be conjured up by the angular 2,000-year-old writing script of Northern Europe called runic. The 24 characters, or runes, of this

A Roman child reads from a scroll, opposite, in a detail from a fresco discovered in a Pompeiian ruin dating to about 50 B.C. An ancient form of the book first used in Egypt, the scroll facilitated the spread of literacy throughout the early Greek and Roman world. At left, an initial F from a 1509 printed edition of the great Greek mathematician Euclid's classic Elements.

alphabet were designed to be carved or incised on bone and ivory, wood and metal, and—most imposing of all—on the great standing stones of Scandinavia. In the millennium from 200 to 1200, runic messages were regularly cut into countless other objects, many of which are still being uncovered at archaeological sites.

Gradually, however, as the Viking world declined, the runic alphabet fell into disuse. Still, the writing persisted on great stones and on fine jewelry passed down through generations. Even when people could no longer read the runes, they suspected that the runestones carried powerful messages. Hold a runic inscription up to your ear, many thought, and it would whisper to you. The belief was so strong it changed our language: the Middle English word for "whisper" is *runeth*.

When we consider the bygone language of the runes and its survival in unreadable artifacts inflated with mystical importance, we are dealing with a no-man's-land between an oral society and a literate one. This shift was crucial, for it meant that life had become so complex that memory alone was not enough; the immediacy—and the permanence—of writing and books was demanded.

The value of writing was so apparent that society was willing to invest heavily in developing this new method of communication, and in underwriting a class of scribes who contributed nothing but their words.

To some extent, writing developed exactly the opposite way art did. That is, it began as a means of recording things realistically, and then moved toward abstraction. The letter "A," for example, was originally the pictograph for a bull, a simplified bull's head that was flipped over and had its eyes plucked out. It

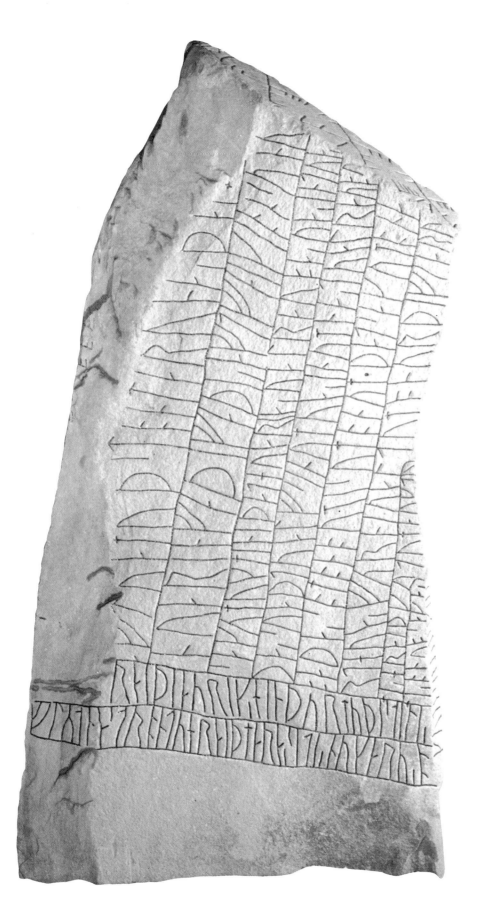

The angular runic script that came into use among the Germanic peoples of northern Europe, Britain, Scandinavia, and Iceland about the second century A.D. may have evolved from the ancient Etruscan alphabet of northern Italy. Runic inscriptions often held religious and even magical significance. The runes accompanying the central motif on a gold bracteate, opposite (top), found at Gudme, Denmark, likely infused this piece with protective powers in the mind of the original owner. Bracteates, perhaps designed after Roman military medals, were the most popular female jewelry of the eighth and ninth centuries in northern Europe. Opposite (bottom), a runic inscription surrounds a depiction of Romulus and Remus being suckled by a she-wolf, from a sculptured whalebone panel on the Franks Casket, discovered in the 19th century in Haute-Loire, France, and dating to the eighth century. Left, short-twig runes on a mighty stone in Rök, Sweden, honor a young warrior who died in battle more than a thousand years ago. This inscription covers the front of the stone, which measures some eight feet high and five feet wide, and is the longest and one of the most important such memorials known.

A view from the top of a ziggurat looks out on a turn-of-the-century archaeological excavation of the temple enclosure at the ancient Mesopotamian city of Nippur, located today in Iraq. These excavations brought to light a number of libraries and their collections of clay tablets bearing cuneiform script, the oldest known form of writing. A system of wedge-shaped characters impressed in clay, cuneiform dates back to the fourth millennium B.C.

should be no surprise that alpha, the Greek forerunner of "A," means bull or ox (*'alpu* in Ugaritic; *'elef* in Hebrew) in several of the old Semitic languages from which the Greek alphabet evolved. Similarly, the letter "N," descends from the wiggly line that represented both a snake and the first letter of the Semitic word for snake, *"nahas,"* which weaves its linguistic way through Ugaritic, Phoenician, Hebrew, Aramaic, South Arabian, and Ethiopian and then on through Greek and Latin.

The trend is from pictograph to syllabary to alphabet. With pictographs, a word is represented by the thing itself. In time, pictography became too cumbersome because theoretically there must be as many signs as there are words. The next step, then, was to simplify the picture so that it represented just the initial sound of the word; but the catalogue of a language's sounds—that is, the combination of all its consonants and vowels, its syllables—can also be quite large. The result was the syllabary, the forerunner to the alphabet. The writing of the ancient Maya civilization of Central America seems to be based mostly on a syllabary, for example, as was the early cuneiform writing of Mesopotamia. Eventually consonants and vowels were separated into distinct symbols and were represented by an alphabet.

Scholars agree that writing originated somewhere in the Middle East, probably Mesopotamia, sometime in the fourth millennium B.C. It is from the great libraries and word hoards of these ancient lands that the first "books" emerge. They were written on damp clay tablets with a wedged stick; since the Latin for wedge is *cunea*, the texts are thus called cuneiform. The clay tablets usually were not fired; sun-drying was probably reckoned enough to preserve the text. Fortunately, however, many tablets survive because they were accidently fired when the buildings in which they were stored burned.

Cuneiform writing lasted for some 3,000 years in a vast line of succession that runs through Sumer, Akkadia, Assyria, Nineveh, and Babylon, and preserves for us 15 languages in an area represented by modern-day Iraq, Syria, and western Iran.

The oldest cuneiform texts record the transactions of tax collectors and merchants, the receipts and bills of sale of an urban society living and dying on profit and margin. They have to do with grain and goats, real estate and realpolitik. But eventually there is a change. Scribes realize they have their fingers on the pulse of Babylonian society: they record the laws and keep the records. Knowledge confers power. As a result, the scribes are assigned their own goddess, Nisaba, later replaced by the god Nabu of Borsippa, whose symbol is neither weapon nor dragon but something far more fearsome, the cuneiform stick.

Cuneiform texts on science, astronomy, medicine, and mathematics abound, some offering astoundingly precise data. One tablet records the speed of the moon over 248 days; another documents an early sighting of Halley's comet, from September 22 to 28, 164 B.C. More esoteric texts attempt to explain old Babylonian customs, such as the procedure for curing someone who is ill, which includes rubbing tar and gypsum on the sick person's door and drawing a design at the foot of his bed. Wrote the scribe: "That is a net and traps any Evil." What is clear from the vast body of books (some 20,000 tablets were found in Ashurbanipal's library at Nineveh) is that scribes took pride in their writing and knowledge. They worked with diligence and care, often ending their texts with the colophon: "Let the learned instruct the learned, the ignorant may not see!"

Cuneiform writing on both sides of a Mesopotamian baked-clay tablet, top, dating to about 2360 B.C., records business transactions regarding the sale and delivery of donkeys, which were used to pull plows. Above, a detail from a relief uncovered in a seventh-century B.C. Assyrian palace in Nineveh depicts scribes with a hinged writing board and a scroll tallying the booty taken from a Chaldean settlement.

The foremost cuneiform tablet or "book," the Babylonian *Epic of Gilgamesh,* deals with humankind's feeble attempts to conquer time. In it, Gilgamesh, king and warrior, is crushed by the death of his best friend, and so sets out on adventures that prefigure those of both Hercules and Ulysses. His goal is not just to survive his ordeals but to make sense of this life—the most important job of any literature. Like the Bible, the story contains an account of the Flood and also of an encounter with a serpent that snatches away the gods' gift of life. Remarkably, versions of *Gilgamesh* span 1,500 years, between 2100 and 600 B.C., making the story the epic of an entire civilization. It would have been lost to us had it not been written on clay. Gilgamesh did conquer time.

The Greeks had a special name for the Egyptian writing in books. They called it *hiero glyphic,* literally "sacred writing." This was language fit for the gods. Perhaps that is Egypt's great contribution to the history of the book: hieroglyphic writing, in use from 3100 B.C. until A.D. 394, created books that were

Nineteenth-century French Egyptologist Jean-François Champollion's decipherment of the Rosetta Stone, above, whose inscription was written about 200 B.C., solved the mystery of hieroglypics. Opposite (top), the hieroglyphic funerary papyrus of the royal scribe Hunefer dates to about 1310 B.C. In this scene, Hunefer, at far left with the jackal-headed god Anubis, watches the weighing of his heart against the feather of Maat, goddess of justice and wife of the god of wisdom, ibis-headed Thoth, at center. Depicted again, Anubis checks the accuracy of the balance, and Thoth, with brush and palette in hand, prepares to record the results. Opposite (bottom right), Champollion's success in deciphering the cartouche for Egyptian queen Cleopatra broke the code to the hieroglyphic language. Opposite (bottom left), from about 2100 B.C. on, a hieroglyph of the crown of Pharaoh, combined with the spiral of life, formed the Egyptian symbol for the letter N.

fine art as well as communication. Egypt gave us the tradition of the scribe not just as sage but as artist and calligrapher.

Scholars have detected some 6,000 hieroglyphs in use over the long run of Egyptian writing, but never more than a thousand in use during any one period. It still seems a lot to recall, but what was lost in efficiency was more than made up for in the beauty and richness of the texts. Writing was meant to impress the eye with the vastness of creation itself.

Each symbol or glyph—the flowering reed (pronounced like "i"), the owl (m), the quail chick (w)—was a tiny work of art. Manuscripts were compiled with an eye to the overall design. Egyptologists have noticed that the glyphs that constitute individual words were sometimes shuffled to make the text more pleasing to the eye, with scant regard for sound or sense.

In July 1799, a group of French soldiers working near Rosetta in the Nile Delta found a four-foot slab of basalt inscribed in three scripts. At the top was hieroglyphic text; across the middle, the same message in demotic, a less formal, more cursive version of Egyptian in use from about 600 B.C. to A.D. 500; and at the bottom, the text in Greek, the common tongue around the Mediterranean just before the birth of Christ. The black stone was a temple decree that can be precisely dated to March 27, 196 B.C.

In 1802, the stone made its way to London as part of the booty from the war between England and France. There, several years later, Thomas Young made a breakthrough in its decipherment. In the Greek text, he recognized the name of the pharaoh Ptolemy, which appeared six times. Among the hieroglyphics, Young discovered a similar repetition, a sequence of characters always encircled with a box called a cartouche. Might they be the Egyptian word for Ptolemy? Knowing the Greek pronunciation of the name, Young deduced the phonetic sounds represented by the glyphs within the cartouche.

Young was unable to decipher completely the hieroglyphics on the Rosetta Stone but published his results in 1819. He was convinced that hieroglyphs were chiefly a series of symbols, not a phonetic writing system at all. But Young did not go far enough. The system was phonetic and its code was broken in 1822 by Frenchman Jean-François Champollion, who claimed to be innocent of Young's work. Using other texts in addition to those on the Rosetta Stone, Champollion compiled the names of many more dignitaries in cartouches: Cleopatra, Alexander, and Caesar, for example. These were used as a test against which his deductions from the Greek and demotic texts could be compared.

Egyptian books were written on papyrus, the precursor of paper, made from the tall, reedy plant that once choked the banks of the Nile. To make papyrus sheets, the stalks were stripped of their rinds, exposing the piths, which were pounded flat. These were laid horizontally and then vertically atop one another to constitute a two-ply sheet. The resulting smooth and durable material revolutionized the book, making it light, portable, and cheap. The strength of papyrus allowed it to be reused, after old texts were washed off. And its flexibility allowed it to be glued together in long rolls; what is known as the *Harris Papyrus I* in the British Museum, for example, measures 133 feet in length.

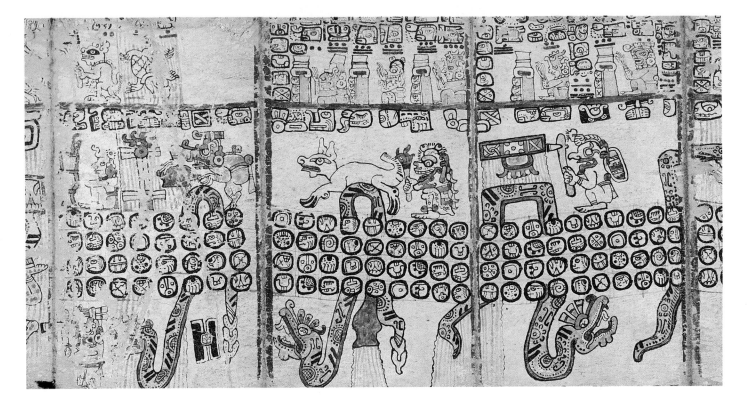

The greatest of the Egyptian books are the funerary papyrus rolls that contain a text called the Book of the Dead, the deceased's personal guide to the afterlife. No one of any importance would consider being buried without this celestial Baedeker, which is why so many of the texts survive among the grave goods in Egyptian tombs.

Immortality was a constant concern in Egyptian culture, a concern that inflated the value of the scribe and his books. Scribes knew they were as important as great men and pharaohs; their writings could triumph over death, as in this elegy from a 19th-dynasty papyrus of about 1300 B.C.:

> *Be a scribe! Put it in your heart,*
> *that your name shall exist like theirs!*
> *The roll is more excellent than the carved stela.*
>
> *A man has perished: his corpse is dust,*
> *and his people have passed from the land;*
> *it is a book which makes him remembered*
> *in the mouth of the speaker.*

Scribes held the key to happiness in both this life and the next; especially in preliterate societies, and in those whose writing was so difficult and so open to interpretation that to understand any text, you need both the book itself and the man who wrote it. In Egypt, the scribe was assigned his own god, Thoth, symbolized by the clever baboon or the ibis.

But there were other early societies, across an ocean of water and time, that also produced books. Their languages appear to have been so complex that reading may have been a royal ceremony; the scribes of at least one society, the Maya, were honored by being assigned—not unlike Egyptian scribes—the howler monkey as their patron of writing.

The societies were those of the Mesoamerican Indians, which flourished between 300 B.C. and A.D. 1500. Their books are some of the most beautiful ever produced, though they may never be completely deciphered. They are written on paper pounded out of the inner bark of the ficus tree and covered with a thin layer of lime plaster to form long, screen-folded manuscripts that we call codices.

The most remarkable part about these codices is their design, the way the scribe controls space. The reader's eye is guided through the manuscript by vertical and horizontal guidelines in red. In some instances, particularly in Mixtec codices, the text is boustrophedon; that is, it reverses direction on alternating lines, like cutting the grass. The Mixtec codices cover the history of tribes and rulers, with excursions into practical matters. Their depiction of warfare is vigorous, with attacking warriors in ceremonial gear brandishing weapons and descending on unsuspecting enemies.

Our knowledge of the Mayan book is based on only four codices, thought to have been written between 1250 and 1450, but possibly copied from earlier books. The first, the *Codex Dresden,* is the handsomest and is about 12 feet long (it sustained water damage in the Allied bombing of World War II). It is followed by the *Codex Paris,* a fragment four feet, nine inches long, and the *Codex Madrid,* which is almost 20 feet long. The *Codex Madrid* is easily the most difficult to read; the scribe may even have been illiterate or dyslexic. The fourth is the recently discovered *Codex Grolier,* which got its name after being exhibited at New York's Grolier Club in 1971. It is thought to have consisted originally of 20 pages, but only 11 pages of this Venus calendar remain. Today, the codex is kept in a vault at the Museo Nacional de Anthropología, in Mexico City.

The job of deciphering these codices is ongoing and difficult. The closest approach to a Mayan "Rosetta Stone" came from Spanish prelate Bishop Diego de Landa, who recorded what he took to be a Mayan alphabet in about 1566. Although Landa's original manuscript, based on interviews with an Indian who spoke a northern version of Mayan, is lost, an abstract of it survives in the Royal Academy of History in Madrid. Unfortunately, Landa was scourge as well as minister to Mayan studies. His duty was to supplant native belief with Christianity, and so he burned a great many of their books. Before he did so, however, he learned as much as he could about their language.

Mayan text appears to be a mixture of phonetic signs, word signs, and art. The existing codices and fragments, which date from the Postclassic period (A.D. 1000—1500), deal mainly with astronomy or are calendars of ritual events. It is possible that earlier codices dealt with such things as genealogies, territorial claims, trade, and other transactions; a strong oral tradition apparently paralleled the texts. We can imagine the books being read on court occasions by scribes or priests wielding decorative pointers, the texts themselves little more than elegant aide-mémoirs to long tales cunningly embroidered in the tropical night.

In the world of the Greeks and Romans, the expansion of literacy owed

much to Egypt. Nile papyrus was sold all over the Mediterranean. Papyrus was so entrenched in Greek and Roman culture that its documents were written mostly on papyrus until the ascent of parchment in the second century A.D. The Greeks, for their part, taught Egyptian scribes to use a reed pen rather than a brush for their writing. The papyrus roll was a *volumen,* Latin for "a thing rolled up," the source of our modern word "volume." *Liber,* the root of our "library," comes from the Latin word for book, meaning "rind" or the inside bark of a tree, the oldest Roman writing material.

Because Greek literature often was written on papyrus, much of it has perished. The statistics are depressing: Sophocles, for example, wrote 113 plays; seven survive. The bulk of our early classical books, however, come from archaeological sites associated with Greco-Roman settlements in the hot, dry Egyptian desert where the low humidity preserved them. These finds are literally the trash heaps of the ancient world, but they tell us much about classical reading and writing habits.

In 1947, a Bedouin boy looking for a lost goat among the cliffs at Qumran near the Dead Sea stumbled upon a cave that hid an ancient library sealed in pottery jars. Dating from the first century A.D., the cache held the oldest Hebrew Biblical texts ever found. Over the next nine years the Qumran caves yielded some 800 manuscripts, many of them unique and many others that attested to the accuracy of succeeding generations of Hebrew scholars in copying the Bible. Though the Dead Sea Scrolls are mostly on leather, a few are on papyrus; two rolls are on copper.

Greco-Roman archaeological sites in Egypt have also given us writing tablets of hollowed-out wooden boards filled with wax. The boards were linked with leather thongs; impressions were made in the wax with a stylus that had a sharp end for writing and a blunt one for erasing. The Romans called such notebooks

Early books—texts on tablets and scrolls—reveal much about antiquity, but often remain swathed in mystery themselves. Rembrandt's Moses With the Tables of the Law *(1659), opposite, depicts the Hebrew prophet, teacher, and leader of the 14th or 13th century B.C. holding aloft the tablet upon which the Ten Commandments are written. Above, a satellite photograph reveals the Dead Sea and its rugged, inhospitable setting. It was here, in 1947, in a cave at Qumran on the sea's northwest shore, that an ancient library of about 800 rare Hebrew manuscripts was discovered. The Dead Sea Scrolls, as these texts are called, date from between the second and third centuries B.C., and include the oldest known versions of the Old Testament. Above (left), a section of the* Isaiah Scroll *(c. 100 B.C.), which contains the complete text of the Book of Isaiah. Controversy continues to surround the history of this priceless cache of documents.*

The Greeks adopted the Phoenician alphabet in the eighth century B.C., subsequently adding their own vowel signs. Above, a page from the Works of Plato, *copied in Constantinople about the year 900. The similarity between the Greek minuscule seen here and the writing on a Phoenician text on a gold sheet, above (right), indicates that they also may have adopted the Phoenician style of script. Raphael's* School of Athens (1508–1511), *opposite (detail), portrays the Greek philosopher Plato, among the great scholars of his day, in discourse with his pupil Aristotle.*

pugillares or *tabulae,* from the Latin *tabula,* meaning "board." An early form of the codex, they look very much like a modern book.

The Roman invention of the codex transformed the book into the form that we are familiar with today. Consulting the tail or head of a papyrus roll, while you were reading it, was inconvenient and distracting. Instead, the roll could be folded into pages, making flipping back and forth much easier. To make this change effective, the text had to be recorded in columns, one or two of which would make up a page. Roman biographer and historian Suetonius tells us that Julius Caesar was the first to do this, in dispatches to his troops.

All that remained was for someone to cut the folded papyrus roll into leaves and bind the leaves together under wooden covers. In the first few centuries A.D., codices were made of both papyrus and parchment, but by the fifth century parchment was the material of choice. To Christianity goes the credit for popularizing the codex, because of the importance of the Gospels.

*An idealized portrait of a youthful Virgil,
seated between his lectern and scroll box,
graces a manuscript created in Italy in the
fifth or sixth century. Virgil's national epic
poem, the* Aeneid, *inspired later writers
from Dante to John Milton.*

The codex was such a good idea that its use quickly spread from theology to all other branches of knowledge. At the same time, literacy was spreading out from under the control of a handful of powerful shaman-scribes to public copyists and finally to the Roman schoolboy with his tabulae.

Today, when we stare at the puzzling and undecipherable images in ancient writings, we are astonished by the brilliance of what the people of long ago

achieved, and we root for latter-day Champollions. Until they come, we are in the same predicament as the illiterate Jo in Dickens's *Bleak House:* "To see people read, and to see people write, and to see the postmen deliver letters, and not to have the least idea of all that language—to be, to every scrap of it, stone blind and dumb! … and to think … what does it all mean, and if it means anything to anybody, how comes it that it means nothing to me?"

Stylus in her right hand and pugillary, a hollowed-out wooden notebook filled with wax, in her left, a Greco-Roman poetess depicted in an ancient Pompeiian fresco pauses thoughtfully as she contemplates her next line of verse.

No book in history approaches the Bible. It's the all-time best seller, published in more than 1,000 languages. Gutenberg invented printing with the Bible in mind. Martin Luther's translation of a single word from the New Testament launched the Reformation. Herodotus gave us ancient history as far back as 450 B.C.; the Old Testament pushes that date back another 1,500 years.

The Bible's power and influence over the past four millennia are incalculable. Both its Testaments, Old and New, have been revered as sacred scripture, as literature, as magic, as the ultimate self-help books. Generations have turned to it for advice both sternly practical—"An eye for an eye, and a tooth for a tooth"—and hopelessly ideal—"Blessed are the meek: for they shall inherit the earth."

We've laughed at its stiffness— "Esau my brother is a hairy man, and I am a smooth man"—and shivered at its perception—"Man is born unto trouble, as the sparks fly upward." We look to it in good times for humility—"For dust thou art, and unto dust thou shalt return"—and in bad times for solace—"O death, where is thy sting? O grave, where is thy victory?"

Consider the story of Shadrach, Meshach, and Abednego in the Book of Daniel. The year is 605 B.C.; the place, the Babylonian court of Nebuchadnezzar. When the three refuse to worship the king's golden idol and are thrown into the fiery pit, they know their Lord is capable of saving them. In any case, they will have done the right thing:

If it be so, our God whom we serve is able to deliver us from the burning fiery furnace, and he will deliver us out of thine hand, O king.

But if not, be it known unto thee, O king, that we will not serve thy gods, nor worship the golden image which thou hast set up.

No righteousness or vanity here, just unadorned humility and resignation. As a result, "But if not" has rattled down the ages, the words crystallizing the stance of good in the face of annihilation. In 1940, the last message from the abandoned Allied troops at Dunkirk was merely "But if not. . . ."

Where does the power come from? Possibly from the Bible's approach to history: the Old Testament sees the past not as a collection of random events but as a patterned, cyclical narrative that can be questioned for clues to the good life; the New Testament tries to advance that position, suggesting not only that history can be questioned but that there is an answer.

The Hebrew Bible, also called the Old Testament, has four categories of books: the Book of Law (the first five books, also called the Torah or the Pentateuch); the Histories (12 books, from Joshua to Esther); Poetry and Wisdom (five books, Job through the Song of Solomon); and the Prophets (the last 17 books, from Isaiah through Malachi).

The New Testament is tripartite. First are the Histories—four Gospels and the Acts of the Apostles; next, the Epistles, written by Paul (13 books) and several other apostles and disciples; and last, a single Book of Revelation, a vision of the future.

THE GREATEST STORY EVER TOLD

❧ FROM THE OLD TESTAMENT TO THE NEW

A depiction of the great Roman senator, author, and scholar Cassiodorus, dressed as the aged Old Testament prophet Ezra, decorates the frontispiece of the Codex Amiatinus, *probably written at the Benedictine monastery of Jarrow in England about 700 as a gift for the pope. Cassiodorus is shown working on his huge* Codex Grandior, *an Old Latin or pre-Jerome version of the Bible. On the shelves of the open book cupboard rests his nine-volume Bible, or* Novem Codices, *and at his feet lies a smaller, one-volume edition of Jerome's Vulgate.*

The study of the Hebrew Bible is difficult because it covers events deep in antiquity and is not always written in Hebrew. It was transcribed by people who were dispersed from Persia to Egypt and is fraught with the hazards of transmitting a changing language across many centuries. The Book of Daniel, for instance, details events of the seventh century B.C., but, according to some scholars, may not have been written down until the third century B.C. Moreover, it's partially in Hebrew and partially in Aramaic.

The oldest complete Bible in Hebrew, the *Codex Babylonicus Petropolitanus,* is dated comparatively recently at A.D. 916. It's written in Masoretic, the language used by a sect of Hebrew textual scholars starting about the sixth century A.D. There are thousands of shorter Hebrew fragments on papyrus and parchment dating from earlier centuries, including a fifth-century A.D. Samaritan text of the Pentateuch: Genesis, Exodus, Leviticus, Numbers, Deuteronomy. There are also many fragments in Aramaic. These versions of the Hebrew Bible were corroborated by the finding of the Dead Sea Scrolls in 1947. Since many Dead Sea texts date from about the first century A.D., they validate the later versions and attest to the care with which the scriptures were transmitted over the next thousand years.

The Hebrew can be tested, however, against much earlier Greek translations. Greek was the literary and scientific language of the Hellenistic period, which dates from the fourth to the first centuries B.C. During that time, the works of the greatest writers the world had ever seen—Homer,

Plato, Aristotle, Herodotus—were in Greek, a sort of lingua franca. In fact, the large Jewish community in Egypt under Ptolemy II Philadelphus, who ruled from 285 to 246 B.C., could no longer understand Hebrew. Legend has it that at the request of Philadelphus each of the 12 tribes of Israel sent six scholars to the library at Alexandria to provide an accurate Greek translation of their sacred writings.

They were quarantined in separate carrels, but in time they all emerged with the same translation, which was taken by many as a sign of divine intervention. Another tradition has it that the scholars were brought to a conference on the island of Pharos, the site of the Alexandrian lighthouse, and that their translation was a collaboration—another kind of miracle. Ever since, this seamless Greek text has been called the *Septuagint*. The word is derived from the Latin *septuaginta,* meaning 70, and it referred— roughly—to the 72 translators, the 72 days it took them to complete their task, or to the 71 members of the Sanhedrin, or supreme council of Jews, who authorized the translation.

American Talmudist and educator Solomon Schechter examines fragments of Hebrew biblical manuscripts in 1896 in the famous Cairo Genizah, or secret storage site for Hebrew books and book remnants, below, which he rediscovered in the attic of the ninth-century Ezra Synagogue. Opposite (top), an ancient coin depicts Egyptian ruler Ptolemy II Philadelphus, thought to have arranged for the translation of the first five books of the Hebrew Old Testament into Greek, and his wife and sister Arsinoe II. Opposite (bottom), a 17th-century vellum scroll of the Book of Esther.

Built on the site where Moses is said to have seen the burning bush, the monastery of St. Catherine at Mount Sinai, above, yielded up a fourth-century codex of the Greek Bible, the oldest known version of the New Testament. The Codex Sinaiticus, *as the manuscript is called, was recovered in the mid-19th century by German philologist Konstantin von Tischendorf, opposite (top). Opposite (bottom), a papyrus page, its uncial hand arranged characteristically in four columns, from the codex's Gospel of John.*

The scholars did not, however, translate the entire Hebrew Bible, but only its Pentateuch. Later translations were added to complete the Greek text in the first century B.C. Although this is often called the *Septuagint* (and labeled LXX, or 70 in Roman numerals), the term should be confined strictly to the first five books. The Christian philosopher Origen (c. A.D. 185–254), determined to have the last word in theological debate, compiled a huge parallel-text edition of the Old Testament in

Hebrew that also included a version with Hebrew transliterated into Greek and four other Greek translations. This complete six-way text, the *Hexapla,* is now lost except for some parts that were copied down in the eighth century.

For the New Testament, the oldest and most important manuscript is the *Codex Sinaiticus,* which is written in Greek and was discovered at the monastery of St. Catherine on Mount Sinai in 1844. It was found in a basket of the monastery's kindling and saved by the German philologist Konstantin von Tischendorf. The text carries a notation by the martyr Pamphilius, who died A.D. 310: "The confessor Antoninus compared it against the *Hexapla* of Origen, and I, Pamphilius, corrected it in prison. It is not easy to find a copy the like of this one."

Sinaiticus covers parts of the Old Testament as well as the entire New Testament, written in a neat uncial hand of the fourth century. It is rivaled in the breadth of its contents only by the *Codex Vaticanus* (Greek, fourth century), which today contains most of the Old Testament and up to Hebrews 9:13 of the New Testament. The *Codex Bezae* (fifth century) has facing pages of Greek and Latin and is a check against St. Jerome's translation of the Greek into the Latin Vulgate. The *Codex Alexandrinus* of the fifth century was considered so valuable that in 1731 a scholar risked his life for it, dashing into a raging inferno at the Cotton Library—one of the foundation collections of the British Library—in his nightdress to save it from the flames.

Greek is the key to the New Testament. It's thought that the Gospels were originally written in a version of

Greek called Koine, the common language ("e koine dialectos"). Palestinian Koine reflects both Greek and Aramaic, the language of Jesus, the language that stands behind the Gospels. Ever since the days of the *Septuagint,* Greek, rather than Hebrew, had been used in theological debate. To give their words the heft and feel of the Old Testament, the writers settled on Greek.

Only two Evangelists, however, are reported as having known Greek. Luke was a Greek from Macedonia, where Paul met him. Echoes of formal Attic Greek occur in Luke's Gospel and in Acts, which he also wrote. Mark also knew Greek and acted as Peter's translator, which is why Peter is so prominent in Mark's Gospel.

In addition to the great uncial manuscripts in Greek, there are thousands of New Testament fragments on papyrus and parchment in Old Latin, Old Syriac, Peshitta (or, later Syriac), Coptic, Gothic, Armenian, Ethiopic, Georgian, Nubian, Arabic, Old Persian, Slavonic, and Provençal. The result was text as battlefield, one on which the struggle was not so much over interpretation and doctrine as simply deciding what the text said.

In the waning of the Middle Ages, the Bible was central to church reform. Revolutionaries wanted to give ordinary people access to scripture in their own tongues rather than just Latin, freeing them from dependence on the clergy. All over Europe in the 12th and 13th centuries anti-clerical sects were being suppressed. By the time of England's John Wycliffe (1330–84), the door could no longer be nailed shut. Wycliffe thundered from Oxford against

church abuse, and his followers, John Purvey and Nicholas of Hereford, made available the first complete Bible in English in 1382.

Two additional innovations together would change both the Bible and the world irrevocably: printing and the study of ancient Greek. In 1516, in Basel (in what is now Switzerland), Desiderius Erasmus printed the first Greek edition of the New Testament in nearly a thousand years. In that book, Martin Luther found his crux, the

47

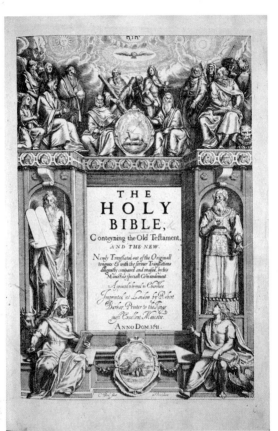

An ornate title page, above, introduces the King James Bible, a major revision of the Bible by six groups of "learned men to the number of four and fifty" that was published in 1611. Deemed the "Authorized Version" and "appointed to be read in churches," the King James Bible owes much to the work of martyr William Tyndale, whose modern English Bible appeared in 1526. Opposite, a detail from the Master of Tolentino's 14th-century fresco The Faithful Listen to the Word of God.

word "justice" in Paul's epistle to the Romans. To Luther, this meant justification—salvation—by faith alone, not good works. The Reformation depended on one word in one book. Luther would then go on to translate his own Bible, using the Greek version of Erasmus.

The modern English Bible begins in Cologne, Germany, the cradle of printing, with William Tyndale's New Testament of 1526. He was followed by Miles Coverdale, whose complete Bible appeared in 1535. Back in England, John Rogers combined the work of Tyndale and Coverdale to produce the Thomas Matthew Bible in 1537. This was closely followed in 1539 by the government of Henry VIII's production of the "Great Bible," which expunged a few troublesome or seditious bits. This work was ordered to be chained to the chancel in every English church, where the public could have access to it.

During the reign of Mary I, or "Bloody Mary" (1553–58), the Catholic monarch, Protestant Bible activity moved back to the Continent. Five years after John Rogers was burned at the stake in London in 1555 for printing the Matthew Bible, the Marian exiles published their own Bible in Geneva. The Geneva Bible is also called the "Breeches Bible" because of its Puritanical view of Adam and Eve (Genesis 3:7), who "sewed figtre leaues together, and made them selues breeches."

The Geneva Bible was immensely popular, and not just with Puritans and Calvinists. Everyone liked it. To counter it, two new versions of the Great Bible lumbered forth from the Church of England in 1568 and 1572,

under the direction of Archbishop Matthew Parker. Too late.

The Geneva Bible's popularity had everything to do with its design and typography. It was the first Bible to number its verses for ease in reference and discussion. It used Roman rather than black-letter type and clearly printed its marginal notes. It was easy to read, use, and comprehend. Church and church-going were changed forever.

In 1607, King James assembled 54 scholars and asked them to revise the 1572 Bishops' Bible. They, like the savants of the *Septuagint,* were impaneled in six groups that were responsible for different sections of the text. Conferring at Oxford, Cambridge, and Westminster, they produced in 1611 the "Authorized Version," the King James Bible. It is hard to imagine how their work could have been bettered. The translators recognized that they stood at the end of a long line of Bible scholars, that they stood on the shoulders of giants.

In the end, whatever else the Bible gave us, it also created an intellectual tradition of close examination of words and their meaning. Minute differences in words can have enormous repercussions in dogma. This is the rabbinical system, which grew into the medieval scholastic universities.

In the best sense, the search for a reliable text is not a mean-spirited but an open investigation of the possibilities of a text, not constrictive but constructive. As the translators of the King James Bible wrote in their preface, their aim was never to repudiate any "bad" book but "to make a good one better, or out of many good ones, one principal good one."

وَمِنْهُمْ جَبْرَئِيلُ

فَإِذَا نَجَّا أَمِينُ الْوَحْيِ وَخَازِنُ الْقُدْسِ وَيُقَالُ لَهُ أَيْضًا الرُّوحُ الْأَمِينُ وَالرُّوحُ الْقُدُسِ وَالنَّامُوسِ الْأَكْبَرِ وَطَاوُسِ الْمَلَائِكَةِ جَاءَ فِي الْخَبَرِ أَنَّ اللَّهَ تَعَالَى إِذَا تَكَلَّمَ بِالْوَحْيِ سَمِعَ أَهْلُ السَّمَاءِ صَلْصَلَةً كَجَرِّ السِّلْسِلَةِ عَلَى الصَّفَا فَيَصْعَقُونَ وَلَا يَزَالُونَ كَذَلِكَ حَتَّى يَأْتِيَهُمْ جَبْرَئِيلُ فَإِذَا جَاءَهُمْ فُزِّعَ عَنْ قُلُوبِهِمْ فَقَالُوا يَا جَبْرَئِيلُ مَاذَا قَالَ رَبُّكَ فَيَقُولُ الْحَقَّ فَنَادَوْنَ لِلْحَقِّ الْحَقَّ وَجَاءَ بِالْجُمَّانِ النَّبِيُّ صَلَّى اللَّهُ عَلَيْهِ وَآلِهِ وَسَلَّمَ قَالَ لِجِبْرِيلَ إِنِّي أُحِبُّ أَنْ أَرَاكَ عَلَى صُورَتِكَ فَقَالَ إِنَّكَ لَا تُطِيقُ ذَلِكَ

PEOPLE OF THE BOOK

READ! IT'S THE FIRST word of the Koran, from a passage that continues, "in the name of thy Lord. . . ." With such a powerful start, it's little wonder that reading is the quintessential act of Islam. ❡ You see them all over the Middle East, men in courtyards reading Korans, following along in the text with their fingers. Their reading is not always silent; the holy words are sometimes audible, making a joyful noise unto their Lord. Those men and their books stand at the end of a long line that stretches back to the Prophet, and beyond. ❡ The book was given to Muhammad, an Arab born in Mecca around 570. He lived at a difficult time for desert nomads; urbanization was overtaking tribal ways, and cities like Mecca, Damascus, and Medina were becoming congested. Muhammad, orphaned at an early age, had overcome hardship and made a name for himself in business. Becoming uneasy about life, however, he began wandering in the hills outside Mecca lost in thought. What answers were there for a society tilting toward materialism? ❡ By the sixth century, most Arabs were aware of, and respected, the earlier prophets who had brought personal messages of hope and glory to humankind, prophets with names like Moses and Abraham and Jesus. Then came the voice. At about age 40, and continuing for more than 20 years, Muhammad received—directly from Allah, as dictated by the archangel Gabriel—the entire contents of the Koran, the Moslem holy book. It was a remarkable performance, not least because Muhammad was illiterate. When Gabriel first appeared, he uttered the single word "Read," and Muhammad did so. He

According to Islamic lore, the archangel Gabriel, depicted opposite in an early-14th-century miniature from Egypt or Syria, was the Almighty's messenger and keeper of sacred intelligence. It was Gabriel who over a period of some 20 years recited the words of God in Arabic to the Prophet Muhammad, who in turn repeated what he heard verbatim to his followers. In the end the message was written down and transmitted as the Koran, the Moslem holy book.

read—or recited to his followers, who copied it down—all 120,000 words of the Koran. With that miracle, Muhammad became the Prophet.

The book is central, for Islam has no priestly class; each person interacts directly with God. The Koran is Everyman's infallible guide. That is why, for Islam, calligraphy is the queen of arts. Everything is subservient to the Word. The best artists became adept not in reproducing, say, the human form or landscape, but rather in illuminating God's Word.

Over the centuries, several styles of Arabic calligraphy, which reads from right to left, evolved for special use in the Koran. Kufic, named after the town in Iraq where it originated, was the first style to achieve classic status. It was copied and recopied throughout the Muslim world beginning in the eighth century A.D. (The Prophet had died the previous century, in 632.) And it was not reserved just for books: its thick and confident strokes were used to post verses from the Koran everywhere—on plates, on metalware, and on mosques.

In the ninth century a calligraphic change called "gliding Kufic" emerged, a smaller, condensed version of the classic hand. Over the centuries, Islamic calligraphers developed a number of more cursive styles that derive from the world

Sitting crosslegged in the open air, Muslim men of Afghanistan silently read and recite from the Koran. When speaking holy writ aloud, followers of Islam continue the example of Muhammad, who became the vehicle for introducing Allah's sacred scripture to the world.

of secular writing. The names of the scripts are exotic and graceful—Naskhi and Rayhani, Thuluth and Muhaqqaq. They create images out of words, images as sensuous and provocative as any representational art form.

The Persian Nasta'liq script, called the "hanging style" because of the sweep and elegance of its letters, had a serious drawback. It was so flamboyant that it was considered unfit for holy writ, although there is a stellar Nasta'liq Koran from 1538 in Istanbul's Topkapı Sarayı Library. In North Africa and Spain, a tightly knotted style called Maghribi (meaning "Western") appeared that was especially suited to fine, dense ornamentation. Christian monks who produced illuminated manuscripts in Europe must have been acquainted with this work.

In the multifoliate patterns of an illuminated carpet page—a page with only decoration, woven like a carpet—we see one of Islam's gifts: abstraction. Islam prized scholarship; early on, it developed a sort of rabbinical tradition of Koranic scholars who delved into the text looking for revelation. Close attention to everything—especially nature—was part of the same quest for enlightenment.

To understand, the scholar must dive beneath the surface of reality, must find the bones beneath the skin. What Islam found was an infinite series of repeti-

Similar in design and use to the girdle books of medieval Europe, a rare Arabian saddle book consists of separate pages of the Koran protected within four nested-leather cases. Hung from the rider's neck or strapped on his mount's saddle, scripture was always near at hand. Easy access to the holy book was vital to the faithful, who believed that answers to all of life's problems resided within the Koran.

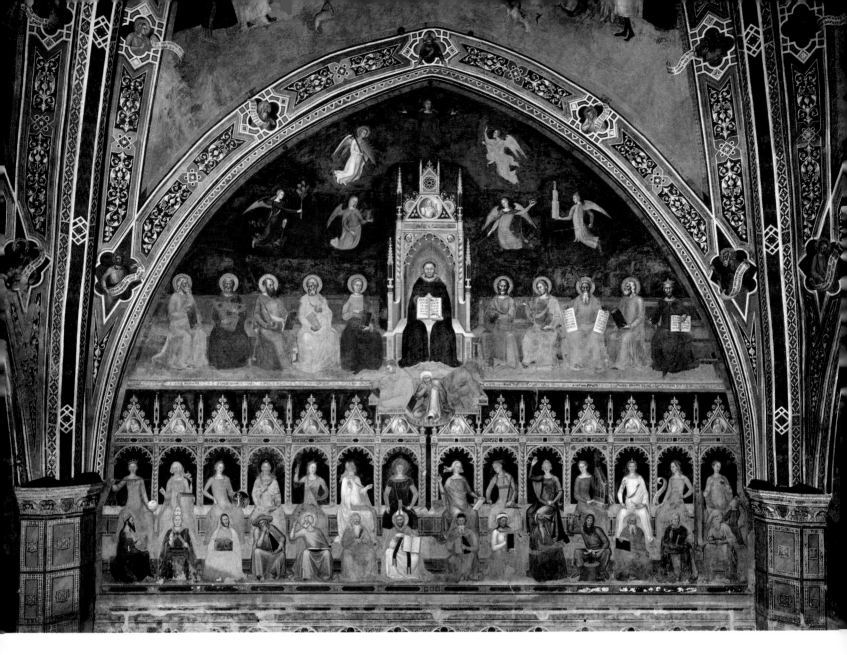

tive structures, interwoven, self-reflective, complex. They discovered the structure of the universe and used it in their art, architecture, and calligraphy.

Islam inherited the books of the Greco-Roman world, preserved them,
refined and improved their ideas, and passed them on to us. At Baghdad and
other scriptoria, thousands of Greek manuscripts were translated and studied.
After an important victory over Byzantium in the ninth century, the caliph al-
Ma'mun demanded just 10 books of Plato, Aristotle, Galen, and other Greek
philosophers, which he then had copied back in Baghdad at his "House of Wisdom," a library, translation bureau, and university.

Plato and Aristotle could have been lost to us without Islam. Scientists and
philosophers like al-Kindi, al-Farabi, and Averroes redefined Greek thought and
made it available to medieval Europe. Without Islam's concern for books, we
would have had no Renaissance.

Geography and navigation were priorities for the Islamic world. In his daily
prayers, a Muslim must know precisely the direction of Mecca. It's not always

east, as Jerusalem was for European Christians: a Muslim in India must bow west; in Russia, south; in East Africa, north. So Islamic books show an early interest in astronomy and maps. Intricate celestial maps were a precise background against which the movements of the planets, moon, and sun could be carefully registered.

Almost 500 years before Copernicus and Galileo, the writings of Muslim astronomers like al-Biruni were questioning the doctrine of the Earth-centered cosmos. The invention of the astrolabe, the forerunner of the sextant and other navigational devices, followed such books. In the West, the single most mentioned Islamic book after the Koran was the *Almagest,* an Arabic text by the Greek astronomer Ptolemy.

In medicine and mathematics, Islamic books led the way. Avicenna, a Muslim who was born in 980 and lived in southern Russia, developed medical procedures used in Europe up through the 17th century. Islamic mathematicians went to old Greek texts to refine something they would call "al-jebr." Meaning "to reunite, restore, and consolidate," it has to do with the analysis of nature, with the breaking down of reality and the restoration of its meaning. Arabs brought the idea to Spain, and so on to the West: algebra.

The Islamic books most attractive to Europeans in the Middle Ages were those dealing with astrology. Islamic science had long surpassed the pre-science of astrology, but its astrological writers had nevertheless amassed a wealth of knowledge about human psychology and behavioral patterns. A translation of al-Bumasar's treatise on astrology, illuminated in Bruges before 1403, is one of the great books of all time.

Where Islam and the West came together, there was fashioned, at least for several centuries before the start of the Crusades, a society of three faiths—Jewish, Christian, and Muslim—that was of the highest intellectual and artistic achievement. In Spain, in Sicily, and even in Cairo, the three religions lived in peace and harmony, united by their faith in a book—the New Testament, the Bible, or the Koran, all revelations given by God to humanity through the prophets. They were all "people of the book."

The Judeo-Christian heritage, then, is a fine concept, but it leaves out a third: "Judeo-Christian-Islamic" is more like it. We should be considered one culture dependent on a common bond of beliefs and observations, all contained in a wide circle of books. The foremost bond is visible in the moral code the books project. In all three religions, God—Allah, the same deity of Moses and Jesus—dictates a moral code, and he who breaks the code offends God.

Islam rejected the idea of printing for a long time, and it was not until the 18th century that books printed from movable type appeared regularly. Somehow, mechanical reproduction was not considered appropriate for the Word of God.

So it's a shock to find a Koran being printed in Venice, with Arabic types, as early as 1537. The book was mentioned in the 16th century, and then dropped from sight. (One should never be surprised by Venice, however. The Venetian empire had close economic ties and trade routes with the Middle East, protected by a string of Venetian fortresses that extended all the way to Constantinople.)

This mathematical jewel, an astrolabe whose brass templates were engraved in Arabic in 13th-century Yemen, could guide caravans across seas of sand and ships across the oceans. Greeks before Christ originated these complex analogue computers, but Arab and Persian technicians kept the art alive, refined it, and transmitted it to Christendom.

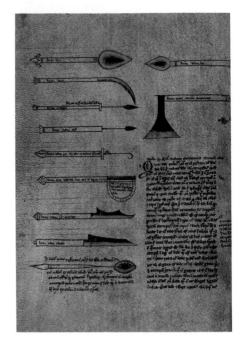

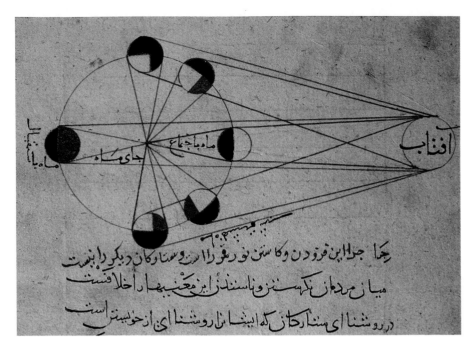

Enthralled by classical science, Islamic masters gathered texts from Europe, Asia, and Africa and furthered the work of the ancients, becoming particularly adept at medicine. Above (left), finely crafted surgical instruments appear in a Latin translation of al-Zahrain's medical text of the 11th century. Al-Biruni's dissection of the sky in an astronomical chart, above, depicts eclipses of the moon. At left, a hemispheric map from 1154 was part of the world's first scientific atlas and gazeteer, the product of a 15-year collaboration between Islamic geographer al-Idrisi and Christian king Roger II of Sicily. Opposite, a pioneering public library as depicted in a 13th-century manuscript from the School of Baghdad.

فقال ايم الله لي حق ارجو ان ينبع واللص لحفين و خفين ان ينبع انذاانوم الحيكم الليلة اليوم فان كان الجماعة

ان نانت بعده وابت تصديق دعوته فوجس في افكارهم واجن في افكارهم وفطن لما بطن من استنكارهم وحذران

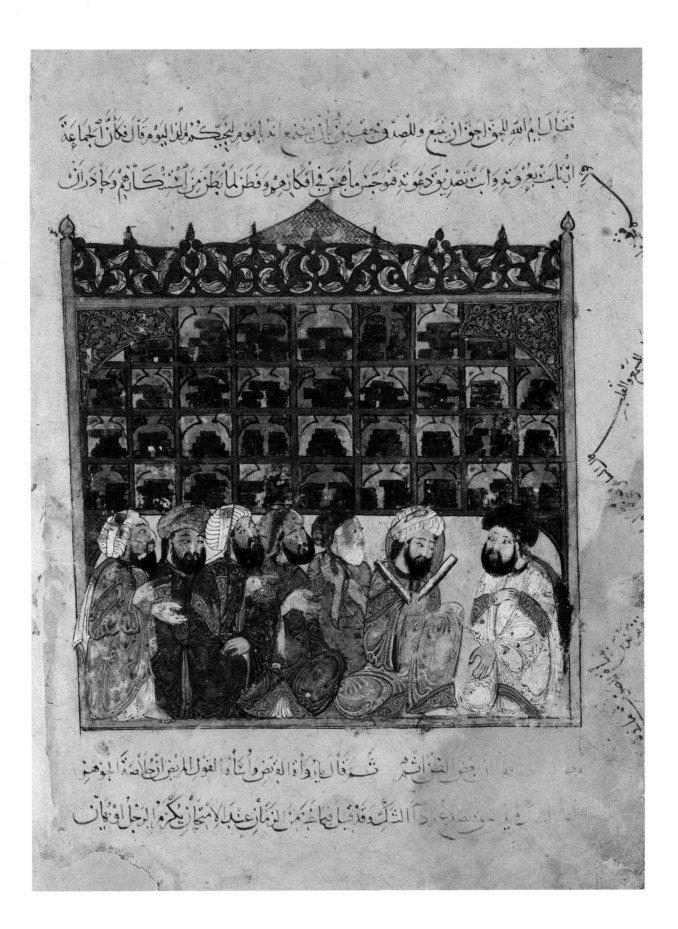

الن بعض الضراثم ثم فقال يا ارواة القطن وشاه القول المربع ان جلاضة الجوهرن

الشكل وقد ناب ما يعظم من لنان ان عبد الامتجاز يكم ارجل اوقان

Hebrew, Christian, and Islamic artistic traditions meld in curious ways in two works of art. Right, Hebrew letters and Arabian-style decoration adorn a manuscript of A Guide to the Perplexed *by Maimonides (1135–1204), a great Jewish jurist, philosopher, and physician who had been born and educated in Islamic Cordoba, in Spain, and later traveled to Cairo to join that city's intellectual ferment. He wrote in Arabic, but his major works were translated into Hebrew. Opposite, pseudo-Arabic calligraphy decorates hems of garments and a cushion in Paolo Veneziano's* Coronation of Mary, *painted in 1362. The appeal was sartorial, not doctrinal, as popes and bishops often wore garments edged with Koranic scripture.*

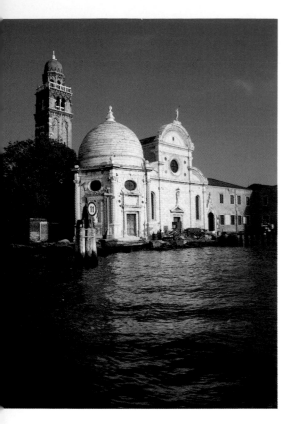

This Koran was printed by Alessandro Paganino, a Christian. At the time, the Koran was listed on the Index Librorum Prohibitorum, meaning that Christians could neither read nor own it. Understandably, some scholars had so distrusted the existence of this printed Koran they'd called it a "ghost" book, the product of wishful bibliographic thinking.

The Franciscan Monastery of San Michele in Isola is just across the lagoon from Venice. In its heyday, the 60 monks who lived there were an economic and intellectual power center. Today, San Michele is chiefly the civic cemetery of Venice, its monastery and fine church manned by a handful of monks.

A few years ago, as Fra Vittorino Meneghin, abbot of San Michele, was cataloguing the 23,000 old books in the cloister library, he rediscovered the missing Paganino Koran. It was just where it should have been, among the rare volumes, its vellum spine labeled "Alcoranus arabicus sine anno" (Koran in Arabic, undated) and clearly shelf-marked "Rari A, V, 22" in a fine italic hand.

It's probably been there—rare bookcase A, row five, the 22nd book—for centuries. It certainly is well made, its 464 pages still bright white after all these years. Like any Arabic or Hebrew book, it starts at what we consider the back and reads to the front. The book makes no concessions to Western readers: no Roman type appears anywhere. Ordinarily, Arabic books have a bit of Roman alphabet on the title page if for no other reason than to help the librarian. Otherwise, such books go astray. A much later hand has added "Coran" on the vellum.

Typographically, the pages are very even, a remarkable achievement for such an early version of Arabic type. There had been attempts at printing Arabic else-

At the Franciscan monastery of San Michele at Isola, opposite (left), just outside Venice, Fra Vittorino Meneghin, opposite (right), discovered the only surviving copy of an edition of the Koran printed in Venice before the press reached Islamic lands. Possibly the first printed Koran, the work appears at left.

where, in Rome and Constantinople, but this was by centuries the first Koran. The volume may have been used for a time by a linguist, for there are occasional interlinear translations in Latin, and the same tiny hand has marked the start of each surah. (The Koran is divided into 114 surahs, which correspond to the books of the Bible.)

According to scholar Angela Nuovo, the entire pressrun was meant for Eastern eyes only. That is why there is no Roman title page. In any case, it would have been illegal and dangerous to sell these Korans in Italy. It was all an export venture. What a financial risk: casting the type, hiring typesetters and proofreaders who could deal with Arabic, investing in paper and press time. And then the books were loaded aboard a Venetian galley headed for the East ... and oblivion—all, that is, save one, picked up at the print shop, cheap, possibly by a scholarly Franciscan.

In *The Merchant of Venice,* as Portia looks out into the Venetian night, a light glints in her eye, like a flare in glass. "That light we see is burning in my hall. How far that little candle throws his beams! So shines a good deed in a naughty world." Stand on the sea wall of the lagoon today and peer out at San Michele. A similar glint comes from the cloister library there. Perhaps it's the Paganino Koran.

In China, books have always had a special power. For it is the written word, not the spoken word, that united that society. I may not understand what you say, but put it on paper, and problems of dialect wither away. In such a context it's no wonder that the Chinese stand first in the use of paper (A.D. 105), lampblack ink (A.D. 400), printing from stone rubbing (A.D. 175), printing from woodblock (8th century), and printing from movable type (11th century).

It is a long and bright record of achievement, and one that the world hardly understood until 1906, when Sir Marc Aurel Stein traveled to Dunhuang in the deserts of Gansu Province and found the "Caves of the Thousand Buddhas." Among them, Stein discovered about 15,000 books, all on paper. There were also 1,130 paper bundles tied up with ribbon, many of which contained a dozen or more scrolls.

He also found the *Diamond Sutra*, the world's oldest dated printed book, whose colophon says it was completed on May 11, 868. The sutra, one of the sermons of Buddha, is printed from a series of woodblocks, each reproducing an inalterable image of an entire page. The sheets were glued side-to-side and rolled into a scroll 16 feet long. The title block shows a serene Buddha on a lotus throne guarded by angels and lions.

Stein's discovery captured the world's attention and transformed conventional Chinese scholarship. Books from all over the world were in the caves, including Old Testament scriptures in Hebrew. (There is a nice arc of coincidence here, for Chinese characters have recently been discovered on the Dead Sea Scrolls.)

Picture and text appear in this section of the Chinese Diamond Sutra, *below, originally a Buddhist work written in Sanskrit. Dated* A.D. *868, the scroll is believed by many scholars to be the oldest complete printed book yet found. Opposite, perhaps returning from India, a Buddhist monk of ninth-century China carries a pack filled with religious manuscripts. The Buddhist devotional act of reproducing hundreds of duplicate images of Buddha, combined with China's early use of the woodblock, may have led to the development of printing in that country.*

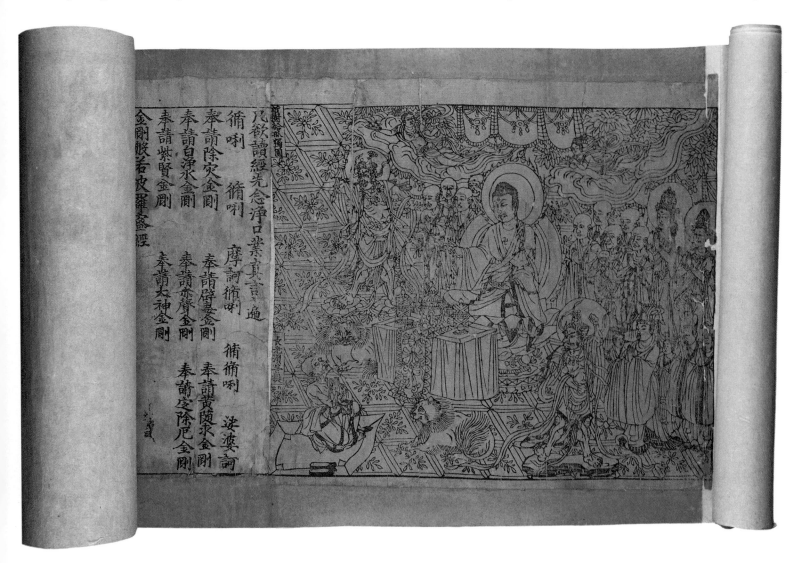

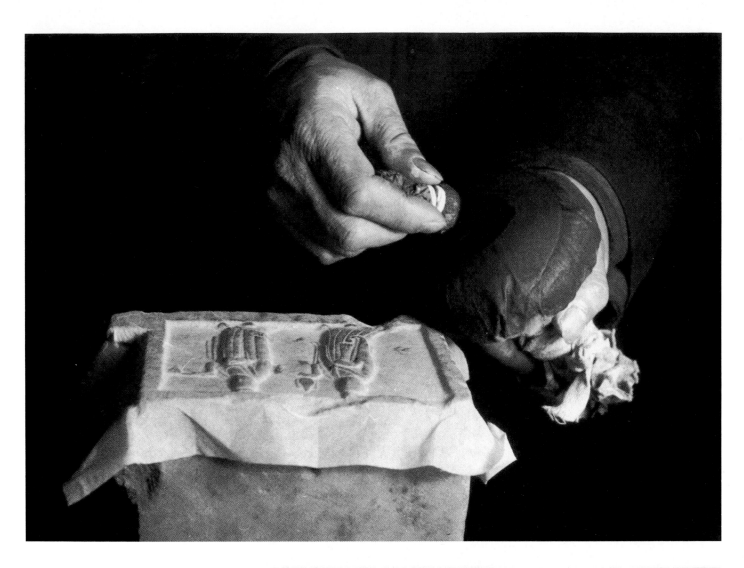

Predecessors of printing, ancient Chinese paper-and-ink rubbings, above, provided accurate impressions of pictures and writing incised deeply in stone or other material. Strong when wet, thin Oriental paper could be pressed into reliefs and would dry holding the contours of the original. Dabs of ink increased legibility. Right, Oriental foundry workers were the first to produce movable metal type. Their heyday came after 1403 when Korea's ministry of books began to cast tons of bronze characters in sand molds, hardly four decades before the German Gutenberg produced his lead-alloy type in steel molds. The text shown here, printed from fine Korean type in the 1600s, displays early technical progress.

Printing in China began with the use of seals made of jade, rhinoceros horn, and copper. In the Han Dynasty (206 B.C.–A.D. 220) these seals were used to make impressions in clay. By the T'ang Dynasty (618–907), when paper documents were common, the seals were dipped in ink to print images.

As early as A.D. 175, the Confucian classics, inscribed in stone, were used in a primitive version of printing. Soft paper was mashed into the text, and ink was rolled across the back of the sheet. The script thus appeared as white letters on a black background. Hordes of the devout could sometimes be seen "making exact copies," the Chinese phrase for stone rubbing.

But stone was expensive, difficult to carve, and not exactly portable. Instead, a text could be drawn on paper, the paper pasted on a plank of wood, and an artisan could carve away the space between letters. The resulting woodblock was then inked, a clean sheet was laid across it, and it was rubbed with a fine brush. There are single sheets—votive pieces, charms, and indulgences—that predate the *Diamond Sutra* by centuries. In about 770, in Japan, Empress Shotoku, in a fit of piety, had a million Buddhist charms printed and distributed.

Clearly, woodblock printing was suited to large projects. In the 10th century, when prime minister Feng Tao ordered a definitive new edition of Confucius, he turned to the new technology. It took 21 years to carve the wood for the 130 volumes. For his pains, Feng Tao is remembered as the Gutenberg of China.

The technology had proved its worth. Less than 50 years later, in 972, the *Tripitaka,* the sacred Buddhist canon, was printed. It was a massive, historic undertaking, akin to building the Great Wall or the Pyramids: 5,000 volumes, 130,000 woodblocks.

Movable type, made of baked clay, was invented by Pi Sheng between 1041 and 1049. Pi Sheng set his type in a sort of iron chase, always keeping two forms in action, one for pulling prints and one for typesetting. Over the next two centuries, tin and wood types followed earthenware type, but the method was destined to falter. China had no printing press; each image was always hand-rubbed, whether from woodblock or movable type. And then there was Chinese itself, a language with some 40,000 ideographic characters.

Fortunately, that did not apply to Korea, which had a more restricted alphabet. The first type foundry was built in Korea in 1392, an experiment that consumed all the bronze in that country. But books were being printed there by 1403. From there the idea spread to Japan, which also had a short alphabet of just 50 characters. From its high-water mark in Korea, printing from movable type also spread back to China, but it was never a success. By the 19th century, woodblocks were again the dominant medium in the entire Far East.

In India, where the Buddhism that originally drove China in the direction of woodblock printing originated, people remained loyal to the manuscript. The subcontinent depended on books of bark and palm leaf—long, thin volumes held together by cords, resembling Venetian blinds. This tradition was so strong that even after the introduction of printing, bookmakers still left space for cord holes. Muslims introduced the making of paper to India, a secret they pried from a group of Chinese captives in 751.

From the beginning, Indian books were celebrated for the richness and quality of their illustrations. Among the most popular stories in the history of the subcontinent is the *Ramayana,* the Sanskrit epic of Rama, the ideal man. The narrative tells of his love for Sita, of her abduction to Lanka, and her rescue. The story has been told throughout South Asia since 300 B.C.

Remarkably, India rejected the block printing common in Buddhist China and Nepal for over a thousand years. It was not until 1556 that printing came to India, and when it did, it came via Europe—namely, the Jesuit mission in Goa. Religious books, however, were not the Jesuits' only product. By 1563, they had contributed to the history of science with Garcia da Orta's *Coloquios dos Simples e drogas,* the first textbook on the botany and medicine of India.

The priests soon adapted their publishing operations to accommodate India's many languages. This included designing and casting new typefaces and training local craftspeople in composition, press work, proofing, and binding. It also occasioned the first modern work in the languages of India, beginning with English Jesuit Thomas Stephens's grammar of the Konkani dialect (1640), the first linguistics book printed in India.

In 1798, the Parsee community in Bombay printed the first book made for and by Indians. The *Khurdah Avesta* was their ancient, sacred text, and was printed in Pahlavi, their traditional Indo-European tongue, using a new Gujarati typeface that was designed by two Parsee compositors. It was a great undertaking, completed, ironically, by pressmen whose apprenticeships reflected two centuries of missionary and colonial control. A big first step. Over the next century and a half, printing would spread throughout India, uniting diverse cultures and making them all "people of the book."

Manuscript books flourished in India well after the Chinese and Koreans had taken the first steps to industrialize printing—though not as successfully as in Europe. On these pages, splendid illumination testifies to the excellence of Hindu bookmaking. Below, in a miniature painting from a 12th-century monastery in Bihar, the enthroned Buddha assumes a posture that stresses his role as religious mentor. Opposite, in a 17th-century copy of the Ramayana, *the monkey-general Hanuman brings healing herbs to revive his weary troops.*

ILLUMINATING THE DARK AGES

T'S KNOWN AS A GIRDLE BOOK. THE leather on its covers and spine smothers it like a great monk's cowl, the excess hide gathered up into a topknot. In turn, the knot slips under your belt, leaving the book dangling upside down at your waist, its words poised to console or inspire. This was the book as *vade mecum*, the perfect traveling companion for a pilgrimage through the countryside or through life itself. ❡ Either way, what a long journey it was: the Middle Ages lasted more than a thousand years, a span of time twice as long as that between the high Renaissance and today. The period starts with the fall of the Western Roman Empire in A.D. 476 and ends with the advent of the Renaissance in the 15th century. ❡ Most of what we know of medieval life and thought comes from manuscripts, not from archaeology or artifacts. The period took its identity from these texts, even from the very beginning, when it inherited two bookish gifts from late-classical times. The first of these was the codex, the book of bound pages rather than a scroll, which was widely available by the fall of Rome. The codex made books cheaper, more portable, and thus more dangerous to the status quo. ❡ The second gift from the classical world was Anicius Manlius Severinus Boethius (480–525), a thinker, a Latin translator of Greek philosophy, and a Roman politician who served in the senate under the first Gothic emperor, Theodoric. Boethius achieved all a man could ask—power, wealth, fame—and then lost it in an instant. Accused of treason, he languished in prison without his books for several months and was brutally executed. He spent his last days wisely, writing the most influential and widely translated book—

Depicted in a 14th-century manuscript by the Dominican friar Nicholas Trivet, medieval Roman scholar, theologian, and statesman Boethius holds his great work De consolatione philosophiae (The Consolation of Philosophy) *as he awaits execution in 524. His* Consolation, *an eloquent argument for a faith in a* summum bonum, *or "highest good," became the most widely read book, excepting the Vulgate Bible, of medieval times. At left, from the late-15th century in Italy, an initial I from Pliny the Elder's* Natural History.

excepting the Bible—available in the Middle Ages, *The Consolation of Philosophy*.

It's easy to uncover the book's value: it offers a message of hope in a cruel world. Boethius is visited in his cell by the goddess "Reason," who explains how injustice, misfortune, and deceit seem to control the world. Why? Because people forget that goodness and love are valuable in and of themselves, not just as insurance for success. People, that is, stop reasoning, and reason is what distinguishes humanity from beasts. Moreover, says Reason, books and ideas are our foremost guides: "I seek not so much a library with its walls ornamented with ivory and glass as the storeroom of your mind, in which I have laid up not books, but what makes them of any value, the opinions set down in my books in times past."

Part of *Consolation's* popularity came from its seductive form, in which long passages of hard-nosed, didactic philosophy are sweetened with poetry:

> *Phoebus sinks under western waves*
> *But by a secret path again*
> *He turns his car*
> *To his accustomed rising.*
> *Each thing seeks its own way back*
> *And coming back is glad;*
> *None is consigned to any ordered course*
> *Save that which links the end to the beginning*
> *And makes the cycle firm.*

Such verse makes it all take wing, like opera: the weary mind relaxes, the heart soars. It's not certain that Boethius was a Christian, but his book embraced one of the hallmarks of the faith, an active acceptance of the rigors and trials of life. His message was eagerly adopted by the entire Christian intellectual world. In essence, the point of view was singular: fortune is most true when she is most cruel. Her symbol was her wheel, on which we all ride, constantly exalted and humbled in turn. Whatever rises must fall.

Because *Consolation* explained and justified the world, and into the bargain offered solace, it went through countless translations. In England, it was paraphrased by two monarchs, King Alfred in the ninth century and Queen Elizabeth I in the 16th. Chaucer's translation, *Boece,* is so important that the rest of his poetry cannot be understood without a firm grounding in Boethius.

The Beinecke Rare Book and Manuscript Library at Yale University has a 15th-century Boethius in the form of a girdle book, its clever medieval binding offering proof that a thousand years after they were written his ideas remained indispensable.

A.D. 480 was a good year. It gave us not only Boethius but also Benedict. If Boethius produced a philosophy for the Middle Ages, then Benedict produced its bread and cheese, a way of dealing with the everyday. As a young man, Benedict sought refuge from the decaying Roman empire. He took to the foothills of Abruzzi, east of Rome, where he lived in a cave, dressed in skins, and ate only enough to keep himself alive.

Swathed in leather and suspended from medieval belts, girdle books, such as this 15th-century copy of Boethius, above, enabled traveling clerics and scholars to keep their manuscripts close at hand. The Benedictine monastery of Saint-Martin-du-Canigou, opposite (top), founded near the precipitous summit of Mount Canigou in the French Pyrenees about the year 1000, typifies the isolated, self-contained medieval monastic community. Many of these communities were based on the "Plan of St. Gall," opposite (bottom), an architectural scheme created by an anonymous Benedictine about 820.

The eremitical lifestyle of the monastic hermit, however, was fraught with hazards, not the least of which was pride, as frenzied monks tried to outdo one another in holiness and feats of self-denial. Instead, Benedict was drawn to the life of the cenobitic monks, self-contained communities of spirit in which peace and harmony as well as food and shelter were the goals.

The order Benedict founded, the Benedictines, was the most successful of all time. In large measure, that success is due to a book, the *Regula monachorum,* or *Rule of Monks.* For the last 15 centuries, groups of monks following the *Rule* have had a chapter of it read to them every day as they gathered for meals.

Moderation is the key, according to this 12,000-word manuscript. Benedict's monks were to eat a proper diet; too much fasting, he saw, led only to lethargy, not godliness. They were to avoid the meat of quadrupeds but could eat poultry on feast days and were allowed one glass of wine a day. "It is better to drink wine with measure than water with hubris," remarked one early commentator.

Monks were expected to spend a good portion of each day reading. For that, they needed manuscripts, and this resulted in the creation of the scriptorium, a writing room where all kinds of literature, secular and divine, were copied for both immediate and future use. Over the years, monks in monasteries stretching from Byzantium to the Outer Hebrides managed to copy out the entire body of classical and medieval literature. They also developed the style of calligraphy that led to cursive writing. And Benedictine ideas emerging from Benedictine scriptoria were a powerful force in early medieval art, architecture, urban planning, education, music, drama, and science.

It was not just the life of the mind that the monks cultivated: their monasteries employed vast numbers of tenant farmers and shepherds and crafts-people. These workers lived efficiently and productively, and it was in this environment that the economics of large-scale agricultural enterprises began.

About 820, an anonymous Benedictine created "the Plan of St. Gall," named after the Swiss monastery where the document has resided since the ninth century. The work is a table-sized architectural scheme that was the paradigm for countless medieval monastic establishments. Historian David Knowles once said that you could drop a blind monk from a monastery in Northumbria into a cloister in Italy and he could easily find his way about.

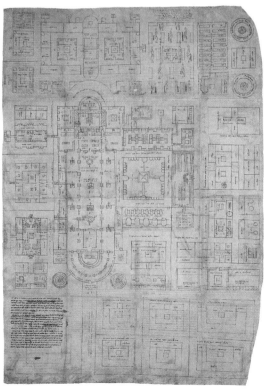

The plan was sketched on five pieces of vellum that were sewn together to make a single sheet 44 inches across. Drawn to scale on a site 640 feet by 480 feet are some 40 monastic buildings, which could house about 120 monks and 170 serfs. A careful hand has annotated the whole with such comments and instructions as "AB ORIENTE IN OCCIDENTE[M] LONGIT[UDO] PED[UM] CC" ("from east to west [this nave is] 200 feet long") and "Between these columns measure ten feet." Around the circular henhouse runs the legend "Here is established the care for the chickens and their perpetual nourishment."

In the 12th century, an anonymous scribe composed a *Life of St. Martin* on the back of this large sheet. Unfortunately, his tale ran too long, and he turned the page over and erased—that is, scraped the ink off—the building on the plan where visiting knights and nobles were housed. The document was then folded

An exquisitely carved 10th-century ivory book cover depicts Pope Gregory I the Great (540–604) composing a text as three scribes copy it for wider dissemination. Venerated as a people's pope and a leader in Christianizing Europe, Gregory believed strongly in monasticism and in Benedictine monastic principles in particular. Monasteries were the power center of books in the Middle Ages. A sequence of decorated letters, opposite, from the Hamburg Bible (1255), illustrates some of the steps in the preparation of parchment, animal skin that was the writing material of choice during this era. At top, a secular parchment maker (left) sells his wares to a monk, identified by his cowl and halo. Between them lie a frame upon which a hide is being stretched and a round scraper used to remove hair. At center, a monk cuts and prepares to rule a sheet of parchment. With the aid of compass and stylus, the monk at bottom divides up space and draws lines.

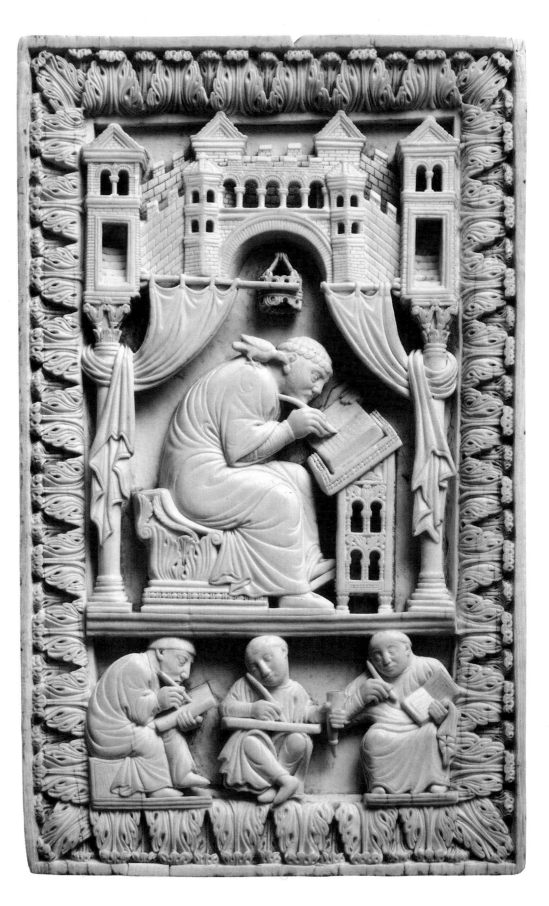

and refolded until it was reduced to the size of a small volume, and placed on a library shelf. Here it remained until its rediscovery in the 19th century.

The nucleus of the plan, as is the case for every monastery, was the church. On the north side of the church was the scriptorium, a long room with seven desks (two monks to a desk) and seven windows. These windows admitted flat northern light, the ideal of every artist since time began and one that was critical to the fine details required by the illuminated manuscript.

Like most art forms, however, illumination and calligraphy had their own special pains. Wrote one scribe in the margin of an eighth-century text: "Writing is excessive drudgery. It crooks your back, dims your sight, twists your stomach and your sides. Three fingers write, but the whole body labors." But another scribe maintained that "To copy books is better than to ditch the vines: the second serves the belly, but the first the mind."

Scribes worked essentially in the same way as from the beginning. You can see them in most portraits of saints at their writing desks, such as the evangelists or Jerome, whose great feat was translating holy scripture from Greek into the Latin Vulgate. His writing desk usually has both books on it, as well as his inkstand, pen, and knife.

These last were part of a scribe's basic equipment, which also included a quill pen, often made from the primary wing feathers of a goose. A knife was used to slice off the quill end obliquely, exposing the hollow canal inside, which through capillary action became a sort of ink reservoir. The knife then carved a broad edge on the pen, which in turn gave the writing thick or thin strokes, depending on the direction the pen was pushed or pulled. Before writing could begin, however, a tiny slit had to be cut in the tip to allow ink to flow whenever pressure on the page opened the slit.

Scribes used both knife and pen constantly. Portraits show them holding the uneven parchment pages down with the knife in their left hand while writing with the pen in their right. Another reason for holding the page steady at knife-edge was to avoid transferring the natural oils from fingers to sheet.

Medieval ink, commonly called "iron-gall," was made from a mixture of tannin, which was obtained from nutgalls, and iron sulphate. Pale in the inkwell, it darkened on the page. It appears to have been used as early as the famous *Codex Sinaiticus* of the fourth century A.D. The alchemy of mixing ink was a delicate one: a poorly executed recipe could result in an ink that would eat into the page. In earlier times, the Chinese, Egyptians, and Romans had refined the use of carbon black for writing ink. In the medieval period, this was sometimes added to iron-gall to make a very dense ink that stood up on the page.

The most important component of the medieval book was parchment, a generic name for animal skin that is cured and used for manuscripts. Technically, parchment was prepared from sheepskin or goatskin and vellum from calfskin, but the terms were interchangeable. After the hides were cured and rubbed smooth, the resulting oblong membranes were cut in the shape of double pages that could be bound into a book through their folds. These sheets, called bifolia, still betray their humble origins in that they have a smooth side, on which

the hair has been rubbed off, and a rough side. And books today take the shape they do—slightly taller than they are wide—because of the way two, four, or eight leaves can be cut out of a hide, leaving a minimum of waste. Even after the invention of printing, the book's shape would remain the same, the new technology copying the best of the old.

Because parchment is a natural material, it took a great deal of skill to write around its flaws and holes. Even the most experienced calligrapher made mistakes, and these mistakes help us understand the workings of the scriptoria. Often we see another hand on the sheet, that of a proofreader patrolling the margins, clucking with superiority. Sometimes the correcting hand belongs to the rubricator, a skilled artisan whose steady hand would insert the great "red-letter" initials or special words in the text.

If a copyist noticed a mistake he put a series of fine dots under the offending word and then continued with his text. This avoided the creation of a horrific black cross-out, which would spoil the normal density of the letters on the page. Mistakes commonly occurred when the scribe was interrupted and then cast his eye forward or backward to a word similar to the one he had just finished. Christopher de Hamel, an expert in medieval manuscripts, says this usually happened when the scribe lifted his pen from the page for more ink (scribes tried to do a single sentence with each refill). The result was a skipped or repeated line, a mistake commonly made by typists today.

Corrections are more common in Bibles than in books of hours, prayer books that usually were made by secular booksellers for wealthy patrons. De Hamel believes this is because the Bibles were actually read, most often by clerics who would note and annotate scribal errors.

During the reign of Charlemagne (742–814) the great Carolingian scripts were developed. When Charlemagne needed help consolidating his world, he turned to the intellectual capital of Europe, the north of England, a land celebrated for the books emanating from its monasteries. From York, in 781, he brought the monk Alcuin to his court and charged him with educating a vast bureaucracy for his empire. Monks and monasteries were at the heart of this effort, as were the scripts that Alcuin helped devise.

Carolingian capital letters, called uncials (from the Latin meaning "an inch high"), were derived from Roman inscriptions. They were used in some of the most beautiful and legible texts ever written, but they required so many lifts of the pen that they were slow and tedious. The next development, called half-uncial, had elegance and pace but was still too slow.

Despite their drawbacks these scripts served Europe well for nearly 500 years. When the humanist scholars of the early Renaissance in Italy began poring over the discarded remains of monastic libraries, they were stunned by the beauty of the writing they found, especially in the Carolingian minuscules, or lowercase letters. From them Renaissance scholars developed a hand that avoided the constant pen lifts required by the earlier styles, a cursive hand that would evolve into several styles, such as italic and chancery cursive.

The humanist Renaissance adopted the letter forms of the Carolingian minuscules and emphasized that the letters in any word should be connected and tilted about eight degrees off vertical. For legibility, each italic letter was given a distinct but simple shape. The Gothic manuscripts, by contrast, used the same pen stroke for many letters, and thus a word like "minimum," with its unrelieved parade of vertical strokes, was almost impossible to read.

For a number of political and economic reasons, monasteries and their scriptoria declined in the 13th century. It's a sad tale: in 1297 at the illustrious St. Gall, not even the prior could write. Instead, the great age of commercial manuscript production had begun. Books had become a big industry, and there

A hollow, jeweled bust of Charlemagne, opposite (top), king of the Franks (768–814) and emperor of the Roman Empire (800–814), was crafted about 1350 to hold fragments of his skull. Charlemagne united and presided over an empire that stretched from the Baltic to the Mediterranean, and, though illiterate himself, sparked an intellectual and cultural renaissance. He engaged the Anglo-Saxon scholar Alcuin of York to serve as master of the palace school at Aachen and later as abbot of St. Martin at Tours, site of one of the most celebrated Carolingian scriptoria. An illustrated page from the Grandval Bible, left, written at Tours around 840, displays the revolutionary Carolingian script inspired by Alcuin. The beauty and clarity of the writing contrast with both an eighth-century Merovingian script, opposite (center), and a heavy Gothic or black-letter hand of the 13th century.

was no lack of scribes: the colophons of Western European manuscripts identify some 23,774 scribes and illuminators by name.

Most scribes had been trained in the universities or had once taken holy orders, but their income was dependent on a large demand for legible books, both sacred and secular. The ability to read and write Latin among the clergy was a holdover from the time of Alcuin. Reading the 51st Psalm in Latin was proof that one was in holy orders and so was exempt from criminal prosecution in civil courts. Ben Jonson, Shakespeare's friend, once used his classical training in this way to escape punishment for manslaughter after a duel. In America this legal device survived into the 18th century.

Fortunately, even in the heyday of the monastic scriptoria, not all their output was directed purely at the soul's needs. History, literature, science, law, politics, and even poetry also came from hands and hearts trained in the monastic

The increasing enrollment of students in cathedral schools and universities during the Middle Ages raised the demand for books. In a miniature, above, from a 14th-century manuscript, Henry of Germany delivers a lecture to students at a university in Bologna, perhaps Europe's oldest. Opposite, a page of medical text from Liber regimenti acutorum, *a late-13th-century translation of a work by Hippocrates, features marginal notes, or glosses, and a miniature depicting two physicians discussing a patient.*

...nde þa gyt hie him asetton segen

denne heah ofer heafod leton holm be

geafon on gar secg him þæs geomor sefa

murnende mod men ne cunnon secgan

soðe sele rædenne hæleð under heofen

hwa þæm hlæste onfeng

.I.

ÐA wæs on burgum beowulf scyl dinga beo

leod cyning longe þrage folcum gefræ

geþæder ellor hwearf aldor of eaþ de

oþ þ him eft onwoc heah healf dene heold

þenden lifde gamol 7 guð reouw glæde scyl

dingas ðæm feower bearn forð gerimed in

worold wocun weoro da ræswa heoro gar 7

hroð gar 7 halga til hyrde ic þ elan cwe

heaðo scilfingas heals gebedda þa wæs hroð

gare here sped gyfen wiges weorð mynd þ

him his wine magas georne hyrdon oðð þ

seo geog oð geweox mago driht micel h

on mod be arn þ hy sæl reced hatan wolde

way. We owe the survival of the most important Old English poem, *Beowulf,* to the monk who copied it down in the beginning of the 11th century, though it had likely circulated in oral form—recited over and over again by generations of Anglo-Saxon singer-poets called scops—for two or three centuries.

Another cleric gave us the *Domesday Book,* whose title had everything to do with collecting taxes in the newly acquired kingdom of William the Conquerer and little to do with the day of reckoning, or doom—except that its tax judgments were said to be as irreversible as Judgment Day. The land William won in 1066 was large and unruly and needed a thorough listing of property, buildings, and livestock. A traveling commission collected the data, but a single cleric copied it all down—including 13,400 place names and all manner of information about the people who lived there—and completed it within 20 years of the Battle of Hastings.

But it was an earlier English King, Alfred the Great (849–899), the translator of Boethius's *Consolation,* among other works, who did the most for English scholarship. He commissioned a standard year-by-year history of England from its beginnings up to his reign. The basic text was copied out at numerous monasteries, which were then to continue the accounts by entering the events of each year even to the edge of doom. The result, the *Anglo-Saxon*

The scribal labors of medieval monks preserved secular as well as religious literature: opposite, a page from the earliest known manuscript of Beowulf, *the great Anglo-Saxon epic poem, transcribed by a monk about the year 1000. Thought to have been composed between 700 and 750, the story relates the exploits of the Scandinavian hero Beowulf. The beautifully embroidered Bayeux Tapestry, below, records the Norman Conquest of England by the forces of William the Conqueror in 1066. In this panel, the Norman cavalry clashes with English foot soldiers at Hastings.*

A page from a 13th-century Bible, right, by William of Devon features a decorative border of animal and human grotesques, or drolleries, a style of manuscript illumination that flourished from the 13th through the mid-14th centuries. Lively imaginations also seized upon the tall tales of travelers to create the monstrous foreign races illustrated in a 12th-century Crusader's handbook, below.

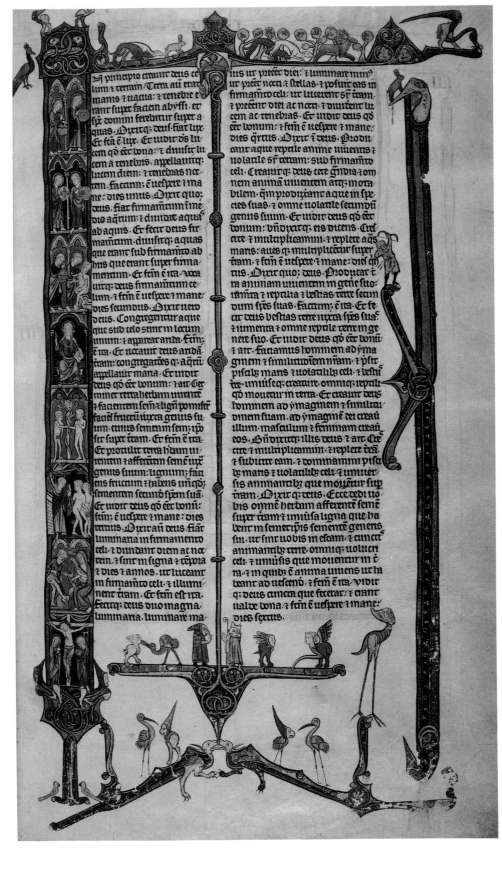

Chronicle—written in Old English rather than Latin—was a valiant effort, finally running out of steam in 1154. The *Chronicle* survives in seven versions and contains such dramatic pieces as *The Battle of Brunanburh,* a poem about a conflict in the year 937; the first short story in English (755); and an account of the arrival of the dreaded Vikings—with 350 warships—at the mouth of the Thames in 851.

The medieval cleric loved to interpret and to draw morals from the natural world. In fabulously illustrated books known as bestiaries, the animals instruct humankind. The ant, for instance, stores up corn (but not barley!) against winter, reminding us that we should stash away good for our wintertime of death.

Ironically, it was the burgeoning availability of books that tended to erode their authority. Contradictions and inconsistencies became more visible. Under closer and closer inspection by more and more people, the frailty of the answers to be found in books was becoming manifest. It became clear that if you wanted to find out about nature, you went outdoors, not to the books. The scientific method was on its way, making early and furtive appearances in philosophical

The first elephant to be seen in England, this "magister bestie" was "drawn from life" by Benedictine monk and historian Matthew Paris in 1255 and featured in his Chronica Majora. *The elephant was a gift from French King Louis IX to England's Henry III. Paris included the animal's keeper, Henricus de Flor, so that "the dimensions of the beast here figured may be imagined."*

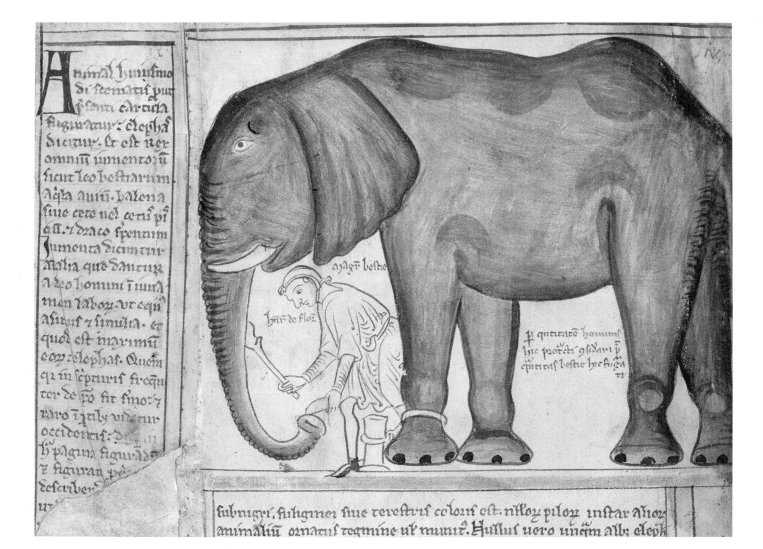

Therfore lordynges alle I yow biseche
If that yow thynke I varie as in my speche
As thus though that I telle somwhat moore
Of prouerbes than ye han herd bifore
Comprehended in this litel tretys heere
To enforce with theffect of my mateere
And though I nat the same wordes seye
As ye han herd yet to yow alle I preye
Blameth me nat for as in my sentence
Shul ye nowher fynden difference
Fro the sentence of this tretys lyte
After the which this murye tale I wryte
And therfore herkneth what that I shal seye
And lat me tellen al my tale I preye

¶ Explicit

Heere bigynneth Chaucers tale of Melibee

A yong man called Melibeus myghty and riche bigat
vp on his wyf that called was Prudence a doghter
which that called was Sophie. Vp on a day bifel
that for his desport is went in to the feldes hym to pleye
his wyf and eek his doghter hath he left in with his hous of which
the dores weren faste yshette. Thre of hise olde foes han it espyed
and setten laddres to the walles of his hous and by wyndowes
been entred And betten his wyf and wounded his doghter with
fyue mortal woundes in fyue sondry places. This is to seyn in
hir feet. in hir handes. in hir erys. in hir nose. and in hir mouth
and leften hir for deed and wenten awey ¶ Whan Melibeus re
torned was in to his hous and saugh al this meschief. he lyk a
mad man rentynge his clothes gan to wepe and crie. And the ¶ Prude
ce his wyf as ferforth as she dorste bisoghte hym of his wepyng
for to stynte but nat for thy he gan to crie and wepen euere lenger
the moore ¶ This noble wyf Prudence remembred hir vp on the
sentence of Ouide in his book that cleped is the remedie of loue
where as he seith. He is a fool that destourbeth the mooder to wepen in
the deeth of hir child til she haue wept hir fille as for a certein
tyme And thanne shal man doon his diligence with amyable
wordes hir to reconforte and preyen hir of hir wepyng for to
stynte After which resoun this noble wyf Prudence suffred hir
housbonde for to wepe and crie as for a certein space and whan
she saugh hir tyme she seyde hym in this wise Allas my
lord quod she why make ye yowre self for to be lyk a fool for so
that it apperteneth nat to a wys man to maken swich a sorwe yow

Geoffrey Chaucer himself makes an appearance in the magnificent 1410 Ellesmere manuscript of The Canterbury Tales, *opposite, the most sumptuously decorated—and reliable—manuscript of this classic. Also from the* Tales, *one of the most important works of early English literature, is a much-married pilgrim, the Wife of Bath, above. Left, an illustration from the 14th-century* Sir Gawain and the Green Knight. *In this dream-like image, the Green Knight's wife pays a secret visit to the bedside of the sleeping Sir Gawain.*

tomes by the mysterious Oxford monk Roger Bacon as early as the 13th century.

Not surprisingly, art played a role in the advancement of science. The medieval historian Matthew Paris, a monk working at St. Albans near London, actually drew a portrait of a real elephant in the menagerie of Henry III and included it in one of his chronicles. Literature, too, began to be illustrated. The great manuscripts of two major English writers of the 14th century—Chaucer and the Gawain-poet—are illustrated. The Ellesmere Chaucer, once owned by Sir Thomas Egerton, or Baron Ellesmere, and now in the Huntington Library in San Marino, California, contains portraits of the 22 pilgrims—and Chaucer himself—on the road to Canterbury.

Four poems written by the Gawain-poet—*Pearl, Patience, Purity,* and *Sir Gawain and the Green Knight*—survive in a single volume in the British Library

A scene depicting Christ's Ascension decorates the interior of an initial C from the ninth-century Drogo Sacramentary, *right. The shift from monastic to secular book production near the end of the Middle Ages sometimes is revealed in the content of illuminations. A decoration of an initial M, opposite, from Jean Miélot's* Miroir de la Salvation Humaine *(1448–1449), is devoid of religious overtones.*

and are accompanied by realistic illustrations, such as those of Gawain feigning sleep as the beautiful temptress comes to his bed and of Pearl's brokenhearted father staring across the magic river toward heaven.

As the demand for illustrated books increased, it caused seismic changes in the way books were produced. The distinction between scribes and craftsmen who decorated books was increasing, and over time the latter were to become more important. Modern art, it could be said, began in the scriptorium in the work of rubricators, who added fancy initial letters, usually in red ink, to the text; of illuminators, who applied gold leaf, silver, or colored paint to the page; and of miniaturists, who peppered each page with flowers and grotesques and painted historiated initials—big letters containing portraits and landscapes.

By the 15th century, the production of illuminated books of hours for wealthy patrons had become the most profitable side of the book trade. Elaborately decorated with miniature paintings, these prayer books were based on the canonical hours, times set aside during the day for devotions. They also featured calendars of saints' days, prayers for the dead, and selected psalms.

The best of these were sumptuous books, prized as jewels from the beginning. As a result, many survive today. But were they read? Judging from the ab-

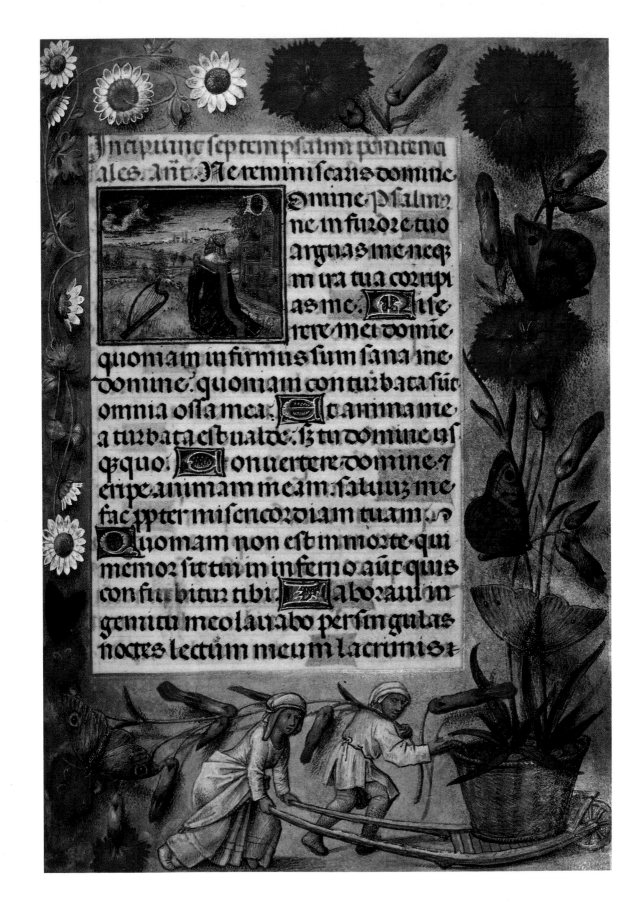

Illustrations in books of hours and other
medieval books provide vignettes both
elegant and simple of life in that era.
A gardener assists his wife in moving a
large, red carnation plant, opposite, in a
depiction from a Flemish book of hours
(c. 1500); the January calendar of the
Trés Riches Heures du Duc de
Berry, left, portrays the opulent lifestyle
of the duke (seated at the table) and his
wealthy guests, while, at top, a luxurious, horse-drawn wagon, the mode of
travel for the ruling class, adorns the text
of the Luttrell Psalter (c. 1335-1340),
and, above, the eternal cat-and-mouse
game, also from the Luttrell Psalter.

Sign of the times: the owner of the breviary above, which dates back to about the year 1400, hollowed out a space inside the front cover to hold his spectacles. The invention of eyeglasses in the 14th century illuminated a world of detail for medieval readers. And detail both secular and religious abounds in this page from the Urbino Bible, opposite, crafted for Federigo da Montefeltro, Duke of Urbino, from 1476 to 1478. The large miniature depicts the children of Israel entering Egypt, and a surrounding floral border holds six medallions with scenes relating to the life of Moses.

sence of scribal corrections in them, such books were perhaps less perused than possessed, serving as portable art galleries that showed status more than piety.

The growing profusion of detail in both art and text demanded an invention that in the next century would improve clarity of vision. This invention was spectacles, which enabled people to read to a much more advanced age and enabled bookmakers to do fine work as well as to cram more and more on every page. On February 23, 1306, Friar Giordano da Rivalto noted in a sermon in Florence "It is not yet twenty years since there was found the art of making eyeglasses, which make for good vision, one of the best arts and most necessary the world has.... I have seen the man who first invented and created it and I have talked to him."

By 1352, spectacles were common enough to appear in art—namely in Modena, Italy, in a portrait of Hugh of Provence, a cardinal who had died almost a century earlier. Hugh is shown at his desk copying a holy book, happily at work and prayer.

HAEC SVNT NOMINA

filioꝝ iſrł̉ qui ingreſſi ſunt in egyptũ cùm Iacob
ſinguli cũ domib, ſuiſ introieruͭt Ruben: Syme
on: Leui: Iudaſ: yſachar: zabulon et Beniamin:
Dan: et Neptalim: Gad: et Aſer: Erant igitur
omneſ animę eoꝝ q̉ egreſſi ſuͭt de femore Iacob
ſeptuagita Ioſeph auté in egypto erat: Quo
mortuo et uniuerſiſ fⁱib, eiuſ: omniq̉, cognatio
ne ſua: filiiſ iſrł̉ creueruͭt et quaſi germinanteſ
multiplicati ſt̃: ac roborati nimiſ impleueruͭt
terrã Surrexit interea rex nouuſ ſuper egyptũ
qui ignorabat Ioſeph: Et ait ad p̃p͛lm ſuũ: Ec
ce populuſ filioꝝ iſrael mltuſ et fortior nobiſ é
Venite ſapienter opprimamuſ eũ: ne forte mul
tiplicetur: et ſi ingruerit contra noſ bellũ: ad
datur n̄r̃iſ inimiciſ: expugnatiſq̉, nobiſ egredi
atur de terra: Prepoſuit itaq̉, magiſtroſ operũ
ut affligereͭt eoſ oneribⁱ: edificaueruͭt q̉, urbeſ
tabernaculoꝝ Pharaoni Phiton: et Rameſſeſ
quãtoq̉, opprimebant eoſ: tanto magiſ multi
plicabaͭtur: et creſcebat: Oderantq̉, filioſ iſrł̉
egyptij: et affligebaͭt illudenteſ eiſ: atq̉, ad a
maritudinẽ perducebant uitã eoꝝ operibus
duriſ luti: et lateriſ: omniq̉, famulatu quo in
terrę opⁱbuſ premebaͭtur: Dixit auté rex e
gypti obſtetricibuſ hebreoꝝ: quaꝝ una uoca
batur Sephora: altera Phua: precipienſ eiſ: Qñ

obſtetricabitiſ hebreaſ: et partuſ tẽpuſ aduene
rit ſi maſculuſ fuerit interficite eũ: ſi femina
reſeruate: Timueruͭt obſtetriceſ deũ: et nõ
fecerut iuxta preceptũ regiſ egypti: ſed con
ſeruabãt mareſ: Quibⁱ ad ſe acceſſitiſ rex ait
quid nã eſt hoc quod facere uoluiſtiſ ut pueⁱoſ
ſeruaretiſ: Quę r̃iderut: Non ſũt hebreeſ ſi
cut egyptie muliereſ: ipſe enim obſtetricãdi
hent ſcientiã: et priuſq̉, ueniamuſ ad eaſ pa
riuͭt: Bene ergo fecit deuſ obſtetricibⁱ: Et cre
uit p̃p͛luſ cõfortatuſq̉, eſt nimiſ: Et qa timue
ruͭt obſtetriceſ deũ: edificauit illiſ domoſ: Pre
cepit auté Pharao omni p̃p͛lo ſuo dicenſ: Q̉cq̉d
maſculini ſexuſ natũ fuerit: in flumé proicite:
q̉cq̉d femini reſeruate: · CII ·
Greſſuſ eſt poſt hec uir de domo leui: accepta
uxore ſtⁱpiſ ſue: q̉ cõcepit et peperit filium:
Et uidéſ eum elegãte: abſcõdit menſibⁱ tribⁱ
cũq̉, iam celare non poſſet: ſumpſit fiſcelam
ſcⁱrpeã: et liniuit eã bitumie ac pice: poſu
it q̉ intuſ infantulũ: et expoſuit eũ in carec
to fluminiſ ſtãte procul ſorore eiuſ: et cõ
deraͭte euentũ rei: Ecce auté deſcẽdebat fi
lia Pharaoniſ ut lauaretur in flumine: et pu
elle eiuſ gradiebãtur p̃ crepidiné alueї: Quę
cũ uidiſſet fiſcellã in papirione miſit unã de

The Irish are nothing if not humorous. This is especially true of the medieval Irish scribes, those cultural warriors who so selflessly labored away in the remotest reaches of the British Isles, meticulously copying and preserving texts of Greek and Latin literature, philosophy, science, and theology. For more than 500 years they braved numbing isolation and, after the eighth century, the constant threat of Viking raids. It must have seemed like the edge of doom.

Still, they saved humanity by the skin of our teeth; into the bargain, they were very human. They liked cats. The *Lindisfarne Gospels,* the powerful illuminated manuscript that contains the earliest Gospels in English, also has the loveliest cat on its pages—in a feline border with images of birds braided into its back.

Another scribe once paused in his serious thought to write a few Irish lines on his favorite pet, a mouser named Pangur:

Pangur is proof the arts of cats
And men are in alliance;
His mind is set on catching rats,
And mine on snaring science.

I make my book, the world forgot,
A kind of endless class-time;
My hobby Pangur envies not—
He likes more childish pastime.

Caught in his diplomatic net,
A mouse jumps down his gullet;
And sometimes I can half-way get
A problem when I mull it.

Today, the books these men produced are known as "insular" manuscripts because they were produced not on the Continent but in the British Isles by missionary monks and scholars. The monks had been sent there to spread Christianity to the "western" lands and in so doing took with them a love for Mediterranean culture. The medium of transmission was Latin, the tongue of the Church and of all European intellectual life.

In the British Isles monks gathered in many centers, but none was more famous than the monastery and scriptorium founded on the island of Iona, off the west coast of Scotland, under the direction of St. Columba (521–597). The combination of piety and scholarship that Columba started on Iona would transform the Celtic north and the north of England into the intellectual center of the Western cosmos, brighter than anything else in Europe at the time. Its light would shine until it was snuffed out by the Vikings in the ninth century.

That grand illumination still glows today in the *Book of Kells,* a sumptuous codex of the four Gospels completed about the year 800 and associated with the monastery of Kells near Dublin. In addition to its glorious decoration, it carries a practical monastic invention called a "canon table"—surely the most beautiful index in book history—which enables readers to compare similar passages in the four Gospels. The walls in Durham Cathedral strongly resemble the decoration of the canon table, with its interlaced arches and columns. Since canon tables are older than the cathedral, the walls are a rare example of architecture following the art of the book.

In the 11th century, the *Book of Kells* was stolen for the sake of its

FROM THE EDGE OF BEYOND

❦ MEDIEVAL GLORIES OF THE BRITISH ISLES

A lavishly decorated canon table from the sumptuous, ninth-century Book of Kells *coordinates parallel passages from the Gospels of Matthew, Mark, and Luke. Above the table appear symbols for the three Evangelists: the man, left, for Matthew; the lion, center, for Mark; and an eagle with a calf's head, right, for Luke.*

William Daniell's *19th-century painting,* The Cathedral at Iona, *above, depicts the ruins of this remote isle, site of the monastery founded* A.D. *563 by Irish missionary Columba. It was from Iona, in Scotland's Inner Hebrides, that Columba brought Christianity to the people of northern England. Opposite, the beginning of the* Breves causae, *or summaries, of Matthew, from the* Book of Kells, *which may have been produced at Iona. Overleaf: also from the brilliantly illuminated* Book of Kells, *an eagle (detail, left), symbol of John; and (right) the genealogy of Christ page from the Gospel of Luke. In the lower-right corner, an artist, brush and palette in hand, appears to be taking a much needed rest.*

golden, jeweled cover, which was savagely torn off along with about 30 of its folios. A note on the reverse of leaf 377 reads: "here lacketh a leafe being y beginnyng of y xvi chapt. of St John." It is followed by a more positive note: "this leaf found 1741." Today the 340-folio manuscript survives at the Library of Trinity College Dublin, a national treasure on a par with our Constitution or the British Crown Jewels.

The *Kells* scribe worked in a script we call "insular majuscule," a script of great orderliness and regularity, consisting of all capitals. It was derived from the handwriting done at Italian and other Continental monastic scrip-

toria and, except for the letters N and G, is very like the Roman alphabet.

The glories of the book are, of course, the opening pages of each Gospel, with their magnificent incipits, and the portraits of the Evangelists. Even obscure passages, Luke 15:10, for example, begin with a riot of curious and fantastic animals—snakes, birds, lions, fish, and dogs—tied up in knots that constitute a few words of Latin. Moreover, the decoration seems to be unconnected with the serious matters in the text. The Christmas story and Good Friday each receive the same playful decoration.

Letters seem deliberately left out of words so their floating insertion above

Natiuitas xpi in bethlem iudse magi munera offerunt
et infantes interficiuntur

8

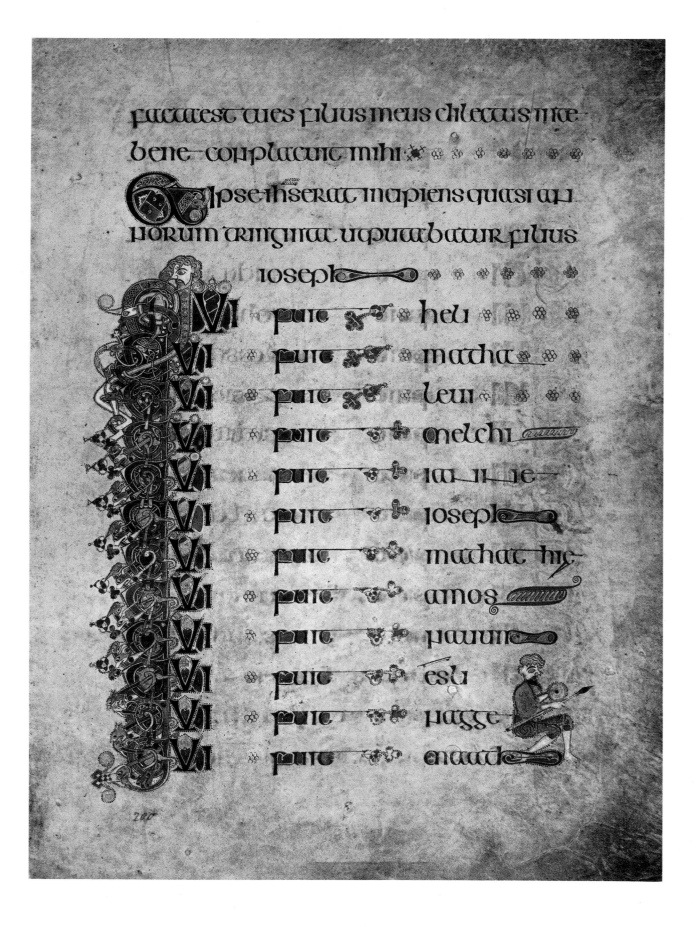

factus est dies filius meus dilectus me

bene complacuit mihi

Ipse ihserat incipiens quasi an

horum triginta ut putabatur filius

ioseph

VII fuit heli

VII fuit matha

VII fuit leui

VII fuit melchi

VII fuit ianne

VII fuit ioseph

VII fuit mathat hic

VII fuit amos

VII fuit nauum

VII fuit esli

VII fuit hagge

VII fuit enauti

Beginning in the eighth century with Viking raids on the British Isles, Celtic motifs found their way into Scandinavian art. Interlace patterns and other details on the animal mace head, above, from the ninth-century Oseberg ship burial in Norway, reflect Irish and Anglo-Saxon influences. Opposite, intricate knotwork and extremely elongated and interwoven birds and beasts adorn the second major decorated initial page—the beginning of the Christmas story—of the Gospel of Matthew from the Lindisfarne Gospels. *Written and decorated at the great monastic scriptorium at Lindisfarne, off the coast of Northumberland in northern England, the* Gospels *was completed* A.D. *698.*

the line can be an excuse for an artist to elaborate the letter into an ornament—an animal or grotesque—of some phantasmagoric kind. Strangely, no gold illuminates the page; orpiment (arsenic trisulphide) is the bright yellow that holds its power even today. The blue is lapis lazuli, which could only have come from Afghanistan in those days, and was as exotic and expensive as gold.

A great many sources have been suggested for the arabesques, interlacings, spirals, and strange flowers and creatures on the pages of *Kells*. They include Celtic and Anglo-Saxon jewelry and stone-carving motifs, Bronze Age artifacts such as the mirror-backs found at Holcombe, England, and runic and Scandinavian designs. The Viking ship-burial treasure discovered at Sutton Hoo in East Anglia is very much in the style of *Kells*. Some scholars have found Byzantine, Islamic, and Coptic influences as well. But no artist had ever weaved them into so unified a whole as the master of *Kells*.

Where was *Kells* made? Tradition associates it with Columba's Iona; the book, which quickly became a holy relic, may have been moved to the more landlocked monastery at Kells in Ireland to safeguard it from the threat of seaborne Viking attack in the ninth century.

But long before this book was written, monks from Iona had begun creating daughter monasteries in the north of England. One of those, on an island called Lindisfarne, off the coast of Northumberland, had a reputation as having the greatest scriptorium in the world. *Kells* could well have come from Lindisfarne, to judge from the

quality of its scribes and scholars—and their books.

Lindisfarne had been founded in 635 by St. Aidan, who had brought to England the austere monasticism of Iona. In 685, a pious man named Cuthbert became bishop of Lindisfarne. Cuthbert was so holy that he often scorned the meager comforts of the monastery to live as a hermit on the Farne Islands, a few tiny rocks in the North Sea. After his death in 687, Cuthbert's body was buried in the Lindisfarne church. When it was exhumed 11 years later, it was said to be perfectly preserved.

Immediately, Lindisfarne became a shrine that attracted pilgrims from afar. They flocked there, patiently waiting on the Northumberland shoreline for the tide to turn each day so they could cross over the dry sands to the little island, its monastery, and its rich collection of books.

The *Lindisfarne Gospels* were completed in 698, possibly as part of the celebration surrounding Cuthbert's saintly reinterment. The book was written by a monk named Eadfrith, who, perhaps because of his skill in producing such a volume, was elevated to the post of bishop of Lindisfarne (698–721). The book is less gaudy than *Kells,* although carpet pages—pages with nothing but interlaced decoration—begin the book and each Gospel. Eadfrith used fanciful, elongated elaborations of real creatures—birds and dog-like quadrupeds—to decorate his text, motifs that reached back into the pre-Christian past of both Celtic and Germanic traditions.

In the 10th century, a monk named Aldred translated the Lindis-

onginneð   godspell   ært   matheus
ÍNCIPIT EUANGELI   um secundum matheu..
                     cníster

ꝥ̅ ꝑ̅
ƕ́ 𝚗 𝚗 ꝺ̅
𝚕̅𝚞 𝚞̅

unꝺ̅lice
ꝑuꞇ ꝑꝁꞃ
cnꝃꝛꝛ cneu
neꞃo

                        ꞃoꝺ lice

AUTE   GE

cꝛnnꝛeccenꝛe ꞇ cnꝁꝑꝛꝛ꞉u   ꝑuꞇ ꝺuꝛ   ꝑꝁꝛ   miꝺ ꝺꝛ

RATIOXILERATCM

ꝑꝁꝛ   bi ꝑoꝛꝛꝛeꝛ ꞇ beboꝺen ꞇ beꝑꝁꞃꞇnuꝺ ꞇ beꞇꝁlꞇ

ꞇoꝛemanne
naller ꞇo hꝁ
bꝁnn e. ꝑꝛꝛ

EXITONBONXAA

moꝺeꝛ   hꝁꞃ

abꝛꝁꞇhꝁn
ꝺe ꝁlꝺonmon
ꝑꝁꞃ inꝺꝁm
ꞇꝛꝺ inhienu
ꞃꝁlem ꝑone
bꝛꝛob. he be
beꝛꝺ mꝁꞃꝁ
ꝛoꝛephꞇ ꞇo
ꞃemenne ꝛ
ꞇobeꝛꝛeonꝛ
ꝁnne miꝺ
clꝁennꝛꝛe

MATTEREIUSMARICUOSEH

The cross motif in the carpet page, opposite, that introduces the Gospel of Matthew in the Lindisfarne Gospels *echoes the shape of a seventh-century Celtic cross, left, on the island of Skellig Michael, Ireland. Medieval monastic communities on such remote insular retreats as Lindisfarne and Skellig Michael produced some of the most magnificently illuminated manuscripts of the era.*

farne text into Old English, carefully inserting the new words in a tight minuscule script between the lines of Latin insular majuscules. This text is important to philologists because it is the earliest English version of the Gospels. These pages also show the evolution of handwriting over three centuries. The insular majuscule has large, curved letters that seem tightly bound between two lines, with only a few ascenders or descenders. The minuscule is far more cursive, has many letters above or below the line, and was much faster to write.

Forty miles to the south of Lindisfarne was another monastic settlement, with twin monasteries at Jarrow and the mouth of the Wear River. The scriptoria there produced the famous *Codex Amiatinus,* a Bible with a detailed portrait of Ezra the scribe at work before his book cabinet and double inkwell (for red and black ink).

The intellectual star of the Wearmouth-Jarrow monasteries, however, was the Venerable Bede, who was asked by Bishop Eadfrith of Lindisfarne to write the biography of St. Cuthbert. Bede (673–735), reckoned the father of English history, is the author of the *Ecclesiastical History of the English People* (731). Although Bede was English, his Celtic training filled him with awe for things Irish. He deferred to them the way the Romans did to the civilization of Greece, and in one case reports on a miracle cure achieved by compounding a medicine from the scrapings from insular holy books.

How persistent is the magic of an Irish book? A thousand years after Bede's report, a 17th-century eyewitness watched in horror as the *Book of Durrow* (680) was dipped in water to make a tonic for a herd of sick cows.

Scribes not only worked on theological and devotional books but also left us important secular works. From Anglo-Saxon monasteries came the bulk of Old English literature, including the only manuscript of *Beowulf,* a work that probably circulated in oral performances by professional entertainers for centuries before it was put on paper by an anonymous monk.

All of Old Irish literature (the oldest vernacular literature in Europe) comes down to us through monastic scriptoria. Perhaps the most influential of these works is *The Tain* (pronounced "Tawn"), a Celtic epic that ranks with the great long narrative poems of Homer and Virgil.

A *tain* is literally a cattle raid, a ritual activity that appears frequently in Irish legend. Although there are a number of versions of *The Tain, Táin Bó Cuailnge (Cattle Raid of Cooley)* is the best known because it introduced the world to the exploits of the hero Cuchulainn (Ka-WHO-lynn), the

Hound of Ulster—a sort of Irish Achilles. Here, for example, is Cuchulainn at work keeping Ulster's cattle out of the hands of a raiding army:

He went into the middle of them and beyond, and mowed down great ramparts of his enemies' corpses, circling completely around the armies three times, attacking them in hatred. They fell sole to sole and neck to headless neck, so dense was that destruction. He circled them three times more in the same way, and left a bed of them six deep in a great circuit, the soles of three to the necks of three in a ring around the camp.

This slaughter had its origin in a debate between King Ailill and Queen Maeve of Connacht over just which of them had the most property. Everything was weighed and found to be equal—except for a magnificent white bull that belonged to the king. Only in the north, in Ulster, was there a similar one, the Brown Bull of Cooley.

The queen immediately sent emissaries to Cooley with a truly generous offer in compensation for a one-year loan of the Brown Bull. The Ulstermen were amazed and readily accepted the offer—until they overheard one of the southerners boast that it was a good thing the loan was agreed to for otherwise Queen Maeve would have stolen the bull. The deal was off, and an army invaded Ulster.

The *Tain* dates from A.D. 300 to 500, though the version of the story we have today is taken from a manuscript written by an Irish scribe who died in 1106. It is the *Book of the Dun Cow,* so called because of its dark cowhide binding. Two other versions—the *Book of Leinster,* copied later that same century, and the *Yellow Book of Lecan,* a book bound in a light leather and written in the 14th century—are obviously based on lost texts. Still, taken together these manuscripts give us a close-up vision of ancient Irish culture. Historian Kenneth H. Jackson has called such legends a "window on the Iron Age."

An anonymous 12th-century Irish scribe added the following colophon to the end of the Book of Leinster:

I who have copied down this story, or more accurately fantasy, do not credit the details of the story, or fantasy. Some things in it are devilish lies, and some poetical figments; some seem possible and others not; some are for the enjoyment of idiots.

In the end, it is neither the sacred nor the profane that brings us back again and again to these books. It's the human part—the notes written beside or below the main text, where the personalities of the writers and scribes are so vivid. There, they sarcastically point to the ineptness of their fellow scribes: "It is easy to know Gabrial's part here . . . [on this page]." Or they complain about the difficulty of a Greek passage they just barely got through: "There's an end to that . . . and my seven curses go with it."

The Irish love of verbal humor of all kinds, especially puns, is on parade, too. The name David, for example, is sometimes laughingly shortened to *v.v.* because its Latin abbreviation, *Da. v.,* sounds like the Irish words meaning "two v's." Part of this instinct for playing with words, which extends straight through from these marginal notes to James Joyce, comes from being adept in two languages, Latin and Old Irish.

There are tears as well. After copying out the *Tale of Troy,* one scribe writes of the death of Hector: "I am greatly grieved at the abovementioned death." Another is sad to see the end of his manuscript: "Goodbye, little book." Yet another recognizes the permanence of the word as compared with his paltry life: "Sad is that, little variegated white book; a day will come in truth, when some one over thy page will say: The hand that wrote it is no more."

Debit

	£.	s.	d.
1 Pork kidney	0.	0.	3
1 Copy Freeman's Journal . . .	0.	0.	1
1 Bath and gratification	0.	1.	6
Tramfare	0.	0.	1
1 In Memoriam			
Patrick Dignam	0.	5.	0
2 Banbury cakes	0.	0.	1

So it went, on June 16, 1904, in the life of Leopold Bloom, the main character of James Joyce's *Ulysses.* In the end, Bloom's total outlay was two pounds, nineteen shillings, threepence; his income, which was listed alongside, precisely the same. Sublime accounting, from perhaps the greatest novel of the 20th century. Joyce balanced Bloom's life in two columns, a form of zero-balance accounting called double entry. While heroes grapple with forces that broaden and illuminate life, attention also must be paid to the mundane.

It was likely for just such purposes that writing was invented some 6,000 years ago. And if great books are prized because they help us come to grips with life, so it is with all manner of records, including accounting books and ledgers—documents that we might scarcely regard as books at all.

Not that this should surprise us, for something so innocuous as double-entry bookkeeping was the spring that drove the Renaissance clockwork. Certainly Shakespeare knew that. In *The Merchant of Venice,* he casts the best and brightest Italians as the men who wield debits and credits. And in *Romeo and Juliet,* when Romeo cries out, "Oh, dear account! My life is my foe's debt," he is complaining about life in general, and about his abysmal choice of girlfriend in particular. But since the scene is set in Renaissance Verona, Italy, Shakespeare fashions his complaint in the language of a trades-man's ledger.

It was the perfection of accounting in the 13th century—and specifically the invention of double-entry book-keeping—that made Italy great. People from all over Europe came to northern Italy to learn the new method, which was based on the principle that every transaction be recorded twice, as a debit and as a credit. Double-entry bookkeeping appeared almost simultaneously in Genoa, Florence, Milan, and Venice; the earliest fully developed and complete double-entry ledgers are from Genoa for the year 1340. From the sophistication of the accounting in these books it's clear that the system had been in use for some time, but a fire in 1339 destroyed the immediate predecessors of these ledgers.

These old ledgers bring to life the commercial world of those times. We see, for example, that in March 1340 Genoa invested in a large shipment of Oriental pepper. As the entries proceed down the pages—debits on the left, credits on the right—over the next few weeks, we can see also that the merchants took a loss on the venture. They bought 80 100-pound lots of pepper at about 24 libre each, and sold them at an average price of only about 22 each.

The need for efficient bookkeeping arose in the 11th and 12th centuries as trade became increasingly complex. The Crusades whetted the appetite for goods from afar, and trade with the Middle East grew. Partnerships and mercantile adventuring in far-flung

DEBITS AND CREDITS

❦ THE KEEPING OF ACCOUNTS

A 16th-century painting of a money lender and his customer by Flemish artist Marinus van Reymerswaele, depicts the use of both eyeglasses and double-entry accounting, two disparate inventions that had considerable impact on the world of books and helped fuel the achievements of the Renaissance.

markets were becoming common, and much of this commerce was controlled by merchants who stayed at home in their counting houses rather than traveling abroad to transport their goods to distant shores. The intricacy of these business transactions—especially those involving speculative loans and middlemen and the shuttling of numerous products and raw materials around the late-medieval world—demanded a highly organized, easy-to-use accounting system, and double entry seemed to fill the bill.

The first printed book of instruction on double-entry accounting was published in 1494, within decades of the invention of movable metal type. The book's title is *Summa de Arithmetica, Geometria, Proportioni et Proportionalita*. Its author was Luca Pacioli, mathematician, Franciscan monk, and friend of Leonardo da Vinci. Writing in Italian rather than Latin, Pacioli emphasized the importance of a thorough inventory of all assets; of starting an account based on that inventory; faithfully recording all transactions; posting to three books—

the memorandum, the ledger, and the journal; keeping trial balances; and always closing smaller accounts by carrying their profits or losses to an overall account. Along the way, he sprinkled his text with such epigrams as "Frequent accounting makes for lasting friendship" and "He who does business without knowing all about it sees his money go like flies"—not exactly Shakespeare's "Neither a borrower nor a lender be," but even though Pacioli fails to mention the bottom line he does note that "Every action is determined by the end in view."

In the end, the Renaissance still shapes up as the product of immeasurable genius, but genius animated by money and the skills essential to commerce. And what of the other kinds of records that have ordered and documented life over the centuries?

Among these are court records, parish registers, wills, and insurance inventories. These books are transforming what we write about the past. They have given us a new kind of history, a history of ordinary people whose stories may never have been reckoned important before.

Consider but a few examples of sleuthing in London's Public Record Office. In April 1983, it was discovered that John Shakespeare, the playwright's father, was indicted twice for usury and once for illegally dealing in wool. Could this family embarrassment have added a personal subtext to the money-lending in *The Merchant of Venice?* The indictment against John Shakespeare is documented clearly on exchequer memoranda rolls for 1570 and 1572, vast scrolls of parchment that went unremarked for more than 400 years.

The identity of Sir Thomas Malory,

Venice bustles with trade in this 1338 painting, opposite. Commerce with nearly all parts of the known world ushered in a kind of golden age for this city-state, as merchant captains sailed for "the honor and profit of the republic." Above (left), Renaissance priest Luca Pacioli uses his pointer to instruct his friend Guidobaldo, Duke of Urbino. Mathematician, lecturer, and friend to Leonardo da Vinci and seven popes, Pacioli wrote the definitive treatise on double-entry bookkeeping, Summa de Arithmetica, *pictured above and also in the right foreground of the painting above (left).*

author of *Le Morte d'Arthur,* remained unknown until the 1920s, when numerous strips of 15th-century legal parchment in the Public Record Office showed him to be a certain Thomas Malory of Newbold Revel, Warwickshire, a "knyght presoner" who spent much of his adult life in jail for breaking and entering, mayhem, cattle rustling, armed robbery of monasteries, and rape. Not a nice story, but the facts indicate that his epic book, full of repentance, was composed in prison before it made its way to William Caxton to be printed.

In 1924, searches through old patent rolls in the Public Record Office brought to light the pardon, by reason of self-defense, of the man who killed playwright Christopher Marlowe in a tavern knife fight. The incident occurred on May 30, 1593, and it was rumored that the two men had fought over a prostitute, that Marlowe had stabbed himself in the eye, and that he had died uttering foul and blasphemous oaths. The true story, however, appears in the coroner's inquest, which remained rolled up for almost 400 years before scholar Leslie Hotson finally laid eyes on it: Marlowe died in a dispute over a bar bill.

From the Middle Ages through the Renaissance, all manner of governmental and legal transactions were documented on parchment rolls, which were stored in courthouses and official residences throughout England. With the opening of the Public Record Office in London in the 19th century, all such records from some 60 sites at last were gathered together at one place. The site had been home to the master of

the rolls, the keeper of the parchment records of the king's chancery, since the 13th century. English diarist Samuel Pepys recalled a visit there in 1669: "I hired a clerk there to read to me about twelve or more several rolls which I did call for; and it was a great pleasure to me to see the method in which the Rolles are kept."

When the Colony of Virginia built its own Public Records Office in Williamsburg in the 1740s, it placed the direction of this office under the Colony's secretary, conferring upon him the medieval title *Custos rotularum* or Keeper of the Rolls, although in fact ledgers had replaced rolls. The Public Records Office was completed in 1748 and replaced the haphazard arrangement of papers in the Capitol building next door. Those records had barely survived a fire the previous year, and many that were recovered already had been "mangled by moths and worms," according to an eyewitness report.

Down Williamsburg's Duke of Gloucester Street from the Public Records Office is the Courthouse. Whereas the Public Records Office handled matters of interest to the Colony, the courthouse was the legal and administrative center of the town and county. Everything that needed to appear in the public record was heard and taken down here. In fact, the importance placed on the gathering of accurate and complete records led to the creation of new kinds of books: solidly bound blank volumes in which the county clerk could enter all the local precedents and have them at hand; and the country's first cloth-bound books, docket books and fee books designed for the record-keeping

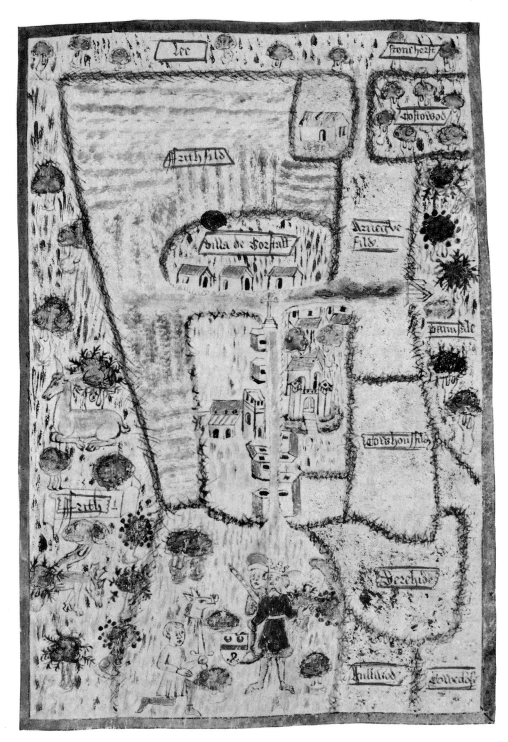

A map of the 15th-century English village of Boarstall, above, highlights an estate plan that dates back to before the Norman Conquest, which began in 1066. Both volumes of the Domesday Book, opposite (bottom), contain the remarkable census and survey of English landowners and their property ordered by William the Conqueror in 1085–86. Named for Judgment Day, or Doomsday, these books detail Anglo-Saxon society after 20 years of Norman plundering. Lambourn Downs, opposite (top), a royal estate in West Saxon, is listed in the Domesday Book.

A bill of mortality tallies the number of deaths by various causes for the week of September 12–19, 1665, in London. Representative of the meticulous accounts kept by the British Public Record Office, the list tabulates deaths at the height of the bubonic plague outbreak that year.

The Diseases and Casualties this Week.

Abortive	23	Grief	1
Aged	57	Griping in the Guts	45
Bedridden	1	Head-mould-shot	2
Bleeding	1	Jaundies	3
Cancer	1	Imposthume	6
Childbed	39	Infants	10
Chrisomes	20	Kingsevil	1
Collick	1	Lethargy	1
Consumption	129	Meagrome	1
Convulsion	71	Plague	6544
Dropsie	31	Planner	1
Drowned 3, one at Stepney, one at St. Katharine near the Tower, and one at St. Margaret VVestminster	3	Quinsie	3
		Rickets	20
		Rising of the Lights	15
		Rupture	4
Feaver	332	Scowring	3
Flox and Small-pox	8	Scurvy	2
Found dead in the street at St. Olave Southwark	1	Spotted Feaver	97
		Stone	1
		Stopping of the stomach	5
French-pox	1	Strangury	2
Frighted	1	Surfeit	45
Gangrene	1	Teeth	128
		Thrush	6
		Timpany	1
		Tissick	4
		Ulcer	1
		Vomiting	2
		Wormes	15

| Christned | Males — 90; Females — 78; In all — 168 | Buried | Males — 3783; Females — 3907; In all — 7690 | Plague — 6544 |

Decreased in the Burials this Week —— 562
Parishes clear of the Plague — 11 Parishes Infected — 119

The Assize of Bread set forth by Order of the Lord Major and Court of Aldermen, A penny Wheaten Loaf to contain Nine Ounces and a half, and three half-penny White Loaves the like weight.

responsibilities of sheriffs and constables. These were informally and unprofessionally bound in one great folio gathering but fit easily into saddle bags.

In England, parish registers constitute another rich source of records, in this case those of such life events as births, baptisms, marriages, and deaths. Such records were required to be kept from 1538 until the establishment of the first national register in July 1837.

Shakespeare's parish, Holy Trinity in Stratford, tells us only that he was baptized on April 26, 1564. Shakespeare's birthday generally is celebrated on April 23, a date that may have been chosen because it is St. George's Day, a day to honor the patron saint of England, and also because it conveniently matches the date of Shakespeare's death, April 23, 1616.

Wills and inventories also offer windows to the past. The former yield insights into the quality of life. From the latter, since they were often room-by-room accounts, we can see the lifestyle of early homes and the kinds of furnishings in every room. Insurance company records and drawings have helped in the restoration of buildings utterly lost above their foundation stones.

Working among such fusty and vernacular accounts over the last generation, historians have reconstructed the existence of the everyday, the ordinary. This kind of historical research reached its peak in France, where it has come to be called the Annales School—from the French word *annales,* meaning records or annals—because of its embrace of journals, diaries, and lists of all sorts. Among the most illustrious historians of this school is Emmanuel Le Roy Ladurie, who documented life in the remote 14th-century village of Montaillou and the surrounding countryside in the Mid-Pyrenees. Ladurie based his history on the records of the trials of Cathar heretics, a pacifist sect that was supposed to have been eradicated during the Albigensian Crusade nearly a century earlier.

The accounts are personal and immediate and in many ways could

have been written yesterday rather than in 1320. Much is made of the reading of forbidden books, the ones that propounded the anticlerical Cathar creed. It's not difficult to imagine the sweat beading up on the forehead of a villager as he succumbs to the prying questions of his interrogator:

"Nineteen or twenty years ago I was sunning myself beside the house . . . and four or five spans away, Guillaume Andorran was reading aloud from a book to his mother Gaillarde. I asked: 'What are you reading?'

"'Do you want to see?' said Guillaume.

"'All right,' I said. "Guillaume brought me the book, and I read: 'In the beginning was the Word. . . .'

"It was a 'Gospel' in a mixture of Latin and Romance, which contained many things I had heard the heretic Pierre Authié say. Guillaume Andorran told me he bought it from a certain merchant."

Clearly this was a case of reading the wrong book at the wrong time. As it turned out, however, the countless peasants who underwent this inquisition survived their ordeal. And the meticulous records of their testimony, translated into Latin and copied into three great volumes, still have the power to open our eyes some 650 years later.

The English carried their tradition of thorough recordkeeping to the New World, constructing halls of public records and other buildings such as the Courthouse in the Colonial capital of Williamsburg, Virginia, for the gathering and recording of comprehensive and accurate accounts.

Incipit liber bresith que̅ nos genesim
In principio creauit deus celu̅ dicim9
et terram. Terra aute̅ erat inanis et
uacua: et tenebre erãt sup facie̅ abissi:
et sps̄ dn̅i ferebat sup aquas. Dixitq̃
deus. Fiat lux. Et facta e̅ lux. Et uidit
deus luce̅ cp esset bona: ⁊ diuisit luce̅
a tenebris. appellauitq̃ luce̅ die̅ ⁊
tenebras nocte̅. Factu̅q̃ est uespe et
mane dies unius. Dixit n̅ deus. Fiat
firmamentu̅ in medio aquax: ⁊ diui-
dat aquas ab aquis. Et fecit deus fir-
mamentu̅: diuisitq̃ aquas que erãt
sub firmame̅to ab hijs q̃ erant sup
firmamentu̅: et factu̅ e̅ ita. Vocauitq̃
deus firmamentu̅ celu̅: ⁊ factu̅ e̅ uespe
et mane dies secu̅d9. Dixit uero deus.
Congregent̅ aque que sub celo su̅t in
locu̅ unu̅ ⁊ appareat arida. Et factu̅ e̅
ita. Et uocauit deus aridam terram:
congregacionesq̃; aquax appellauit
maria. Et uidit deus cp esset bonu̅: et
ait. Germinet terra herbã uirente̅ et
faciente̅ seme̅: ⁊ lignu̅ pomifex faciēs
fructu̅ iuxta genus suu̅: cui9 seme̅ in
semetipo sit sup terrã. Et factu̅ e̅ ita. Et
protulit terra herbã uirente̅ ⁊ faciente̅
seme̅ iuxta genus suu̅: lignu̅q̃; faciēs
fructu̅ ⁊ habe̅s unu̅qdq̃; seme̅te̅ secu̅m
specie̅ suã. Et uidit deus cp esset bonu̅:
et factu̅ est uespe et mane dies tercius.
Dixitq̃; aute̅ deus. Fiant luminaria
in firmame̅to celi: ⁊ diuidãt diem ac
nocte̅: ⁊ sint in signa ⁊ tpa et dies ⁊
annos: ut lucea̅t in firmame̅to celi et
illumine̅t terrã. Et factu̅ e̅ ita. Fecitq̃;
deus duo lumi̅aria magna: lumi̅are
mai9 ut pe̅sset diei et lumi̅are min9
ut pe̅sset nocti ⁊ stellas: ⁊ posuit eas in
firmame̅to celi ut lucere̅t sup terrã: et

pe̅sset diei ac nocti: ⁊ diuidere̅t luce̅
ac tenebras. Et uidit de9 cp esset bonu̅:
et factu̅ e̅ uespe ⁊ mane dies quartus.
Dixit eciã de9. Producãt aque reptile
anime uiuentis ⁊ uolatile super terrã
sub firmame̅to celi. Creauitq̃; deus cete
grandia: et omne̅ aı̅am uiuente̅ atq̃;
motabile̅ quã pduxerãt aque i specie̅s
suas: ⁊ omne uolatile scd̅m genu9 suu̅.
Et uidit deus cp esset bonu̅: benedixitq̃;
eis dicens. Crescite ⁊ mltiplicamini: ⁊
replete aquas maris: auesq̃; mltipli-
ce̅t sup terrã. Et factu̅ e̅ uespe ⁊ mane
dies quitus. Dixit quoq̃; deus. Pro-
ducat terra aı̅am uiuente̅ in gene̅ suo:
iumenta ⁊ reptilia: ⁊ bestias terre scd̅m
species suas. Factu̅q̃; e̅ ita. Et fecit de9
bestias terre iuxta species suas: iumenta ⁊ omne reptile terre i genere suo. Et
uidit deus cp esset bonu̅: et ait. Facia-
mus hoie̅m ad ymagine̅ ⁊ similitudine̅
nostrã: ⁊ presit piscib9 maris: et uola-
tilib9 celi ⁊ bestijs uniue̅rseq̃; terre: omni̅q̃;
reptili qd̅ mouetur i terra. Et creauit
deus hoie̅m ad ymagine̅ ⁊ similitudine̅
suã: ad ymagine̅ de̅i creauit illu̅: ma-
sculu̅ ⁊ femina̅ creauit eos. Benedixit-
q̃; illis deus: ⁊ ait. Crescite ⁊ mltiplicamini ⁊ replete terrã: et sbicite eã: et dn̅a-
mini piscib9 maris: et uolatilib9 celi:
et uniuersis animãtib9 que mouent̅
sup terrã. Dixitq̃; de9. Ecce dedi uobis
omne̅ herbã afferente̅ seme̅ sup terrã:
⁊ uniu̅sa ligna que ha̅t in semetipı̅s
seme̅te̅ genis sui: ut sint uobis i esca̅:
⁊ cunctis aı̅antib9 terre: omni̅q̃; uolucri
celi ⁊ uniuersis q̃ mouetur in terra: ⁊ i
quib9 est anima uiue̅s: ut habea̅t ad
uescendu̅. Et factu̅ est ita. Viditq̃; deus
cuncta que fecerat: ⁊ erãt ualde bona.

THE GUTENBERG REVOLUTION

IMAGINE THE GREAT FRANKfurt Fair of 1455. There, on a plain trestle table, under a canvas awning, were row after row of Bibles. Some were on vellum, most on paper. There had been more handsome Bibles before, and more sumptuous ones, too. But here the magic was in the calligraphy: perfectly regular, no variance whatsoever. Truly, the scribe who penned this must have sold his soul to the devil. ❡ It must have been a shock. An Italian visitor named Piccolomini recorded that there were very many customers for this new and perfect kind of book, one that was so clear it could be read without spectacles. Its cost? About 30 florins, a clerk's wage for about three years. ❡ The man who made the magical Bibles was a middle-aged businessman named Johann Gensfleisch, who, in the customary way of patrician families in that era, was known by his mother's family name, Gutenberg. From his printing shop in the cathedral town of Mainz, on the Rhine River about 20 miles from Frankfurt, Gutenberg had raised the fledgling "secret arts" of printing to a level of perfection that would never be attained again. He also went broke. ❡ Gutenberg was born in Mainz about 1397, but was forced to flee in his youth because of political troubles. Up the Rhine, in Strasbourg, he began experimenting in metallurgy and in the mass-production of souvenir mirrors for pilgrims to the shrine at Aachen. Gutenberg saw a large market for mirrors and knew that the key to that market was inexpensive production. ❡ But the pilgrimage was not the only path to heaven or riches. There was also the indulgence, a small slip of paper offering sinners

Preceding pages: A 19th-century painting recreates a 15th-century visit by King Edward IV to the printing shop of William Caxton, publisher of the first book printed in English. Opposite, hand-painted illuminations decorate a page from a 15th-century Gutenberg Bible printed on vellum in Mainz, Germany. This copy now resides at the Huntington Library in California. Gutenberg's Bibles were the world's first identically printed books. At left, an initial I from the Biblia Germanica (German Bible), printed in 1483 by Anton Koberger in Nuremberg, Germany.

Johann Gutenberg's gothic type, above, remained true to scribal models: his 290 type punches reproduced all the quirks of this style of medieval handwriting. An engraving of the imagined likeness of goldsmith-turned-printer Gutenberg, above (right), appeared in a French book in 1584, many years after his death.

some remission from time spent in Purgatory before entering Heaven, usually in return for a small sum of money. By selling these indulgences, the Church raised money for special projects—crusades, hospitals, or cathedrals. It was a system so open to abuse that it would be a special target of Martin Luther's reformative wrath in the next century.

Gutenberg saw that printing would lend itself perfectly to this business. Since indulgences usually consisted of a single page, they could be printed far faster than the local church registrar or scribe could handwrite them. His instincts proved to be correct. Indulgence pressruns of 200,000 became a regular feature of 15th-century printing.

In Strasbourg, some time before 1434, Gutenberg took his first steps in printing. Printing was not unknown: woodblock printing, or xylography, had been practiced in the Orient for centuries. And in Europe, woodblocks were used for the printing of textiles and playing-cards.

S NVREMBERGA S

S. Lorencius.

S. Sebaldus.

Gutenberg took pains not to reinvent the wheel. He used the best technologies of his day. For his press, he followed the basic structure of the winepress, adding some features from textile presses and the hand presses used by papermakers and bookbinders. He also learned from the techniques for making playing cards and woodblock pictures. In fact, some scholars have associated Gutenberg with a mysterious figure known as the Master of the Playing Card, suggesting that he was printing cards before he turned to Bibles.

The problem with the woodblock was that it yielded a single, unalterable image. Making a pack of cards required cutting 52 different woodblocks. Unless, of course, the basic blocks were made so that the number of pips (the suit signs--hearts, clubs, diamonds, and spades) could be changed. One woodblock with changeable pips could be used to print a whole pack of cards. And if pips in a playing-card woodblock could be changed, why not the letters of the alphabet in a text woodblock?

Towers rise over the city of Nuremberg in this woodcut from Hartmann Schedel's Liber chronicarum, *commonly known as the* Nuremberg Chronicle, *which was printed by Anton Koberger in both Latin and German editions in 1493. Six hundred and forty-five woodcuts were used in this work—some multiple times—to produce 1,800 illustrations. An early publishing entrepreneur, Koberger employed more than 100 people, including a promising apprentice named Albrecht Dürer.*

Gutenberg may have printed thousands of these 31-line letters of indulgence, right, which Catholics of the time bought in hopes of reducing their term in Purgatory. Presumably Gutenberg profited from this and other printing endeavors, but in 1455 he defaulted on a loan and lost his press. Printing was hard work. Compositors and proofreaders, such as those in the 16th-century engraving below, worked 12-hour days, during which a pressman might pull the bar 3,000 times.

The 1430s and '40s were years of experiment for Gutenberg. Perhaps his real genius was in managing a large enterprise that depended on the services of a great many people. Carpenters, chemists, metallurgists, designers, calligraphers, pressmen, binders—perhaps as many as 20 people worked for Gutenberg in his two Mainz shops. His other talent, of course, must have been fund raising: he needed to find money and sponsors for his enterprise.

To keep his creditors happy, he had to show a profit, which meant a careful selection of projects. Thus, the earliest surviving page of a Gutenberg book printed with movable type is a student's Latin textbook by Donatus called *De octo partibus orationis (On the eight parts of oratory),* from 1448. The same type was used to print papal indulgences granted by Pope Nicholas V to raise money for a crusade to Cyprus; they bear the dates MCCCCLIIII (1454) or MCCCCLV (1455).

Both these projects were probably highly profitable; every student needed the Donatus, and the single-sheet indulgence was bought in bulk for later sale to the public. (Fifty of the indulgences survive; the Donatus school book, however, was so well used by students that it is known only from single sheets.)

Gutenberg's great invention was not printing, but printing with movable, metal type (since wooden letters were too fragile). Essential to this was the invention of an adjustable hand-mold, one that would allow the casting of thousands of letters efficiently and with precision.

Originally trained as a goldsmith and thus familiar with metalwork, Gutenberg devised the basic steps used to make a piece of type. First, the letter was carved in relief and in reverse in the end of a steel punch. The punch was driven with a hammer into a soft copper blank, stamping an impression of the letter into the metal; this piece of copper was called the matrix.

Next, the matrix was inserted into a hand-held mold, and molten metal of a special alloy—a combination of lead, antimony, and bismuth—was poured into the mold. This alloy was chosen not only because it melted at a low temperature (300 degrees Celsius), but because it also cooled rapidly, allowing the mold to be opened quickly and the letter—again a reverse image perched atop a rectangular block of lead—to be dropped into a tray and handled in just minutes. The process was less complicated in practice than it sounds. Once all of the necessary punches and matrices were made, even the early typecasters could turn out a letter every 10 seconds—up to 4,000 a day.

The hand-mold was covered in wood, insulating the typefounder's hands from the heat created by the molten metal. The mold could be adjusted to allow the typefounder to vary the body-widths of his pieces of type according to the size of the letter being made. For example, the skinny letter i stands on top of a much thinner piece of metal than the wide capital W.

Varying the widths to fit each letter meant that the printed page could be seen as groups of words, not individual letters. If every letter had a standard amount of lead around its base, words would look   l i k e   t h i s .   And Gutenberg might not have sold a single book. It has been said that the adjustable hand-mold, not the printing press, is what made printing work.

Gutenberg's goal was always to have his books resemble fine calligraphic

manuscripts written in gothic hands. As a result, he took great care with his alphabet, which—incredibly—has some 290 alternate characters. There are eight versions of the lowercase a, for example, a valiant attempt by Gutenberg to give his text the authentic look of one produced by a scribe. He also invented the type ligature, double letters that look better linked together (ff, æ, ɛt). He must have found that ugly gaps disrupted the blackness of the line whenever these were set as two separate letters.

Likewise, Gutenberg used as many abbreviations as medieval scribes did. *Dominus,* for example, appears as *dn̄s*. (Not much risk of misinterpretation: the line over the "ns" indicates an abbreviation, but the context also demands "Lord.") Gutenberg also found that his light, double-hairline hyphens at the end of lines looked better if they extended out beyond the right, justified margin. As a crowning touch, Gutenberg hired rubricators to add initial letters and color to his printed pages.

Gutenberg developed many of the print-shop routines we still use in hand-printing today. He used pinholes in the paper to make sure each sheet was properly aligned for the press. And he used "catchwords," printing the first word of one page on the bottom of the previous page as an aid to compositors, pressmen, and binders alike. His ink formula, oil paint with a high copper and lead content, was one of the best ever. Print made with this ink is still black and glossy after 500 years.

What we know of Gutenberg's life is derived from only 30 contemporary documents, mainly legal and administrative records. We know, for instance, that

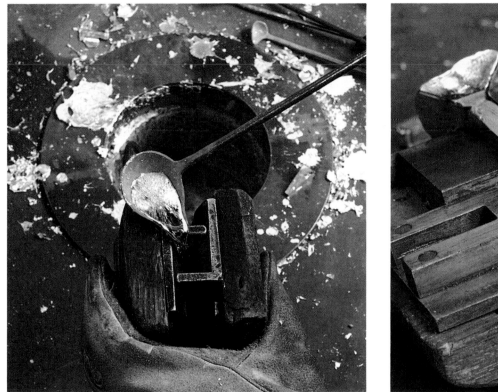

by 1448 he had returned to Mainz from Strasbourg, and that he soon was borrowing large sums of money (in 1450 and 1452) from Johann Fust, a Mainz financier and goldsmith.

By 1452, the huge Bible project—a two-volume edition of more than 200 copies—was underway. It's unlikely that the pressrun was much more than this because of the high risk involved. Perhaps 35 to 50 of these were printed on vellum, which would have required 5,000 animal skins! Who knew if there was a market for something so grand? (Today, 48 Bibles survive, 12 on vellum, a remarkable 25 percent survival rate.)

In any case, the Bible was complete by 1455. Actually, there are two distinct Gutenberg Bibles from this period. One appears in a two-column format with 36 lines to the column; another has 42 lines. A copy of a 42-line Bible bears the earliest date of any printing, because the rubricator, Heinrich Cremer, took the trouble to add the date, August 15, 1456, upon which he finished his work.

Ordinarily these Bibles are undated and have neither title pages nor colophons. Again, this probably reflects Gutenberg's wish to have his printed volumes resemble manuscripts, which were signed by the scribe only at the end of the text. Yet Gutenberg's name never appears.

The Gutenberg Bibles are so well printed that they must be the end result of a long history of development. Something so perfect cannot have been a first. As a result, the year 1440, not 1455, is traditionally considered the birth date of printing.

For Gutenberg, however, 1455 was the best of times and the worst of times.

Gutenberg's genius lay in his method of casting type, demonstrated here by National Museum of American History specialist Stanley Nelson. Steel punches were used to strike letters into copper blanks called matrices, such as these crafted by Nelson, opposite (left); a two-piece adjustable mold, opposite (right), fits around the copper matrix; molten type-metal, above (left), a mixture of lead, tin, and antimony, is poured into the mold; the finished piece of type, seen above in half of a mold made by Nelson, appears silvery. The hardened alloy from the funnel of the mold, called a jet, will be broken from the type and thrown back into the melting pot.

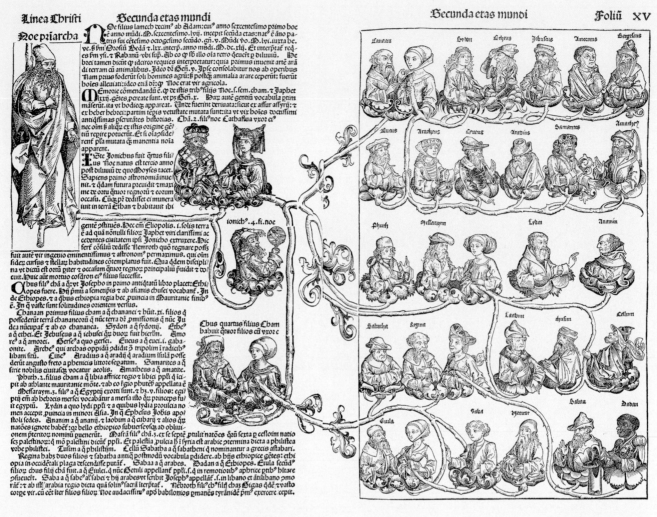

Although his Latin Bible was completed, Gutenberg defaulted on a loan from Fust and subsequently lost a suit brought against him. His printing establishment collapsed, and the "secret arts" that he had perfected over 20 years were made public.

Little more is known of Gutenberg's later career, though some scholars have speculated that he was involved with a Bible produced in Bamberg about 1460. He received some financial relief in 1465 when he was made a *hofmann*, or courtier, by the Archbishop of Mainz. The award was tendered in response to Gutenberg's services to the church, which may have been either political

Opposite (top), the Tree of Noah, from Anton Koberger's 1493 Liber chronicarum. *Koberger's presses alone produced 227 titles by 1500. The technology of printing spread rapidly. A Swiss-printed triptych (c.1490), opposite (bottom), with a hand-colored woodcut of the Lamentation, served as a traveling altar. A Dutch woodcut, left, from Jacob Bellaert's 1485 printing of* De proprietatibus rerum (The Properties of Things), *includes realistic peafowl, geese, cranes, spoonbills, and a rooster together with a griffin. Bellaert's book was produced in Haarlem, in the Netherlands, in time for Christmas.*

or typographical; we may never know. He died three years later, in 1468.

Gutenberg was buried in the Mainz church of St. Francis, and there is a record that the following tablet was erected: "To Johann Gensfleisch, the inventor of the art of printing and deserver of the highest honors from every nation and tongue...." But the church was razed in 1742, and Gutenberg's remains have never been found.

When Gutenberg lost the suit to Fust in 1455, his equipment and operation (and probably many of the employees he had trained) came into the possession of Fust and Fust's future son-in-law, Peter Schoeffer, a printer and typefounder. It is possible that before 1455 all three worked jointly. After that year, Gutenberg was out, though it is clear that his Bible projects were completed.

In 1457, the first printed book bearing a date and a printer's name appeared. It was a Psalter, or a book of Psalms, printed in Mainz by Fust and Schoeffer on the eve of the feast of the Assumption (August 14). That book is also the first example of color printing, a Schoeffer experiment in which a second and third ink were added to certain letters in the chase and all the colors were printed at once.

The Fust and Schoeffer Bible of 1462 is the first book with a printed date, though it had no title page. However, title pages would soon become important marketing tools. In the past, scribes had often known the customer for whom they were producing a book. But when a printer made more than 200 copies of a book he couldn't be sure who his customers might be. Since most texts looked alike to browsers, there had to be a way, in effect, of shouting the name of a book and where another like it could be obtained. In 1470, Schoeffer printed the first book catalogue and the first type-specimen sheet as well. He and Fust continued in the printing business until Fust's death in 1466. With his three sons, Peter Schoeffer remained a fine printer until his death in Mainz in 1502.

Gutenberg and his German followers and workshop assistants carried the torch of printing throughout Europe. Even before 1500, printing had spread to 60 German towns, and German printers would take the technology to England, France, Holland, Italy, and Spain.

Gutenberg's achievements are startling. He perfected the handpress for printing, and it remained essentially unchanged for 350 years. He invented typography, along with a brilliant, adjustable hand-mold and a new alloy. And his Bible, the world's first large-scale book project, would turn out to be the finest, most technically perfect book ever printed.

Until recently, Gutenberg was considered to have been a brooding, romantic loner. Today, we see him as an inventor as well as a motivator of a team of experts and craftsmen, an Organization Man. Something of the industrial world started with him, as did the modern financial world. Printing was the first enterprise in which a large initial investment in research and development, followed by constant operational costs (paper, ink, rent, and wages), would be recouped through sales. Making Bibles in Mainz did not differ fundamentally from making Fords in Detroit.

An allegorical frontispiece from an 18th-century French book on the history of printing depicts the press descending from the heavens, accompanied by Athena and Hermes. Germany is to be the first recipient of the spirit of printing, with Holland, England, Italy, and France next in line. Opposite, colored letters highlight a page from the Mainz Psalter printed in 1457 by Gutenberg's former partners, Johann Fust and his son-in-law, Peter Schoeffer. This was the first book printed in color.

Regē magnū dñm venite adoremus, ps Venite·
Dñicis diebz post festū ephie Inuitatoriū·

Adorem9 dñm qui fecit nos, Ps venite aū Seruite·

Eatus vir qui
non abijt in   Euouae·
consilio impiorū   et in
via pccorū nō stetit: ⁊ in
cathedra pestilēcie nō se-
dit, Sed ī lege dñi vo-
lūtas ei9: et in lege eius meditabit die ac
nocte, Et erit tanqã lignū qd plātatū iste
secus decursus aqrū: qd fructū suū dabit in
tpe suo Et foliū ei9 nō defluet: ⁊ oīa qcūqã
faciet psperabūt, Nō sic impij nō sic sed
tanqã puluis quē picit vent9 a facie terre,
Ideo non resurgūt impij in iudicio: neqã
pctores in cōsilio iustorū Quī nouit dñs
via iustorū: ⁊ iter impiorū pribit, Glia P

Here begynneth the squyers tale

At surrey in the londe of Tartarye
There dwellyd a kynge that warryed wyssy
Thorow whyche there dyde many a doughty man
Thys nobyl kynge was cleppyd Cambuscan
Whyche in hys tyme was of so greet renoun
That ther was nowhere in no regioun
So excellent a lorde in alle thynge
He lackid nought that longede to a kynge
As of the secte of whyche he was born
He kepte hys lay to whyche he was sworn
And therto he was hardy wyse and ryche
Pytwus juste and alwey ylyche
Soth of hys worde benygne and honourable
Of hys corage as ony center stabyl

The thumbprint was first spotted by Lotte Hellinga. The year was 1976. As Dr. Hellinga was examining the manuscript of Sir Thomas Malory's *Le Morte d'Arthur* in the British Library, she noticed some smudges of printer's ink on the parchment, including ink from type transferred to the page via a printer's or compositor's thumb.

The presence of oil-based printer's ink, in contrast to water-based scribal ink, meant that this manuscript had been handled by a typesetter, making it the oldest printer's copy ever found. The thumb could well have been that of William Caxton, who printed Malory's classic in 1485.

Today, we honor the memory of Caxton (1422–1492) for two reasons: he brought printing from the Continent to England and, in editing and publishing his books, he transformed the English language.

Caxton first saw printed books on the Continent, probably in the Low Countries—Holland, Flanders, Zeeland—where he worked as a merchant in the wool trade for more than 30 years, eventually rising to the post of governor of the English merchants in Bruges in 1462. It was a time when printing technology was taking the world by storm. Between Gutenberg's Bible in 1455 and the end of the century, a mere 45 years, more than 10 million books would be printed.

In 1468, "to keep himself from idleness," Caxton began translating a French book, *The Recuyell of the Historyes of Troye,* an entertaining summary of Greek legend. For some reason unknown to us, Caxton was exiled to Germany in 1471, thus interrupting his translation. He settled in Cologne, a city in which several active presses were turning out books for the university, the church, and the public. There, during a period of enforced leisure, he finished translating his book of Greek legends on September 19, 1471. It must have been favorably received, for Caxton immediately began thinking about ways to reproduce his text. He resolved to learn printing.

His period of exile over, he returned to Bruges, set up his own press in 1472, and began printing in earnest. There he published seven books, including his *Recuyell* and the first sports book printed in English, *The Game of Chess,* before sailing for England in 1476.

For the last 15 years of his life, Caxton's shop was situated near London at Westminster, under the sign of the "Red Pale." Though the exact location of his print shop has never been found, it was certainly on the grounds of Westminster Abbey; a lease shows that Caxton rented "una shoppa" there starting at Michaelmas (September 29) 1476.

There he published about 100 books, a number of which will live forever. *The Canterbury Tales* (1476–1478) was nearly a century old when Caxton printed them (Chaucer had died in 1400). He probably printed them not because they were "literature" but because they contained popular, appealing stories. Caxton was a businessman. Entertainment was more important to him than erudition.

At the time, Caxton was also a bookseller, importing Latin and French books. He limited his own printing to books that would not

CAXTON AND ALDUS

❧ MASTERS OF THE PRESS

A woodcut of a handsome young squire on a caparisoned steed introduces "The Squire's Tale" from Geoffrey Chaucer's The Canterbury Tales *in a 1484 edition printed by William Caxton, the father of English printing. Caxton published the original version of the* Tales *in 1476–1478, and then printed this later edition with revised text and woodcut illustrations.*

The early woodcuts in William Caxton's 1481 Mirrour of the World, *below, seem crude in comparison with the complex scene, opposite (left), from Johann Froben's edition of Sir Thomas More's* Utopia, *printed in Basel, Switzerland, in 1518. Opposite (right), a monstrous and mobile siege-engine in the shape of a dragon is one of 82 such illustrations featured in Robert Valturius's 1472 technical manual on military science,* De re militari, *printed in Verona, Italy.*

directly compete with cheap and well-printed ones from abroad. Instead, he specialized in English books, ripping yarns intended to appeal to a market that he and his press were creating.

But it was not just by selecting appealing titles that Caxton was nurturing English readership. He was editing as well. In March 1471, a mysterious figure named Sir Thomas Malory had died in Newgate prison, leaving a compendious manuscript containing stories surrounding a mythical King Arthur and his round table of knights. Somehow the long, rambling manuscript made its way to

Caxton (and his inky thumb?) in Westminster.

Instead of merely printing it, however, Caxton edited the text, tightening Malory's language and, what is more important, dividing the manuscript into eight chapters or "books," thus making it more palatable and readable. Caxton issued the book in 1485 as *Le Morte d'Arthur,* instantly popularizing a story still in print (and on stage as *Camelot*) even today.

The English of Caxton's time had advanced somewhat from Middle English, the language of Chaucer. But it was far from Modern English. In

1490, Caxton complained in the introduction to *Eneydos,* his translation of the *Aeneid,* that English was too unsettled and varied so much from shire to shire that people were having trouble communicating.

To prove his point, Caxton tells of two Englishmen who stopped for breakfast near the mouth of the Thames:

One of theym named Sheffelde, a mercer, cam in-to an hows and axed for mete; and specyally he axed after eggys. And the goode wyf answerede, that she coude speke no Frenshe. And the marchaunt was angry, for he also coude speke no Frenshe, but wolde have hadde egges, and she understode hym not. And thenne at laste a nother sayd that he wolde have eyren. Then the goode wyf sayd that she understood hym wel! Loo, what sholde a man in thyse days now wryte, egges or eyren?*

In his books, Caxton selected the diction and the spelling (and thus the pronunciation) that he felt most comfortable with, based on his life in London and his 30 years working on the Continent. So the English of southeast England, of London and Kent (Caxton's birthplace), with a sprinkling of French here and there, replaced the more difficult northern or Old English (Anglo-Saxon). Caxton's English became the linguistic coin of the realm.

Over the length of his printing career, Caxton's typography grew more confident. Before about 1480, his margins were often ragged; they became more regular after that date. Caxton used eight type fonts, bringing one with him from Bruges and probably importing the later faces from Europe. All were the so-called "black letter" fonts, derived from the Gothic faces first used by Gutenberg and spread throughout Europe by the migration of German printers.

After Caxton died in 1492 his

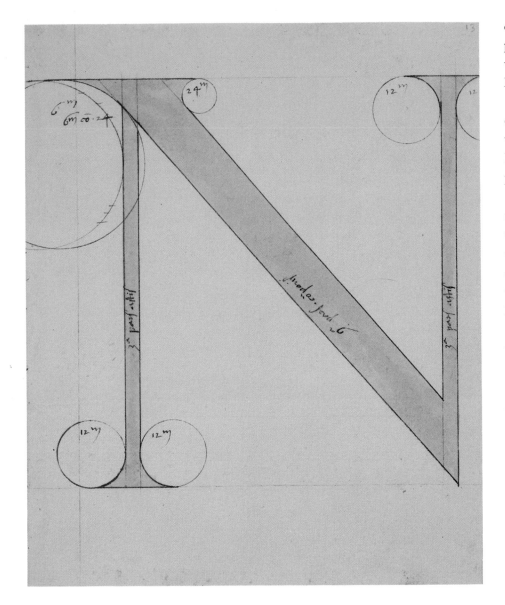

An illustration, above, from a late-15th-century guide to letter design reflects the influence of ancient Roman letter shapes on Renaissance scholars and printers. French master engraver Nicolaus Jenson's roman type, seen opposite on a page from his 1472 printing of Historia Naturum *by Pliny the Elder, appears modern even today.*

work was continued by his assistant, Wynken de Worde (d. 1535). Wynken, an Alsatian printer who came to London in the 1470s, took over the firm and continued to reprint Caxton's classics as well as many of his own editions. His *Polychronicon* (1495) contains the first page of music printed in England. Wynken also made a significant business change. He moved his shop from Westminster, where Caxton had relied on printing for Parliament and the court, to Fleet Street, on the edge of London, where commercial printing was in demand. This area would become the printing center of England for the next five centuries.

Richard Pynson, the third of the early English printers, may also have worked with Caxton. Pynson was a Frenchman from Normandy who printed in London between 1490 and 1530. He seems to have imported his type from either Paris or Rouen and thus introduced England to the easy-to-read roman typefaces. Before the end of the century, roman faces would drive black-letter books out of England.

Oddly enough, German printers were the first to experiment with roman fonts, beginning perhaps in Strasbourg in 1467, with the books of Adolf Rusch, and moving on to Italy. There, the émigré Germans Conrad Sweynheym (d. 1477) and Arnold Pannartz (d. 1476) developed a partially roman face at their press, set up at the Benedictine monastery in Subiaco.

Theirs was the first press in Italy, begun in 1465. At their later establishment in Rome in 1467 the pair used the first purely roman typeface. The name roman reflects both the site of Sweynheym and Pannartz's shop and an acknowledgment that the face was based on the letter shapes of ancient Roman inscriptions.

In Florence, the Medici feared that printing would corrupt the fine manuscripts in their libraries. As a result, Venice instead became the center of Renaissance printing. The city's prominence in printing derives largely from the roman typefaces designed by Nicolaus Jenson (1420–1480), a French master of the mint at Tours who learned printing in

CAII PLYNII SECVNDI NATVRALIS HISTORIAE LIBER .I.

CAIVS PLYNIVS SECVNDVS NOVOCOMENSIS DOMITIANO SVO SALVTEM.　　　PRAEFATIO.

LIBROS NATVRALIS HISTORIAE NO-
uitium camœnis quintium tuorum opus natum
apud me proxima fœtura licentiore epistola nar-
rare constitui tibi iucundissime imperator. Sit.n.
hæc tui præfatio uerissima:dum maxio cōsenescit
in patre. Naq; tu solebas putare esse aliqd meas
nugas:ut obiicere moliar Catullum conterraneū
meum. Agnoscis & hoc castrése uerbum. Ille enī
ut scis:permutatis prioribus syllabis duriusculū
se fecit:q uolebat existiman a uernaculis tuis:&
famulis. Simul ut hac mea petulātia fiat:quod
proxime nō fieri questus es:i alia procaci episto/
la nostra:ut in quædam acta exeāt. Sciantq; omnes:q exæquo tecum uiuat impium
Triumphalis & censorius tu sextumque consul ac tribuniciæ potestatis particeps. Et
quod iis nobilius fecisti:dū illud patri pariter & equestri ordini præstas præfectus præ-
torii eius:omniaq; hæc reipub. Et nobis quidem qualis in castrési contubernio? Nec
quicq mutauit in te fortunæ amplitudo in iis:nisi ut prodesse tantundem posses:&
uelles. Itaq; cum cæteris in ueneratione tui pateant omnia illa:nobis ad colendum te
familiarius audacia sola superest. Hanc igitur tibi imputabis:& in nostra culpa tibi
ignosces. Perfricui faciem:nec tamen profeci. Quando alia uia occurris ingens. Et
longius etiam submoues ingenu facibus. Fulgurat in nullo unq uerius dicta uis elo-
quentiæ. Tibi tribunitiæ potestatis facūdia. Quāto tu ore patris laudes tonas? Quāto fratris amas? Quantus in poetica es? O magna fœcunditas animi. Quēadmodū
fratrem quoq; imitareris:excogitasti. Sed hæc quis posset intrepidus æstimare?subi-
turus ingenii tui iudicium:præsertim lacessitum? Neque enim similis est conditio
publicantium:& nominatim tibi dicantium. Tum possem dicere:quid ista legis imperator? Humili uulgo scripta sunt:agricolarum:opificum turbæ:deniq; studiorū
ociosis. Quid te iudicem facis? Cum hanc operam condicerem:non eras in hoc albo.
Maiorem te sciebam:q ut descensurum huc putarem. Præterea est quædam publica
etiam eruditorum reiectio. Vtitur illa &.M.Tullius extra omnem ingenii aleam po-
situs. Et quod miremur:per aduocatum deféditur. Hæc doctissimum omniū Persiū
legere nolo. Lælium Decimum uolo. Quod si hoc Lucillius qui primus códidit stili
nasum:dicédum sibi putauit. Si Cicero mutuandū:præsertim cum de repub.scribe-
ret:quanto nos causatius ab aliquo iudice diffidimus? Sed hæc ego mihi nunc patro-
cinia ademi nuncupatione. Quáplurimū refert:sortiatur ne aliquis indicé:an eligat.
Multumque apparatus interest apud inuitatum hospitem & oblatum. Cum apud
Catonem illum ambitus hostem:& repulsis tanquam honoribus ineptis gaudentem:
flagrantibus comitiis pecunias deponerent candidati:hoc se facere:pro inocétia:quod
in rebus humanis summū esset:profitebāt. Inde illa nobilis.M.Ciceronis suspiratio.
O te fœlicem.M.Porti a quo rem improbam petere nemo audet. Cum tribunos ap-
pellaret.L.Scipio Asiaticus:iter quos erat Gracchus:hoc attestabat:uel inimico iudici
se approbare posse. Adeo summum quisq; causæ suæ iudicem facit:quécunq; eligit:
Vnde prouocatio appellatur. Te quidem in excelsissimo humani generis fastigio po-
situm summa eloquentia summa eruditione præditum religiose adiri etiam a saluta-
tibus scio. Et ideo immensa præter cæteras subit cura ut quæ tibi dicātur:cum digna

Italian Aldus Manutius, shown opposite (top) in a contemporary portrait, perfected 15th-century scholarly printing. His 1499 printing of Francesco Colonna's Hypnerotomachia Poliphili, *below, remains one of the world's most beautiful books. The frontispiece to his 1500* Epistole *of St. Catherine of Siena, opposite (bottom), contains the first use of italic type.*

Germany. Moving to Venice, he designed type for the first Venetian printer, Johannes de Spira (d. 1470), and then produced his own masterfully designed volumes. His edition of Eusebius's *De Evangelica Praeparatione* (1470) is as clear and readable as any book ever printed.

With Aldus Manutius (1450–1515), the world of printing achieved a level of excellence not approached

since the days of the great medieval scriptoria. For Aldus was not only a printer, he was a scholar. He knew Greek and Latin and vowed to produce new and dependable editions of works by Aristotle, Plato, Euripides, Pliny, Plutarch, Dante, Petrarch, Erasmus, and many others.

Not only would these books be widely available in small, affordable editions, they would be easy to read.

TRIVMPHVS

ce ligatura alla fistula tubale, Gli altri dui cũ ueterrimi cornitibici concordi ciascuno & cum gli instrumenti delle Equitante nymphe.

Sotto lequale triũphale seiughe era laxide nel meditullo, Nelqle gli rotali radii erano infixi, deliniamento Balustico, gracilifcenti seposa negli mucronati labii cum uno pomulo alla circunferentia. Elquale Polo era di finissimo & ponderoso oro, repudiante el rodicabile erugine, & lo'incédioso Vulcano, della uirtute & pace exitiale ueneno. Summamente dagli festigianti celebrato, cum moderate, & repentine riuolutióe intorno saltanti, cum solemnissimi plausi, cum gli habiti cincti di fasceole uolitante, Et le sedente sopra gli trahenti centauri. La Sancta cagione, & diuino mysterio, inuoce cósone & carmini cancionali cum extrema exultatione amorosamente lauda uano.
✶✶
✶

PRIMVS

EL SEQVENTE triũpho nó meno mirauegliofo đl primo. Impo che egli hauea le đtro uolubile rote tutte, & gli radii, & il meditullo defufco achate, di cádide uéule uagaméte uaricato. Ne tale certamẽte gestoe re Pyrrho cũ lenoue Muse & Apolline í medio pulfáte dalla natura ípffo.

Laxide & la forma del dicto đle el primo, ma le tabelle erão di cyaneo Saphyro orientale, atomato de fcintilluledoro, alla magica gratiffimo, & longo acceptiffimo a cupidine nella finistra mano.

Nella tabella dextra mirai exfcalpto una insigne Matróa che dui oui hauea parturito, in uno cubile regio colloca ta, di uno mirabile pallacio, Cum obstetricce stu pefacte, & multe altre matrone & astante NympheDegli quali ufciua de uno una flammula, & delaltro ouo due fpectatiffi me stelle.
✶ ✶
✶

Working with the type designer Francesco Griffo (1450–1518), Aldus developed fine roman types and a Greek typeface. In 1500, he and Griffo brought out the first italic type, a cursive, or tilted, script-like face. The 1501 small-format edition of Virgil's *Works* was the earliest book printed entirely in italics.

The Virgil was the first of many small Aldine volumes, the ones often seen in the hands of people of stature and degree in the great portraits of Renaissance Italy. These little books became part of the national character.

The Aldine book that was fixed for all time in the hearts and minds of typographers, designers, and printers, however, was a larger book, a work of fiction by the Dominican Francesco Colonna, *Hypnerotomachia Poliphili* (1499). This volume, an allegorical search for a lost mistress named Polia, is celebrated for the grace with which type, white space, and illustrations (by an unknown artist) work together— one illustration to a page, exactly the width of one column of type.

In 1896, when English poet William Morris wanted to revive the arts of the book with his Kelmscott Press *Chaucer,* he modeled his ideal book on the *Hypnerotomachia Poliphili,* a book printed perfectly nearly 400 years earlier.

Today, nothing remains of the Aldine press in Venice. Its location, however, is known. A 10-minute walk from the Rialto along an impossibly twisty route brings you to a limestone plaque that states flatly, in Latin, HOC LOCI ARTE TIPOGRAPHICA EXCELLVIT: "In this place the art of typography was made excellent."

After the incunable, or "cradle,"

period of printing, from 1455 to 1501, the genius of printing passed from Venice to France. Claude Garamond (1480–1561) and Robert Granjon (d. 1579) were typefounders who did not print. Instead, they sold type to the printers of Paris and Lyons and brought an end to printing as a one-person craft.

The printing dynasty of Henri Estienne (d. 1520), Robert Estienne (1503–1559), and Henri Estienne II (1528–1598), working near the Sorbonne and later in Geneva, set new standards for scholarly works, which they produced in Hebrew as well as Latin and Greek.

In the Netherlands, Christophe Plantin (1514–1589) established the largest printing office in Europe, with 160 employees manning 20 presses. The family printing firm founded by Louis Elzevir (1540–1617) was renowned for its cheap vest-pocket editions, a development reminiscent of Aldus a century earlier.

In Britain, the typefounder William Caslon (1692–1766) produced a clean face based on Dutch models. It was influential in Europe but was greatly in demand for American presses. Colonial printers sent to London for type rather than making it themselves.

John Baskerville (1706–1775), a typographer and printer from Birmingham, printed an edition of Virgil's poetry in 1757 that reminded the world what printing was about— paper, ink, and pressmanship. Simplicity was elegance. John Baskerville's *Virgil* and William Morris's *Chaucer* are often reckoned the crown jewels of English printing. Neither would have appeared without Caxton and Aldus.

SANCTA CATHARINA DE SENIS.

A BRAVE
NEW
WORLD

❡ PRINTING
IN THE AMERICAS

Applying ink to metal type, Tim McMahon prepares Colonial Williamsburg's letterpress, a reproduction of an 18th-century original, for printing. Print shops such as this were a focal point of American Colonial towns, and often served as post office, advertising firm, and local newspaper.

A death's head set in type hardly represents the distinguished career of Jonas Green, but for the annals of American printing it serves very well. Green (1712–1767) had come to Annapolis, Maryland, to be near its bureaucrats and lawyers, the delegates to a legislature that badly needed printing. Like any printer, Green loved the dull thunk of type biting into pliant sheets of paper. He liked even more the crinkle of bank notes in the cash box.

As printer to the province, Green kept Annapolis awash in paper and books. His masterpiece is a 1765 edition of the *Laws of Maryland at Large,* in more than 700 folio pages. It took four years to print. The book is dignified and stately, with MARYLAND set triumphantly in a grand parade of letter-spaced italic capitals. Inside, Green used black-letter or gothic type to set off all the introductory legalistic phrases—"Whereas," "Enacted," "And be it further Enacted"—an old-fashioned face for deadwood diction. In the margins, he printed notes that compress the dense prose into simple phrases; thus, 217 words on the militia became "Persons to behave at Musters decently, etc. Penalty for Misbehaviour to be determined by two Field Officers." Plain speaking.

Simple truth simply expressed has always been a very American trait, one that seems to have arrived on these shores with the first printing press. Certainly the person setting the type is in a good position to clarify it, edit it, fix it. In America, printers did that from the beginning. They learned to speak their minds, plainly.

Printers were not just book makers. They published newspapers as well. In 1745, Jonas Green revived the Maryland *Gazette,* the longest-running act in American printing, still coming out of Annapolis today. In 1765, however, choked with choler at the Stamp Act, which increased the cost of printing and thus lowered demand, he brought out special editions of his paper—such as *The Apparition of the Maryland Gazette, which is not Dead but Sleepeth*—with a skull and crossbones, rather than the now offical British revenue stamp, printed on page one. Plain enough.

Green had come to Annapolis from Boston, then a hotbed of radical printing. His great-grandfather, master printer Samuel Green, was a link to the dawn of the press in British America. He had come from England in 1633. In 1638, the first press arrived on the ship *John of London,* along with locksmith Stephen Daye and his family, including his son Matthew, a printer's apprentice. The press was set up in Cambridge on the grounds of Harvard College, and within a year the Dayes were recorded as having produced a broadside and an almanac. The first book that survives from their press is *The Whole Booke of Psalmes Faithfully Translated into English Metre* (1640). The Dayes were not great printers. The "Bay Psalm Book," as the volume has come to be called, has countless errors, but it is solid and serviceable. Out of a pressrun of 1,700, 11 are known to survive, despite long and hard use at church services.

In 1649, Samuel Green took over the operation of the Cambridge press and, over the next few decades, made its imprint famous. His most remark-

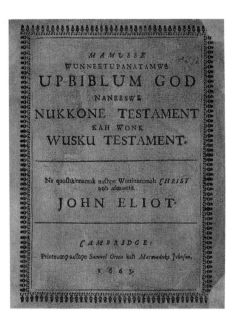

able production, however, was the first Bible printed in the 13 colonies, a work that appeared in 1663. No ordinary Bible, it was the first book printed in any Native American language as well. Its Algonquian title page reads *Mamusse Wunneetupanatamwe Up-Biblum God.* This was no easy job, and it bears all the earmarks of a labor of love. John Eliot, the missionary and translator among the infidels, might well have been able to read this transliteration, but it is unlikely that either Green or his compositors, proofreaders, pressmen, or collators recognized Algonquian on the page. And in making a book for people then generally considered to be savages, was not Green committing a social, if not technical, felony?

Of course, Green printed many books dearer to the hearts of the Massachusetts oligarchy as well. One of them was Increase Mather's *An Arrow Against Profane and Promiscuous Dancing, Drawn Out of the Quiver of the Scriptures* (1684). This is a small book, but it is confidently and generously set in a manner that is not at all small-minded, as you might expect with such a humorless text.

It would be convenient to report that the "Bay Psalm Book" was the first book printed in America, as is often said. But that would be wrong, by far. The Spanish had set up the first printing press in the New World within decades of Columbus's arrival. Like their counterparts to the north, they, too, were in the conversion business. And so, in 1539, more than a century before the Bay Psalms, Mexico City saw the first book printed in America: *Breve y más com-*

pendiosa doctrina christiana en lengua mexicana y castellana.

The society of New Spain, centered in Mexico City, was sophisticated and literate. Its presses poured forth a torrent of poetry and philosophy, theology and science. Not all the writers were Spaniards: in 1690, Carlos de Sigüenza y Góngora (1645–1700), a mestizo, published his *Libra Astronómica* a scientific explication of the appearance of a comet over Central America in 1680. In printing this clear-headed account, full of tables of observations, he crossed swords with the famous priest Eusebio Francisco Kino (1644–1711), whose own book *Exposicion astronómica de la cometa* (1681) had predicted dire effects for an unrepentant populace.

Intellectual squabbles carried out in print are always invigorating. Latin America's most famous such debate ended badly for one of its participants but at the same time gave the Americas their first feminist writer. Sor (Sister) Juana Inés de la Cruz (1648–1695) was a bright light among New Spain's intelligentsia. She was a playwright, a poet, and a scientist who is said to have corresponded with Sir Isaac Newton. As a nun, however, she risked all by writing a strong rebuttal to a sermon given a number of years earlier by a highly regarded Portuguese Jesuit. The bishop of the Puebla de los Angeles, impressed with the rigor of her thought, had her essay printed under the title *Carta athenagorica* (1690). When he sent her a copy, however, he included a letter under the pseudonym Sor Filotea making it clear that as she was a woman and a nun her time would be better spent in prayer. Her reply was swift but

John Eliot's Indian Bible, whose Algonquian title page appears opposite (top), was printed in Cambridge, Massachusetts, in 1663, by master printer Samuel Green. The first Bible produced in the 13 Colonies, it was also the first book printed in a Native American language. America's first print, the woodcut of Puritan elder Richard Mather, opposite (bottom), grandfather of clergyman and author Cotton Mather, was carved by John Foster, of Massachusetts, in 1670. Above, the title page of Juan de Zumárraga's Dotrina breve, printed in Mexico City in 1544 and one of the first products of a New World printing press. Spanish American printers also published the writings of early feminist and intellectual Sister Juana Inés de la Cruz, left, in the late 1600s.

measured; within months she had written *Respuesta a Sor Filotea de la Cruz,* a "Here I stand" that detailed her struggles as a female intellectual in the 17th century. It did her little good. She was silenced and denied the use of her 4,000-book library for the remaining four years of her life.

Latin America, of course, was not the only place where the establishment kept a wary eye on printers and intellectuals. Sir William Berkeley, who served as governor of Virginia from 1642 to 1652 and again from 1660 to 1677, is said to have remarked in 1671, "I thank God we have not free schools nor printing; and I hope we shall not have these hundred years. For learning has brought disobedience, and heresy, and sects into the world, and printing has divulged them, and libels against the best government. God keep us from both." Berkeley distrusted his Colonists; his overly harsh response to Bacon's Rebellion in 1676 cost him his office.

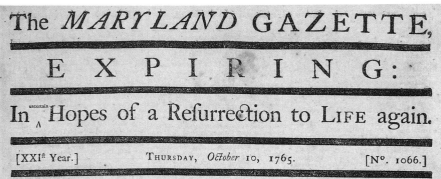

Printing was banned in Virginia until 1690. We were a rebellious, loud people. Printing made us louder.

There's a strange inconsistency here. Printing and typography are the most conservative of trades. The printing press hardly changed at all from Gutenberg until the 19th century, but consider how many revolutions its books fueled over that same span. In the deepest sense, books have two parts. The first has to do with ink, type, paper—the two-dimensional, controllable elements. The second is content, the uncontrollable, potentially volatile ideas contained in a book that can make it a time bomb. Printers are perhaps more aware than the rest of us of the inherent power and danger of books, which makes them a little more circumspect about content. When books cause trouble, the person who set the type and printed the sheet is often found just as culpable as the writer. Printers want to be considered the medium, not the message. But they never are.

The communications revolution in 18th-century British America heightened the dramatic role of printers. Newspapers fanned the fire. Everyone wanted the "freshest Advices both Foreign and Domestick," the Colonial term for hot news. Printers always put that first, at the beginning of their little four-page or broadside weekly papers. They filled out the rest with dense columns of tiny Caslon type, imported from England. The text listed all manner of advertisements and notices, the everyday matters that let us in on real life.

None of it was highbrow stuff. In fact, historian J. H. Plumb says that horse racing gave rise to English newspapers; people wanted race results. So it was in America, in its 10 or 11 colonial "rags," a word first applied to newspapers in 1734. The Virginia *Gazette* for October 17, 1755, announced, among other matters, that Tarpley's store in Williamsburg had just received a shipment of linen and gingham, that its old customers would be sued if they did not discharge their accounts, and that Tarpley's also sold "Rum, Sugar, and Melasses."

The same page listed houses for sale and for rent, noted that the almanac for 1756 had been published (seven and a half pence a copy; five shillings a dozen), and described several runaways, including Jimmy, "about 5 Feet 10 Inches high, of a yellow Complexion, very sly and crafty, speaks seldom, tho' tolerable good *English;* about 35 Years of Age; had on when he went away, a close double-breasted grey Bear skin Coat, with a black Velvet cape, and Twist Buttons . . . and carried with him a Gun."

The Colonial print shop was Eyewitness News and more, an information center. Papers were printed once a week, but people couldn't wait. They constantly wandered in for the latest news and notices. Williamsburg printers were so eager for dispatches that they sent post riders to the port of Norfolk to get the London journals. The best stories were culled from these pages and reprinted in the Virginia *Gazette.*

Much of what passed as "news" was too much for some people. John Custis, the cultured owner of an elegant Williamsburg house with ornamental gardens (and father-in-law of Martha Custis, later to be Mrs.

George Washington), sniffed, "I never have had any news papers in my life nor ever desire any. I do not regard who has lost a Spaniell bitch, who has died of the pox, and such stuff as Gazetts are stuff'd with."

But the traffic in news—in the "freshest Advices"—was so strong that print shops doubled as post offices and newspaper printers also had to be postmasters, a tradition followed by Isaiah Thomas, the Revolutionary War printer in Worcester, Massachusetts; by Samuel Green in Annapolis; by William Parks, the Williamsburg printer; and by Ben Franklin.

Ben Franklin's life revolved around ink and paper. As a youth, he was apprenticed to his brother's print shop in Boston. Fleeing that confinement, he traveled to New York and England before fetching up in Philadelphia, where he received the bulk of his education with a composing stick in his hand. He loved books, of course, but there is nothing like the discipline of typesetting to make someone really come to grips with and understand a text.

Franklin taught himself to write by trying to re-create essays out of Joseph Addison and Richard Steele's *Spectator,* the literary high-water mark for journalism, and then comparing his versions with the original. In his *Autobiography,* Franklin consistently uses printing terms—such as "one of the first Errata of my Life"—and at age 28 he composed the following bookish epitaph: "The Body of B. Franklin, Printer; Like the Cover of an old Book, Its Contents torn out, And Stript of its Lettering and Gilding, Lies here, Food for Worms. But the Work shall not be wholly lost: For it will, as

Printer Jonas Green, great-grandson of Samuel Green, used a special title and a skull and crossbones on his October 10, 1765, Maryland Gazette, *opposite, to show his outrage at Britain's Stamp Act. The death's head appeared where the tax stamp should have gone. Green's former employer, Benjamin Franklin, above, was official printer to Pennsylvania and Delaware. He printed laws, money, literature, the highly successful* Poor Richard's Almanack, *and the Pennsylvania* Gazette, *then retired to become a statesman and diplomat. The portrait above was painted in London in 1767.*

he believ'd, appear once more, In a new and more perfect Edition, Corrected and amended By the Author."

Franklin printed wonderful books that showcased his curiosity and love of language. His most profitable venture was *Poor Richard's Almanack,* which sold thousands of copies each year from 1732 to 1757 and made him a rich man. Cicero's *Cato Major* (1744) is regarded as Franklin's most handsome piece of printing, its title page featuring lines of type in black and terra-cotta.

Franklin was a quick writer and a tireless contributor to knowledge. On one trip across the Atlantic he wrote scientific papers on the stove, on navigation, and on chimneys. Such tracts were models of clarity and common sense; he experimented carefully and entered what he saw in clear prose. "The electrical spark will strike a hole thro' a quire of strong paper," he wrote in a 1751 paper on electricity—once again using a printer's term, a "quire" being 24 or 25 sheets of paper.

The phrase "self-evident" may be the one that helps us understand Franklin most. That's what his prose sought. When Franklin reviewed Thomas Jefferson's draft of the Declaration of Independence, he changed "We hold these truths to be sacred and undeniable" to "We hold these truths to be self-evident." In no small way, that was America. A people who depended on style and rhetorical flourish were old-fashioned, European. We were new Adams and Eves set free in a new Eden, and could do what we wanted. You could see it in our books: plain speaking.

The American writer who learned the most from Ben Franklin is Mark Twain. He, too, had been a printer's devil, apprenticed to the printer of his brother's paper. Twain knew what it was like to transform confused drafts into crisp prose that could persuade and move.

He detested perfumed writing and was constantly on guard against pretension. We can see his vigilance today in the manuscript of *Huckleberry Finn* (1885). "You do not know about me without you have read a book by the name of *The Adventures of Tom Sawyer,*" he penned, and then quickly changed the opening to "You don't." He wanted the sound of real speech, the way it was spoken outside the salons of literary New York and Boston. "I have never tried in even one single instance, to help cultivate the cultivated classes. I was not equipped for it, either by native gifts or training. And I never had any ambition in that direction, but always hunted for bigger game—the masses."

Twain was irreverent about the printing trade, especially when he recalled his stint as frontier editor in Nevada (where, by the way, editors all wore guns). "Ever since I survived my week as editor, I have found at least one pleasure in any newspaper that comes to hand; it is in admiring the long columns of editorial, and wondering to myself how in the mischief he did it!"

He tells us in *Roughing It* (1872) that he just invented Nevada news whenever reality let him down. But when there was real action, he soared. "When things began to look dismal again, a desperado killed a man in a saloon and joy returned once more. . . . I said to the murderer: 'Sir, you are a stranger to me, but you

Pictured at top in 1850 as a young printer's apprentice, Samuel Clemens would adopt the pen name Mark Twain. Above, the first page of the recently discovered Huck Finn *manuscript; opposite, Thomas Hart Benton's portrayal of Huck and Jim on the Mississippi.*

have done me a kindness this day which I can never forget."

Plain speech is the key, a thread that runs back through Ben Franklin and Jonas Green. If people think and speak clearly, their attempts to evade the truth—to tell themselves only what they want to hear—are frustrated. When they are not tested, pride, hypocrisy, and self-delusion always win.

The most powerful scene in all fiction, to my mind, occurs when Jim, the runaway slave, confesses to Huck that it was his own ignorance that made him hurt his young daughter. The incident, as Jim recalls it, happened when the child was four and seemed to be disobedient, not responding to his commands. When he asked her to shut the cabin door, she did not move, even after several requests. So Jim hit her, hard. As she stood before him, tears streaming down her face, a gust of wind slammed the door behind her. The child stood stark still. Could she be deaf?

Petrified, Jim tried an experiment, sneaking up "behine de chile sof' en still en all uv a sudden, I says *pow!* jis' as loud as I could yell. *She never budge!* Oh, Huck, I bust out a-cryin' en grab her up in my arms, en say, 'Oh, de po' little thing! de Lord God Almighty fogive po' ole Jim, kaze he never gwyne to fogive hisself as long's he live!' Oh, she was plumb deef en dumb, Huck, plumb deef en dumb—en I'd ben a-treat'n her so!"

A great writer once said that American literature began with a little book by Mark Twain called *Huckleberry Finn*. His name was Hemingway. Plain spoken.

"YES, WE HAVE NOW BANANAS!"

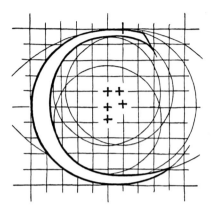

ENTRAL TO THE PRINT REVOLUTION is the lowly piece of type, a rectangular casting from molten lead with the shape of a letter protruding from its top. In this little block of metal Gutenberg's real genius is congealed, for it brought flexibility and rigidity at once to the page. This is no oxymoron. And anyone who has seen a page of his or her handwriting transformed into print knows it. ❡ Type is flexible in that it can be shrunk or expanded by changing type size or the leading between lines to fit any available space. The rigidity of the letter shapes, endlessly repeated in a text, lends a kind of regularity and clarity that prompt belief. The printed page thus assumes the authority of holy writ. ❡ The casting of type in the adjustable hand-mold results in a font—that is, a collection, in a single typeface and type size, of all the upper- and lowercase letters of the alphabet, and numerals, punctuation marks, accents, and any special symbols (ampersands, asterisks) and ligatures (pairs of letters such as ſt or fl, connected for stylistic reasons on one piece of type). ❡ Early on, printers managed their own type foundries. It was soon discovered, however, that a single typefounder could supply many printers, and the craft quickly separated from printing. Typefounders sold type by the bill, a measure of type by weight. In 1960, for example, a 1,000-pound bill of 12-point Caslon type would contain 4,200 m's weighing 34 pounds, 6 ounces, and all the other letters in proportion to the frequency of their use in the English language: 9 pounds of k's, 56 pounds of A's, 2 pounds, 3 ounces of Z's, and so on. ❡ When a bill of type arrived at the

Stored in their respective partitions in a type case, opposite, these pieces of type are 48-point Caslon, a typeface designed by William Caslon of England in the early-18th century. The type, which was cast in the United States in the 1890s, and the type case now reside in the Smithsonian's National Museum of American History. Originally an engraver of guns, William Caslon revived the art of type casting in England. His 1734 roman typeface remained one of the most popular book types for some 200 years; in 1776 America's Declaration of Independence was printed in Caslon type. The initial C at left is from Frenchman Geoffroy Tory's 1529 Champ Fleury, *an effusive study of language and letters. The Italian-trained Tory is considered the founder of French Renaissance book decoration.*

printer's shop, it first was sorted or distributed in type cases, shallow wooden boxes with partitions for particular letters. Each type font was stored in two basic trays or cases: an upper case for capitals and numerals and a lower case for small letters and punctuation marks.

Joseph Moxon's *Mechanick Exercises,* a 1683 compendium of English printing-house practice, illustrates the layout of the cases, based on a traditional arrangement dating from Gutenberg's day. When it is said that Gutenberg began the modern industrial world, the type case is offered up as Exhibit A: primitive time-and-motion studies contributed to its efficient design.

Distributing type in the case accurately, a job for the shop's apprentice, or printer's devil, was critical. Type in the wrong case, or the wrong partition of the right case, caused typographical errors. Like typists who memorize their keyboards, compositers knew by heart the location of the type in the trays before them, so they could concentrate on the copy they were setting.

Standing before a rack that held the lower case at a shallow angle and the upper case at a sharper angle above it, the 17th-century compositor began picking up letters and placing them into a composing stick, an adjustable type holder

held in the left hand. Each letter of type—reversed, of course, so its image would reverse again when printed—was placed upside down in the stick. (Typesetters quickly learned that the easiest way to read reversed type was upside down, because the letters then still read left to right.)

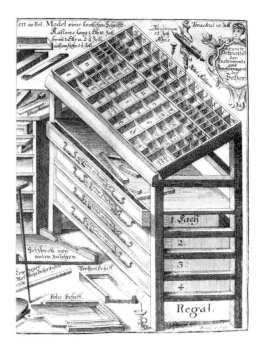

This meant the first letter would be inserted in the lower left-hand corner and the text would work its way right until the end of the line was reached. The second line of text, which of course would print below the first, was actually set above the first line in the composing stick.

To ensure that words were being placed in the stick upside down, each piece of type had a nick cast in its bottom side. The compositor could feel for the individual nicks as he reached into the case, and—after he had finished an entire line—could look for an uninterrupted row of nicks.

Nicks were time savers because, while it's easy to tell whether an A is upside down, for letters such as I, O, N, and S it is somewhat more difficult to determine that they're right side up. If compositors neglect to pay attention to their nicks, the name IOѴNNIS can appear completely upside down (except for the A), looking a little askew but still readable. The value of the nick was

discovered early: a 1498 copy of Sebastian Brandt's *Stultifera navis (Ship of Fools)* bears the accidental imprint of a piece of type lying on its side; the nick is clearly visible.

Six to eight lines of regular type would be composed in the stick before the type was transferred to a tray in which whole pages could be fashioned. A compositor who set more than a few lines at once ran the risk of making the stick too heavy to handle, or of dropping the stick and "pieing" or mixing up the type. Pied type was swept up by the printer's devil for redistribution in the type cases.

The compositor added spacers between words and between the letters of words to equalize the line lengths, a process called justifying. Of course, in those pre-spelling-bee days, another way of making a line the proper length would be to alter the spelling of some words, adding or subtracting letters. Knowing that he could set either "queen" or "queane" gave a 17th-century compositor a great deal of flexibility.

Something should be said here about the confusing "s" and "f" of early typesetting. Close inspection of a word such as "ufefull" set before the 19th century will show that on its second letter the crossbar does not actually cross; it is not an "f" at all, but an alternative form of "s." Further, this form of the letter is not used at the end of a word: thus, "excefs." Needlefs to fay, the letter always founds like an "s."

Another job of the compositor was to make lines of type look lighter by inserting strips called leading (if metal) or reglets (if wood) between the lines of type. In time, leading was cast onto the type body. Compositors then could choose a 10-point type on a 12-point body, yielding two points of leading between each line. This page is set in 11-on-14 Bembo.

In typography, the basic linear measure is the point, equal to 1/72 of an inch. Six lines of 10-point type with two points of leading—72 points—would occupy one inch of a column of type. The point system of measurement was developed in France by Pierre Fournier in 1737.

In the 19th century, trays called galleys that held about three pages of text in one column came into regular use. Earlier printers probably went right to page makeup, using pieces of wood called type furniture to hold the lines and

A complete form of type, opposite, including an engraving, is locked in the chase, or frame, of this mid-20th-century cylinder proofing press at the National Museum of American History. Above (left), "Glory to God, Honor to the King, Salute to Arms" reads type illustrated in the 18th-century Encyclopédie, *the great compendium of knowledge compiled by French philosopher, critic, and dramatist Denis Diderot. The lines of type contain letters of different styles as well as punctuation and spacers of various widths to control letter and word spacing. Above, a hurried compositor forgot the word "not" in line 14 of the Ten Commandments, creating the so-called Wicked Bible of 1631.*

columns of type in place. When the type for several pages was ready, it was locked into a chase (the printing frame) by quoins (metal or wooden wedges). The chase was then ready to be carried to the bed of the press for printing.

Type stands 0.9186 inches above the bed of the press. Everything expected to print had to be exactly that tall, or type-high. To ensure evenness in the final print, the type in the chase was pounded with a mallet, sometimes breaking pieces of type whose flawed images can still be traced from book to book.

A factotum was a type-high ornamented holder into which a letter from any font could be inserted, thereby creating an instant decorated initial letter. Until the invention of the factotum in the 16th century, printers often would leave a square space at the beginning of the first column of each chapter, so the book's owner could hire an illuminator to fill it with a fine initial.

Typesetting changed little for 500 years and added phrases to our language that are still with us. Like good compositors, we watch our p's and q's. We specify uppercase and lowercase letters. And even when we order computer-set type, we still wait for galley proof.

Mechanical typesetting began in the 19th century, first with the Monotype machine, which combined a typewriter-like keyboard with a lead-casting unit. Depressing any key automatically selected a matrix for that letter, into which the machine poured molten lead. Perfected in the 1890s, the invention produced individual letters that could be melted down after use and cast again as new letters later. In 1886, the Linotype machine was invented in New York by Ottmar Mergenthaler. It cast a whole line of type at once as a single slug of lead. The slugs or lines of type were then composed into columns and pages for printing.

The keyboard of a Linotype machine was arranged differently from that of a typewriter, with the letters s, h, r, d, l, and u on the top line, instead of the typewriter's q, w, e, r, t, y, and so on. Newspaper typesetters sometimes marked the end of a piece by running a finger across the top row of keys. If this last line of type escaped the eyes of the proofreaders and went on to be printed, people enjoying their morning newspaper would shake their heads at yet another appearance of the mystery word "shrdlu."

Linotype machines making "hot" type dominated typesetting until the 1950s, when photographic processes for making "cold" type began to replace them. In phototypesetting, the typesetter's keystrokes produce letters to make up columns of type on photosensitive "repro" paper, which is then pasted up into pages and photographed. The resulting film is used to make plates for printing.

Today, computer-controlled typesetting has taken the world by storm. Not only does it save money, but the printer's devil doesn't have to come into the shop at 4 A.M. to begin melting the day's lead. The best of these computers can make type of remarkable sharpness and can give designers almost unlimited freedom. With appropriate software, a designer can choose from an almost unlimited variety of typefaces, lay out pages of type on the screen, store the pages on a disc, and then use the disc to make film.

In 1886, American inventor Ottmar Mergenthaler, top, introduced a machine that allowed a keyboard operator to set complete lines of type automatically in single pieces of cast lead. Known as the Linotype, above, the device revolutionized printing: composition was fast and the type never wore out because it was melted down and recast for each new job.

Devices of the current printing revolution have fewer moving parts than the Linotype: tiny microchips on circuits, left, have made the computer indispensable to the publishing industry. Designers use screens and computer keyboards for typography and layout. A desk-top software program such as QuarkXPress, below, can create, display, and store illustrations and type for each page, not on paper but on a magnetic disk.

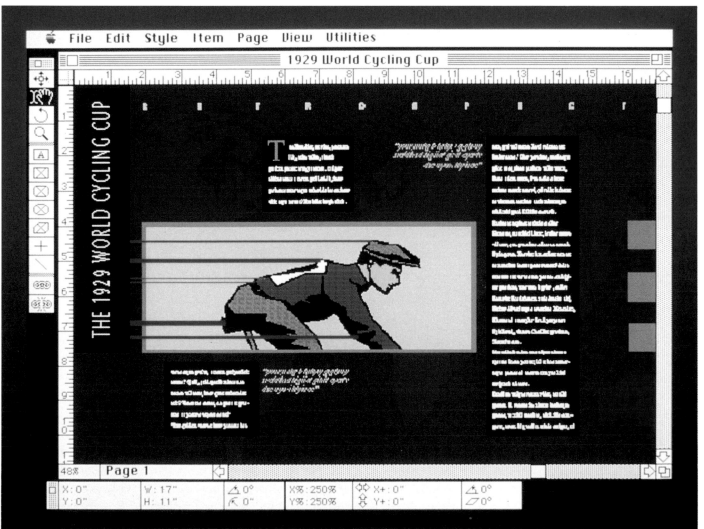

Geoffroy Tory's 1506 illuminated manuscript, Les Heures de Jean Lallement, *features the roman letter forms which he had studied in Italy and which later influenced his design of printing types.*

Although they have been made obsolete by the last century's advances in typesetting, the old factotums and woodcuts and printers' ornaments, distinctively broken and worn pieces of type, and compositor's errors and misspellings all have proved valuable to the science of analytical bibliography, literary sleuthing based on the study of printing-house practice. Its goal is to improve the study of literature by carefully noting changes made to a text during the printing process. For instance, in Herman Melville's *White Jacket* (1850), his

Black Letter
Old Style
Transitional
Modern
Slab Serif
Sans Serif
Decorative
Script

The black-letter or gothic family of type-faces is derived from northern European scripts of the 12th century. Gutenberg's printing type was black letter.

Old style is a 19th-century adaptation of the roman type devised by Aldus Manutius in the 15th century and based on Italian Renaissance handwriting.

Transitional was devised by 18th-century English printer and type designer John Baskerville. Old-style serifs are combined with the exactness of modern type.

Modern typefaces have contrasting thick vertical and thin horizontal lines. First used in France, they are derived from letters engraved on copperplates.

The family of slab-serif or egyptian type-faces maintains a consistent thickness of both lines and serifs. Also called antique, it is often used as display type.

Sans-serif typefaces also are often used for display. Their uniform lines and lack of serifs give them a bold, geometric quality but make them unsuitable as book type.

Decorative or display types come in many styles. Often seen in headings and adver-tisements, these faces are used relatively large and not for an entire text.

Script describes any face that suggests handwriting. Printing types had a profound influence on the way people wrote; this type reverses the process.

"soiled" fish of the sea, once thought to refer to evil under the waves, was dis-covered to be a typographical slip for "coiled" fish—eels.

Similarly, when Hamlet said he knew "a hawk from a handsaw," what did he mean? Was the compositor misreading "heronshaw," the name of a bird, from the manuscript, an easy mistake? And what did Horatio mean when he re-called that King Hamlet once "smote the sledded Pollax on the ice?" Did he mean that Hamlet's father whacked his heavy or "leaded" poleax on the ice, or

A spread from Theuerdank, *above right, an extended poem about Holy Roman Emperor Maximilian I that was printed in 1517 by Johann Schönsperger. The unique typeface, Fraktur, was Germany's answer to the classic roman face. Opposite, French illustrator Gustave Doré spun a web of typography to make this anti-Russian cartoon for his 1854* Histoire de la Sainte Russie. *The animated letters seen below were published in the 19th-century magazine* Rebus Charivariques.

that he attacked the Poles (Polacks) while they were crossing the ice on their sleds? Scribal or compositor's or proofreader's errors are all possibilities.

The greatest of the bibliographic detective stories is a 20th-century one, involving forged copies of books, printed and sold over many years by one of the leading rare-book dealers and scholars of his day, the legendary T. J. Wise (1859–1937). Wise was tripped up because he used a "kernless" font in printing bogus 19th-century pamphlets supposedly written by Elizabeth Barrett Browning, John Ruskin, and other writers.

Kerned letters are pieces of type, typically f, j, and y, that hang over the edge of the type body. In 1775, John Smith's *Printer's Grammar* had warned compositors about them: "Kerned Letters being attended with more trouble than other sorts, founders are sometimes sparing in casting them; whereas they rather require a larger number than their casting bill specifies, considering the chance

which Kerned Letters stand, to have their Beaks broke, especially the Roman f, when it stands at the end of a line."

Late in the 19th century, typefounders, discouraged by the damage that high-speed presses were doing to kerned letters, began designing fonts in which the problem letters were squeezed onto the body of the type, with no overhang. These were called kernless fonts. Such faces were very distinctive, the hook of the f being as curvy as a question mark.

Wise's downfall was an "Elizabeth Barrett Browning" pamphlet that was said to have been produced by a mysterious printer in 1847 but that used a kernless font not available until years later. The discovery was made by the bibliographers Graham Pollard and John Carter. Pollard is said to have noticed the deception as he left the British Museum one Saturday afternoon in the early 1930s. Walking down Museum Street, he stopped at a bookstall offering another pamphlet with the same curious font as the Browning pamphlet. Turning to the title page he discovered the book had been seen through the press by T. J. Wise—which meant the kernless font was a fingerprint placing Wise at the scene of the crime.

Carter and Pollard's book on the affair is a model of reserve—after all, they were accusing a bibliographic demigod of shenanigans. Its title: *An Enquiry into the Nature of Certain Nineteenth Century Pamphlets* (1934).

In general, early compositors and proofreaders had far more latitude in changing copy than they do today. Important texts sometimes were given to outside scholars to proofread and supervise through the press. A book printed at Naples in 1472 concludes with this boast:

> Sixtus the copies printed with much care,
> Now twice revised by Dr. Oliviere.
> The happy purchaser in vain shall look,
> Yet find no error in this faultless book.

Proofing during the pressrun often detects mistakes that only a compositor would catch. For example, a wrong-font error results when a piece of type belonging to another face finds its way into the wrong type case. People untrained in typography often miss wrong-font mistakes. Conversely, printers will correct a wrong-font mistake while ignoring misspellings that totally confuse the meaning of a passage.

A one-letter substitution—f for d—in the title of Tom Stoppard's award-winning 1966 play transformed it into *Rosencrantz and Guildenstern Are Deaf*. A similar change in a line by poet Walter de la Mare—"the leaves rusted in the hedgerows," meaning that they turned brown in the fall—was changed to "rustled in the hedgerows" by some unimaginative proofreader or typesetter.

Of course, it could be that literary researchers worry too much about such things. The eminent scholar W. W. Greg observed that a bibliographer hearing the Depression-era song "Yes, We have No Bananas" would be tempted to emend the title to "Yes, We Have Now Bananas," figuring that some dim-witted printer had been at the text. But that would be wrong.

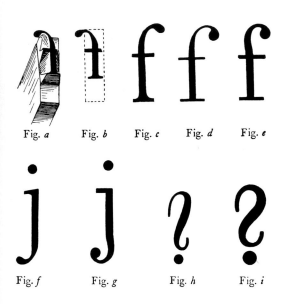

Fig. *a* Fig. *b* Fig. *c* Fig. *d* Fig. *e*

Fig. *f* Fig. *g* Fig. *h* Fig. *i*

British typographical sleuths Graham Pollard and John Carter exposed bibliographic scholar Thomas J. Wise as a forger of rare editions. In An Enquiry Into the Nature of Certain Nineteenth Century Pamphlets *(1934), above, they revealed Wise's use of 20th-century letter styles in his printings of what were supposedly 19th-century books of poetry. Opposite, American artist Robert Rauschenberg incorporated both relief and intaglio printing on fabric into his collage* Platter.

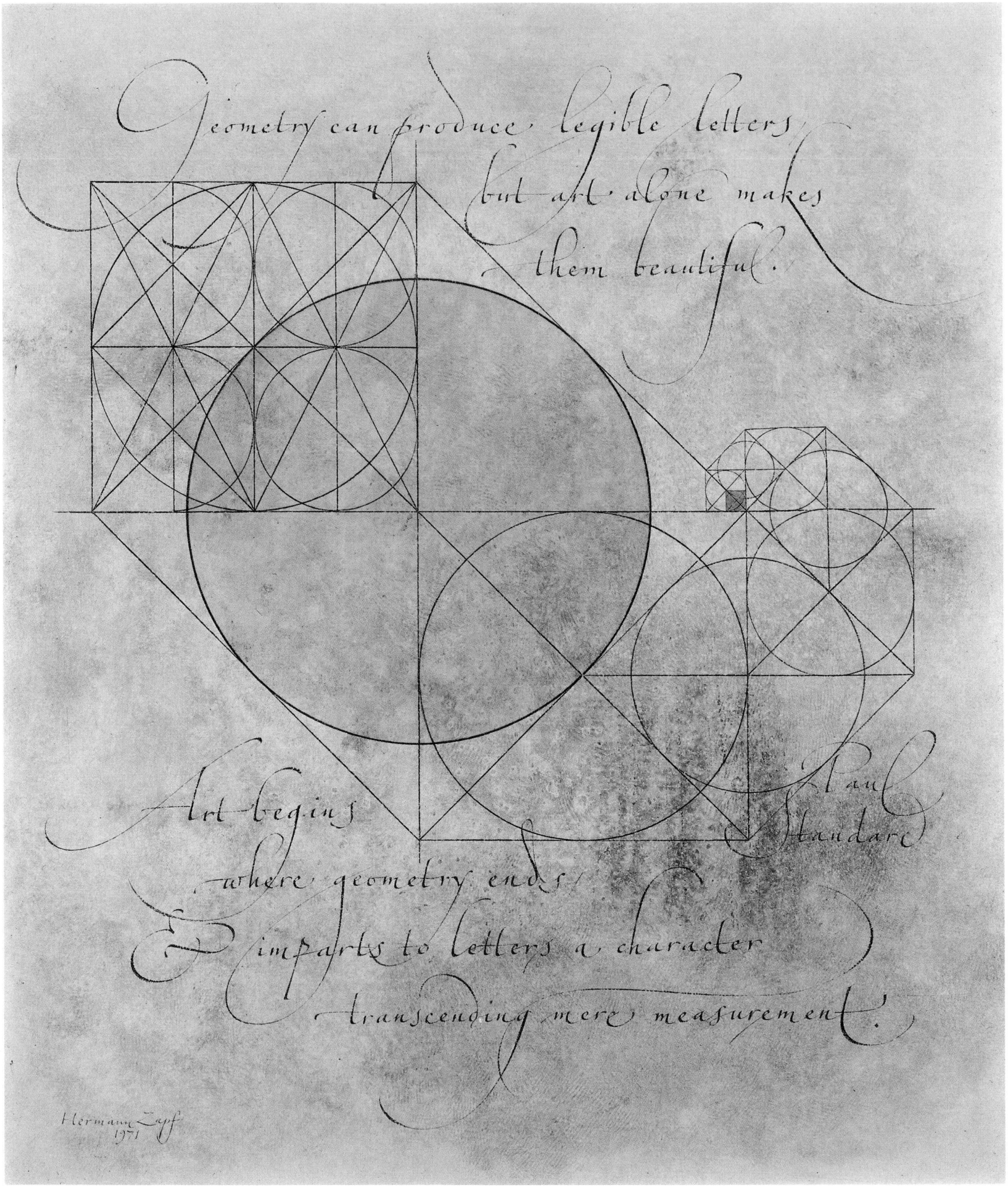

Geometry can produce legible letters,
but art alone makes
them beautiful.

Art begins
where geometry ends,
imparts to letters a character
transcending mere measurement.

Paul
Standard

Hermann Zapf
1971

The 20th century has produced its share of great typographers, designers who will always be counted with Janson and Aldus and Caslon. Three modern masters, however, stand out. The careers of Stanley Morison, Hermann Zapf, and Eric Gill are similar in that all had a solid understanding of the history of bookmaking, all came to typography through calligraphy, and all were influenced by the work of William Morris and the craft-printing movement.

Stanley Morison (1889–1967) began his typographic quest in London at the age of 23, when he happened to notice the Printing Supplement in the September 10, 1912, edition of the *Times.* Morison was completely captivated by the elegantly designed pages and printers' and typefounders' advertisements. He set out to devour everything about book and type design. He developed an italic hand for his own handwriting using a broad-edged pen and spent his leisure hours at the British Museum studying old books.

This almost monastic dedication yielded a philosophy of type and printing that he would carry with him for the rest of his life: "The chief function of the typographer is to interpret a text visually rather than to make attractive patterns on the page." This credo distinguished him from his forebears in the craft-printing movement, some of whom seemed to see the book more as a work of art rather than as something that was meant to be read.

Morison's research sensitized him to the pitfalls of modern typography. In 1913, for example, the Monotype Corporation of London issued a "his-

torical" face supposedly based on a design by the printer Christophe Plantin (1520–1589). Unfortunately, the type model that Monotype chose had never been used by Mr. Plantin. Morison was determined to prevent such gaffes while ensuring that classic type would be available for the high-speed press.

Type was not Morison's only interest. He was a devout Catholic and a Marxist who was jailed as a conscientious objector for two years during World War I. During those years he published a number of booklets and broadsides on war and peace.

After the war, at the Pelican Press in London, Morison designed fine books that attracted international attention. In 1923, he became typographical adviser to the Monotype Corporation, the same company that had erred with the Plantin face 10 years earlier. Soon his new types, all updates of faces from classic printers—Garamond, Baskerville, Poliphilus, and Fournier—began to revolutionize the look of books.

During this time, too, Morison was the force behind the *Fleuron,* the influential typographic annual published from 1923 to 1930. Each issue was chock-a-block with bibliographic research on type and antique printers and often served as the vehicle for the introduction of new faces.

At the *Fleuron,* Morison's purpose was "to improve the quality of printing, not by improving the printer, but by improving that much more important man, the printer's customer." He succeeded so well that before the 1920s were out, he was flooded with offers. In the United States, Doubleday wanted him to design books; in

Morison, Zapf, and Gill

❦ MODERN MASTERS
OF TYPOGRAPHY

German type designer Hermann Zapf created this celebration of the art of letter forms in Frankfurt in 1971. The quotation by Paul Standard is from Zapf's superb 1954 Manuale Typographicum. *Deeply committed to all aspects of the graphic arts and type composition, Zapf has been a fundamental force in 20th-century type design.*

Baskerville
Baskerville
Fournier
Fournier
Times New Roman
Times New Roman

Three classic typefaces revived by the English Monotype Corporation appear above. In reintroducing these typefaces, Monotype followed the advice of its brilliant type historian Stanley Morison, opposite right (top). Baskerville (1923) and Fournier (1924) were based on 18th-century types. The enormously popular Times New Roman (1932) was modeled after a 16th-century face. Opposite, the title page to Morison's 1933 book on Renaissance mathematician Luca Pacioli was designed by American typographer Bruce Rogers, as was an ornament, opposite right (bottom), used throughout the book.

England, both Oxford and Cambridge University presses wanted him for special projects. When Cambridge asked Morison if he'd like to join them, he boldly responded, "Yes, if you're interested in good printing." Clearly they were.

Morison's response to the hectic pace of the Jazz Age was to create a quiet and patient life of printing and design, manufacturing new typefaces and writing monographs on the history of type. It was a life so obviously full of unexcelled craftsmanship and care that William Morris himself would have approved.

Peacefulness, however, had a way of evaporating under the crush of people who wanted his talent. The *London Times* engaged him to completely redesign the newspaper: text, headlines, the lot. The task took him two years and resulted in the appearance in 1932 of a triumphant new typeface, Times New Roman, based on a face used by the 16th-century French printer Robert Granjon. Immediately after the type change, Morison began writing the definitive history of the *Times,* a massive job whose four volumes appeared from 1934 to 1952. Up until the end of his life he produced a stream of important books on typography, from *'Black Letter' Text* (1942) to *Politics and Script* (from a series of lectures, 1957–1972) and, finally, *John Fell: The University Press and the 'Fell' Types* (1967). Morison died on October 11, 1967. Nearly a quarter-century after his death, Morison is now in print again (thanks to the editorship of his former pupil, Nicolas Barker), with *Early Italian Writing-Books* (1991), a tribute to the calligraphic influences that

shaped his career and his life.

The triumph of Hermann Zapf is a trio of elegant faces—Palatino, Melior, and Optima—that are so sensible and beautiful that book designers and advertising executives alike have flocked to them over the past quarter-century.

Zapf was born in Germany in 1918 and spent much of his youth teaching himself italic letter forms, living laborious days copying the old masters. He was so self-taught, in fact, that it was several years before he discovered he was holding his pen the wrong way. Zapf's early enthusiasm was for modernistic calligraphy, but his ideas changed abruptly when he came across Edward Johnston's *Writing and Illuminating and Lettering* (1906). Reading those pages, Zapf realized that traditional italic letters—faithfully copied and thus deeply understood—would determine his future.

In a very real way, Zapf seems to be a descendant of the 16th-century Italian writing masters who perfected the art of italic lettering. In Zapf's Palatino typeface, the v, y, z, k, uppercase Y, Q, and the ligatures Th and Qu share their sense of grace and playfulness.

Remember that there are basically two kinds of type in common use: roman and *italic.* Roman is upright, orthogonal; *italic tilts,* like cursive writing. Most modern typefaces are designed with a matching italic font. Some are not, however. The Doves type of Emery Walker had no italics, and so books using it had to rubricate, or print in red, any lines to be emphasized. The Arrighi italic face was designed in 1929 by Frederic Warde to match the Centaur roman face of Bruce Rogers. Stanley Morison's

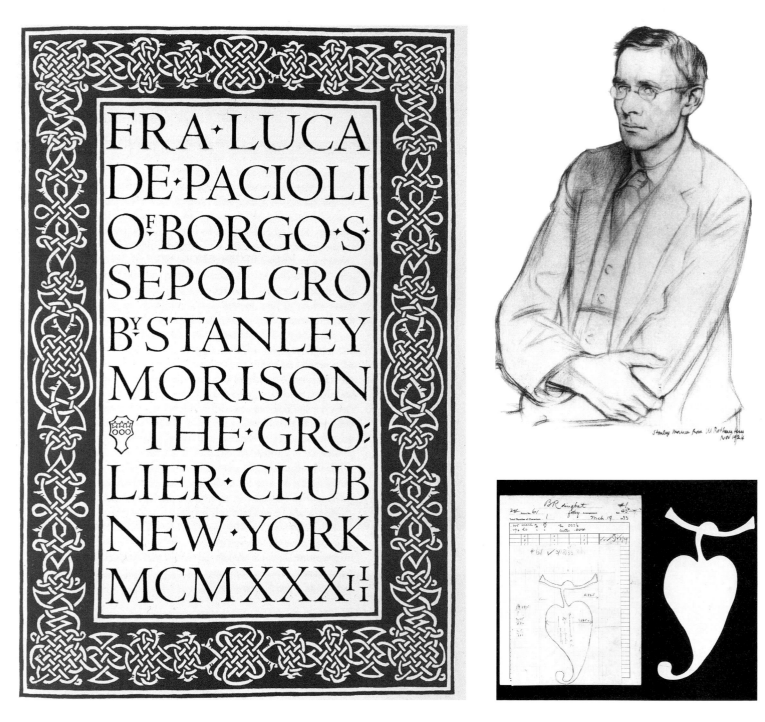

FRA·LUCA
DE·PACIOLI
O⸍BORGO·S
SEPOLCRO
B⸍STANLEY
MORISON
THE·GRO-
LIER·CLUB
NEW·YORK
MCMXXXII

Stanley Morison from W. Rothenstein
Nov 1924

Blado is an italic face that complements his Poliphilus.

Italic type evolved in three stages. The first stage centered on the Renaissance humanists, who rediscovered and adapted the Carolingian minuscule hands to their handwriting needs. Scholars such as Poggio Bracci-olini wanted their handwriting to be elegant, legible, and fast. The second stage coincided with the introduction of printing; in Venice, Francesco Griffo cut the first italic typeface for printer Aldus Manutius in 1501, and handwritten italics were no longer needed for book production.

The third stage was a post-printing development in which italic handwriting became an art. The three Italian writing-masters—Ludovico degli Arrighi, Giovanni Antonio Tagliente, and Giovanni Battista Palatino—wrote guidebooks to the italic hands that were the rage in all the courts of

Europe. Young Queen Elizabeth I of England mastered the italic hand, also known as the chancery hand. Stationery stores still do a lively business in italic pens. Stanley Morison once wrote of his own italic hand:

When I took my own script in hand I formed it on a certain, as I thought, rational basis and decided that, as far as capitals were concerned, I would stick to CAPITALIS QUADRATA *[broad roman caps]. And for the lower case I stuck to humanistic pretty closely, but not absolutely. I abandoned humanistic which has a straight "q" in favor of the capital form which has the tailed "Q." I did this for the reason that the tail seemed to give the shape more dignity, and I got more fun out of it.*

More than any other present-day typographer, Hermann Zapf seems to take advantage of the robust history of italic. One of his latest faces, Zapf Chancery (1979), was designed for computerized phototypesetting, vaulting over five centuries of printing. It does not exist in metal type. By slightly extending the serifs on the lowercase letters so that the letters appear to run together, Zapf allows the photoset page to have the look of handwriting, an effect that would be impossible to achieve in lead.

On its appearance in 1950, Palatino was a hit not only with designers but with the reading public as well. The *New Republic,* for example, has been set in Palatino since the 1950s. To accompany Palatino, Zapf designed an all-caps "titling" face called Sestina, which still can be seen on everything from title pages to movie credits. His Melior, designed for newspapers, is a squarish face also well suited to book design.

But Optima was the path-breaker for Zapf. With it he created a typeface that appears to be sans-serif (without serifs) but on closer inspection is not. It has faintly suggested serifs, those thicks and thins at the ends of letter strokes that are the remnants of the brushwork and pen lifts of the ancient calligraphers. Optima's serifs hold groups of letters together in word units. No other sans-serif alphabet works together in that way, and for that reason none is suitable for texts longer than advertisements. Optima is the most graceful sans-serif ever made.

Only one other sans-serif face has ever vied with Optima for grace and readability, and that is Gill Sans, designed by Eric Gill (1882–1940).

IT CAME TO PASS IN THOSE DAYS, THAT THERE WENT OUT A DECREE FROM CÆSAR AUGUSTUS, THAT ALL THE WORLD SHOULD BE TAXED. (AND THIS TAXING WAS FIRST made when Cyrenius was governor of Syria.) And all went to be taxed, every one into his own city. And Joseph also went up from Galilee, out of the city of Nazareth, into Judæa, unto the city of David, which is called Bethlehem; (because he was of the house and lineage of David:) To be taxed with Mary his espoused wife, being great with child. And so it was, that, while they were there, the days were accomplished that she should be delivered. And she brought forth her

137

Gill came to typography through his interest in art and sculpture. He trained as a calligrapher and was a student and friend of Edward Johnston, whose 1906 book had such an effect on Zapf.

Over and above typography, Gill retained a lifelong enthusiasm for making engravings and calligraphic inscriptions in stone or slate. In fact, the paper hat that became his trademark was not the traditional printer's hat but one he wore to keep stone dust out of his hair. It is unclear whether Gill ever set type or pulled a sheet from the handpress.

But he knew type. In the decade between 1925 and 1935, no fewer than seven important faces came from him. Gill Sans (1928) took England by storm, arriving on the scene just after the popular new German sans-serif, Futura.

Gill developed the Perpetua face and its italic counterpart, Felicity, for the Monotype Corporation and its typographic adviser, Stanley Morison. The face was announced in the 1930 edition of the *Fleuron*. Though Perpetua is Gill's, the face would never have seen the light of day had Morison not been there to cajole and stimulate Gill, as well as to get the punches properly cut and to wrestle with internal politics at Monotype. Perpetua was the first original design, as opposed to one based on a classic face, that Morison and Monotype sponsored. Gill's other faces—Golden Cockerel (1929), Joanna (1930), Aries (1932), Bunyan (1934), and Jubilee (1934)—were critical successes, but none achieved the wide use of Gill Sans.

For Gill, God was in the details,

especially in the details of his type designing. When he saw the first proof of Perpetua, he wrote to Morison that "a very nice font can be made from these letters," providing:

(i) The y must be altered—the blob removed . . .
(ii) The tail of the 'g' is rather heavy. You see it all over the page . . .
(iii) I think the bow of the lower case 'r' is too heavy.
(iv) I agree the space between the letters is too great.
(v) I agree that the capitals are too short . . .

On all typographical matters, Gill had strong opinions. "The title page should be set in the same style of type as the book and preferably in the same size," Gill wrote in his *Essay on Typography* (1931). "The title of a book is merely the thing to know it by; we have made of the title page a showing-off ground for printers & publishers. A smart title page will not redeem a dully printed book any more than a

Type designer Eric Gill created the Golden Cockerel Press version of The Four Gospels, *opposite, in 1931. Above (at left), Gill appears before the nameplate he designed and painted for the British Great Northern Railway's famous locomotive, the* Flying Scotsman. *His typeface Gill Sans, seen below with his Perpetua and Joanna, assured his fame.*

Gill Sans
Gills Sans

Perpetua

Perpetua

Joanna

Joanna

Palatino
Palatino
Melior
Melior
Optima
Optima

With his 1950 typeface Palatino, above (top), Hermann Zapf displayed an intuitive knowledge of Italian Renaissance letter forms, while his Melior (1952), above (center), and Optima (1958), above, were unique in their elegance. At right, children touch water flowing over carved letters at the Civil Rights Memorial in Montgomery, Alabama. Stone carver John Benson named this wall face John Stevens Sans Serif Roman after his 286-year-old company.

smart cinema will redeem a slum."

Gill worried about economics and its deleterious effect on both the health of society and the quality of the goods it produced. Printing was one of those goods. He sought to turn printing away from the production of vast amounts of ugly advertising, newspapers, and worthless books toward a craft-oriented society. Gill's ideal was in the unification of work and life.

It was a lesson straight from John Ruskin via William Morris, and it centered around the life in the print shop, the world of the typefounders, the engravers, the carvers of woodcuts. In more than 300 pamphlets and articles, Gill hammered away at his theme: "It is not true that a hand operated printing press is essentially the same as one automatically fed and operated by what they call 'power,' any more than it is true to say that a hand loom is essentially the same kind of machine as a power loom. It is not a proper use of words to call the work of Caxton 'mass' production; and least of all is it true to say that the early printers were simply men of business." For Gill, work was the crown of life, too precious to be wasted on the frivolous or tawdry.

Together, Morison, Gill, and Zapf were committed to the best of the past. They may look out of place to our eyes, with their broad-edged italic pens, their chisels, and their paper hats, but they refused to admit defeat at the hands of industrialism. They presided as printing made the shift from the mechanical to the electronic age. Any beauty remaining in the world of print today is due in no small measure to these three.

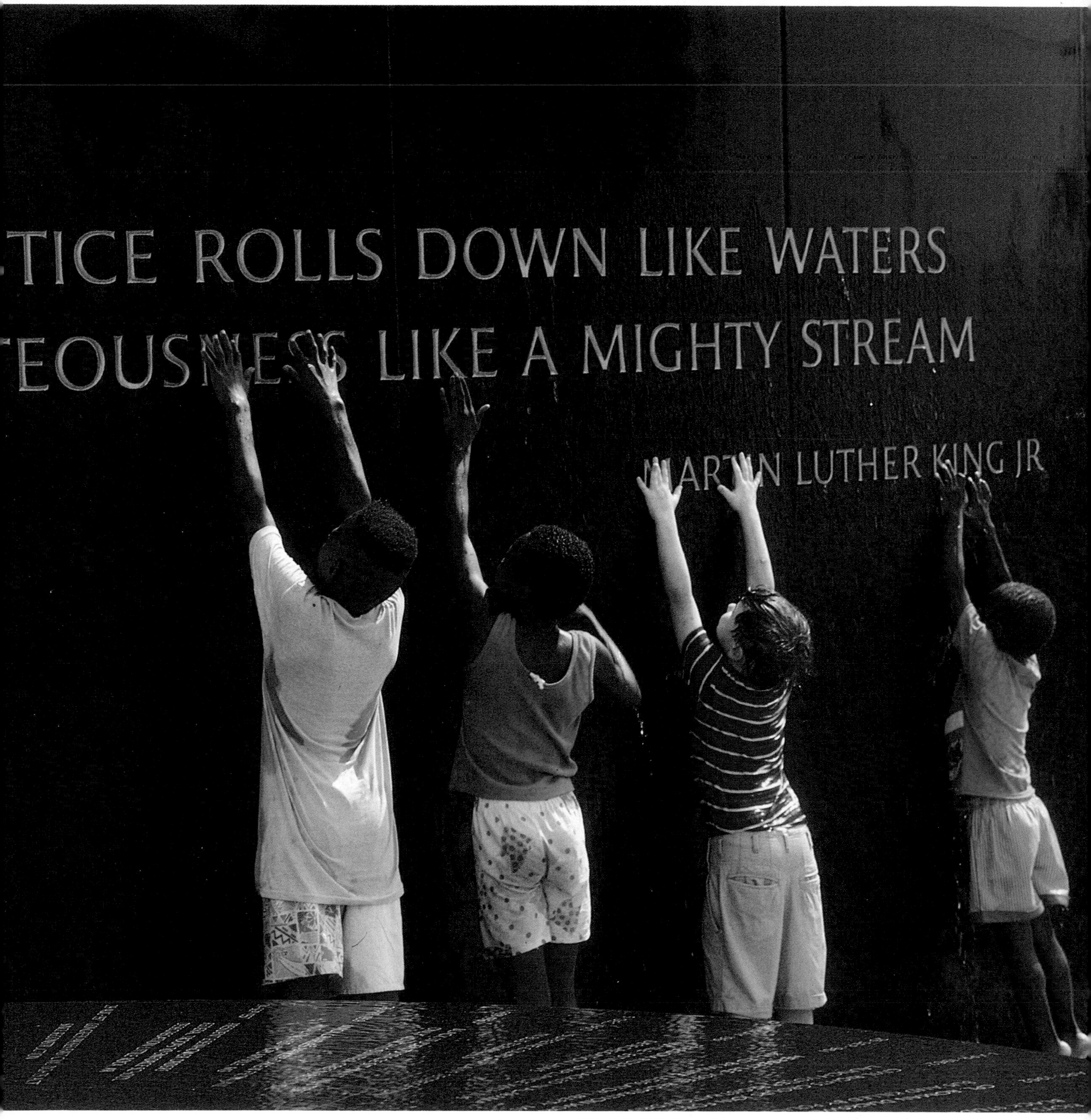
TICE ROLLS DOWN LIKE WATERS
EOUSNESS LIKE A MIGHTY STREAM
MARTIN LUTHER KING JR

THE BOOKMAKER'S CRAFT

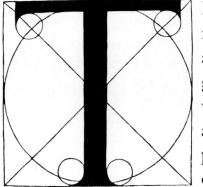

HE HANDPRESS THAT DOMI-nated printing for 400 years is, in essence, a device for bringing type and paper together. Its active ingredient is a bar, which, when pulled hard with both hands, turns a screw that drives a spindle down onto a plate, or platen. The platen presses a sheet of paper onto inked type lying in the bed, or coffin, of the press. Returning the bar to its original position raises the platen from the paper, which now bears an inked impression of the type below it. What could be simpler? ⁋ Before the machine could be used, however, the printer faced an important decision: what format to print in? The choice determined how much paper would be used and affected both the cost and size of the book. The printer also had to fix the shape of the book by deciding how many times each printed sheet that came off the press would be folded (a printed page to each fold). Paper was made in more or less standard oblong sizes; 22 inches by 15.75 inches was the largest sheet used by Caxton. If you fold that sheet once, it yields a book format of two leaves called a folio; twice, a quarto. ⁋ Of course, sheets do not have to be folded. An unfolded single sheet, often printed with a folk ballad or the account of some riveting scandal, was called a broadside. However, books could not be made easily from broadsides; the binder needed a fold for the thread to pierce to sew the book together. Even if broadsides were bound, the result was a large, ungainly volume that was difficult to read, especially in comparison with the more convenient folded format of the folio, which was the same as the *bifolium,* the format of the medieval parchment manuscript. ⁋ For a folio, two pages

While Columbus encountered the New World, printers in the Old World discovered the power of the press. In 1511, when famed artist Albrecht Dürer sketched a printer's shop, (detail) opposite, printing technology was still so novel that he recorded it incorrectly. He reversed the threads of the press's great screw, so that when the pressman threw his weight on the bar, the press would back up instead of pressing down. About this time printers stopped trying to make their books look like medieval manuscripts. This new identity came from mechanical typography, based on the clean, classical lines of Greek and Roman inscriptions cut in monuments. Such was the origin of the initial T at left, from De Divina Proportione *by Italian mathematician Luca Pacioli (died c.1520), whose work inspired generations of typographers.*

were printed on one side of the sheet, then the type in the coffin of the press was changed and the sheet was turned over and printed again. This is referred to as perfecting the sheet.

The printer then took the perfected folio sheet off the press and folded it once down the center. This yielded the unit of a book called a signature, and in this case the signature could be pages one through four. If so, the printing sequence on the press was this: on the first pass through the press, the sheet was impressed with pages one and four; this is called the outer form of the sheet.

If the printer was making 500 copies of a book, he would print 500 copies of the outer form, and then change the type. He would then perfect the 500 copies of the outer form by turning over its sheets and printing pages 2 and 3 on their inside, called the inner form.

In a quarto book, the sheet is folded twice. The result is a book unit, or signature, of four leaves or eight pages. Since the sheet still makes only two passes through the press, four pages are printed with each pass (modern printers refer to this as "printing four-up"). The pages must be printed so that they are in sequence after the sheets on which they are printed are folded and cut. This order determines which pages are printed next to, above, or below others. Thus,

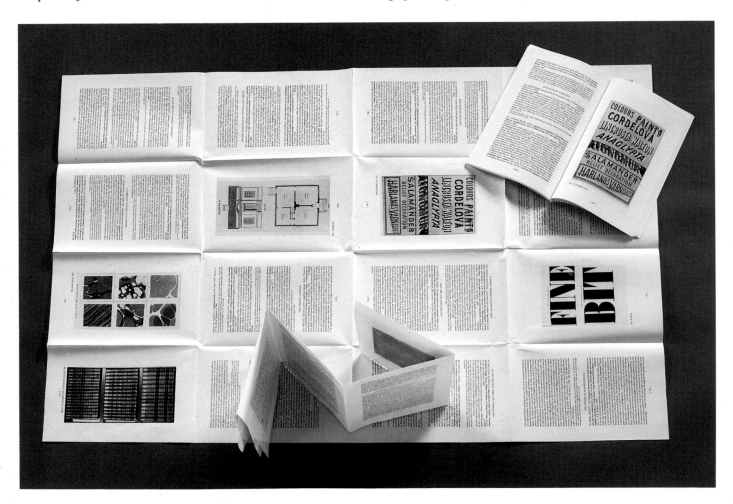

for a quarto, the four pages of its outer form would be 8 and 1 and, upside down above them, 5 and 4. The sheet would then be turned over to print the inner form: 2 and 7, 6 and 3. After the sheet is folded, the top folds are cut, making a gathering of eight pages.

The folio, a large format, was used for expensive presentation volumes and for important religious books. Quartos, half the size of a folio, were for more popular books, such as the short Elizabethan novels, plays, and tracts of all kinds.

Efficiency governed everything in the print shop. For a quarto, the common practice was to print the inner form (2, 7, 6, 3) first, since printing could begin as soon as the compositor finished page 7.

There are other formats as well. Folding the sheet again yields an octavo (three folds, eight leaves, 16 pages). Its outer form holds pages 4, 13, 16, and 1, with 5, 12, 9, and 8 above them. By continuing to fold, the printer gets a sexto-decimo (or sixteenmo, abbreviated to 16mo), a 32mo, and a 64mo (which, depending on the size of the original sheet, can result in very small pages). Combining the octavo and a special half-octavo format gives a duodecimo or 12mo (12 leaves, 24 pages) and a 24mo (24 leaves, 48 pages).

Folio books were often bound in quires, which means a gathering of two or three sheets folded once and slipped inside each other. The chief advantage of this format—called folio in fours, or folio in sixes—was that it saved time at the binder's and prevented an ugly buildup of sewing thread on the book's spine. For a folio in sixes, the outer form of the first sheet printed would consist of pages 1 and 12. The disadvantage of this format, as for all multi-page signatures, was that it required the printer to have enough type to set at least the first 12 pages at once.

If there is not enough type, then the compositor must be very good at casting off, or estimating how much type will occupy each page. A skilled typesetter might be able to set and print pages 1 and 12 (first outer form) and 2 and 11 (first inner form), and then distribute that type back into the typecase to be used in pages 3 through 10. But this left little room for error.

Naturally, casting off is far easier to do accurately if a printer is following a printed text rather than handwriting, a fact that may have affected the printing of Shakespeare's First Folio (1623). In that work, as many as nine compositors were constantly adding white space or crowding text when their estimates were off.

Once the book's format was settled, the printer could begin laying out his pages of type. This involved adding a running head or chapter title to each page and then a catchword at the lower right-hand corner of the page. An aid to printer and binder alike, the catchword is the first word of the next page repeated on the bottom of the page before. Catchwords offered a quick visual check on the order of the pages, not a bad idea for a book whose type was set upside down and read in reverse and whose pages were often upside down on the press.

The next task for the compositor was to add a signature to the first printed page of each sheet. Typically, signatures were letters of the alphabet (excluding J, U, and W)—although they could also be numbers—that indicated to the binder the order in which the book should be assembled. If a book was longer than 23 signatures, a second pass through the alphabet would list the signatures as A1, A2, etc. The word "signature" did double duty here; it meant both the gathering of leaves in a book and the identifying mark on each gathering.

John Smith's *The Printer's Grammar* (1755) contains tables of just where each signature will fall. Thus, in a quarto, sig. C will fall on p. 9, sig. N on p. 89. (Most books start with sig. B as p. 1; sig. A is reserved for preliminary pages and the table of contents, which is almost always the last page to be set.)

After all these decisions about page makeup had been made, the type was imposed—that is, arranged in inner and outer forms and locked in the chase. It then could be carried safely to the carriage of the press. On the carriage was a hardwood plank with a rectangular opening called the coffin, floored with a smooth piece of marble or limestone. Into this coffin would go the chase with its form. By turning a crank, the pressman could slide the carriage with its type under the platen of the press to make an impression.

Because of the size of the platen, typically 9 inches by 14 inches, two impressions were needed to print each form. For a folio, one pull of the bar would print the first page and then the crank would be turned, moving the type farther under the platen. One more pull of the bar would impress the second page of the form.

The crank would be turned again, the coffin would slide from under the platen, and the printed sheet could be removed. When it came time to perfect that sheet—that is, to print its other side, its inner form—there had to be a way of ensuring that the back of the sheet was aligned, or in register, with its front.

Two pins provided registration. They protruded from the center of the tympan, the hinged wooden frame that held the paper over the coffin. Every sheet was folded to determine its center line before it went on the tympan; the two pins, called press points, punched little holes in the sheet during its first press-run. When he perfected the sheet, the printer put it back on the tympan using the same holes, thus ensuring registration. Since the holes were in the folds, they would be hidden by the binding.

To protect the margins of the sheet from being fouled by ink that had accidently smeared on the furniture in the chase or on the coffin, another hinged wooden frame, called the frisket, was attached to the tympan. The frisket held a sheet of heavy paper with cutouts wherever type was supposed to print. All other parts of the sheet were protected.

According to Joseph Moxon's *Mechanick Exercises* (1683), the apprentices who removed sheets from the tympan were often covered in ink—"whence the Workmen do jocosely call them [Printer's] Devils; and sometimes Spirits and sometimes Flies."

Printing ink was greasy and sticky, very different from the water-based inks of the scribes. It was smeared onto a flat stone mounted beside the press and transferred directly to the type in the coffin with one or two ink balls covered in lambskin and filled with wool.

For the type to bite into the paper—to make the sharpest print—the paper had to be dampened. Every third sheet was wetted and the pile left overnight. Next morning, the damp paper would also require less pressure from the pressman to make a crisp impression.

When all was ready, a sheet of paper was placed on the tympan, the frisket was flipped down over it, the tympan was folded over the coffin, the crank was turned, the carriage slipped under the platen, the pressman pulled the bar, the spindle drove the platen down, and the platen mashed the paper onto the inked type—a chain reaction that changed the world.

After both sides of the sheets were printed, they were hung up to dry on ropes that stretched across the ceiling of the printing house. These ropes, strung with folded sheets hanging like laundry, are visible in numerous early prints. And so is the paddle-like tool, called a peel, that was used by the printer's devil to put up and take down the sheets.

Throughout history, the press and paper have been closely tied. Graham

A page from the Biblia Polyglotta, above, an eight-volume, multi-lingual Bible printed by Christophe Plantin from 1569 to 1572, displays parallel Greek and Latin texts. Opposite, Cornelius Kiel, one of Plantin's many famous scholars, proofread Dutch manuscripts and is considered the father of lexicography for the Netherlands.

Pollard's influential 1941 essay, "Notes on the Size of the Sheet," suggested that changes in press design usually were linked to attempts at printing on larger paper. Efficiency was the goal: 250 impressions per hour was the standard rate of printing in the 17th and 18th centuries. If both the platen on the press and the printing sheet could be made larger, productivity could skyrocket, with no change in the number of impressions.

Paper predates printing by almost 1,400 years, originating in China in A.D. 105. Papermaking came to Spain in 1150, to Italy in 1276, to Germany in 1390, to England in 1495, and to Philadelphia in 1690. As with every new technology, however, paper was distrusted at first: important documents continued to be written on vellum up to the 19th century. For the same reason, the Vatican used papyrus, with its ancient and honorable heritage, until the 11th century. Both Gutenberg and Caxton printed on paper and vellum. Still, the cheapness of paper made it widely available in Europe before the invention of printing.

Today, most paper is made from wood pulp in large mills that are equipped with giant vats, drums, rollers, and dryers. However, the chief ingredients of handmade paper historically (and currently) made in Europe and the United States are linen and cotton rags, which are beaten in water into a smooth, milky pulp. Dipping into a vat of pulp with a rectangular tray, the papermaker pulls up about an inch of the liquid, which slowly drains through a wire and screen mesh in the tray's bottom. As draining proceeds, the vatman gently shakes the tray, causing the matted fibers in the remaining liquid to interlock.

Sheets of partially solidified raw pulp are taken from their trays and placed in a press between layers of felt to squeeze out the last traces of water. At this point the paper is more like blotting paper, and so must be sized by being dipped in animal gelatin. It is now ready to hold ink on its surface.

The wooden frame around the tray, called the deckle, determines the shape of the sheet. Depending on its height, it also determines the sheet's thickness by limiting the amount of pulp lifted out of the vat. The uneven edge still seen on handmade paper and imitated by machine-made paper is known as the deckle edge, after the traces of pulp that seep between the screen and the deckle of the tray.

The mesh and wires in the tray bottom leave a crisscross impression on the paper. These impressions—called laid lines or chain lines, depending on which way they run—are visible if handmade paper is held up to the light. Papermakers advertised their product by weaving symbols and initials in wire and fixing them in the tray bottoms. Because these caused a slight thinning of the fibers settling over them, these watermarks are still visible today.

Laid lines, chain lines, and watermarks are important bibliographic tools. When they are out of place, it is a clear sign that a book has been tampered with. For example, chain lines are always parallel to the shorter side of the sheet, which means they will appear vertical in a folio and horizontal in a quarto. From page to page, from signature to signature, the chain lines should match up.

Moreover, since the watermark always appears in the top half of a broadside sheet, it will be visible only on the first leaf of a folio, only in the middle of the

Asian artisans transform raw materials from nature into fine paper. In a painting from 19th-century China, above, a worker gathers bamboo, a source of cellulose fiber. Opposite, Japanese women depicted by Hokusai (1760–1849) pound fibrous bark, separating individual filaments to make pulp, which is molded into sheets.

At Auvergne, France, in Europe's only paper factory to continue medieval craft traditions, employees combine old-time machines and manual skills. Opposite (left), a worker sorts and shreds rags, the source of cellulose that will be pounded into pulp by a battery of water-powered hammers to his right. Opposite (bottom), a vatman dips his woven-wire mold into a thin soup of water and cellulose fiber. When water drains from the mold, the coucher interleaves soft sheets with felt-like cloth, building a pile for the "Samson," or paper press, below (left). Everyone works the windlass to squeeze excess water from the couched paper, which is finally separated from the felt, at left. Below, sheets hang in the drying loft.

A magnificent watermark, right, produced by the Pietro Miliani mill in Italy depicts Raphael's Madonna of the Chair. Unlike earlier watermarks formed by soldered wires embedded in the mold, this watermark was first incised in wax from which an electrotype was made. The electrotype was then impressed on the woven-brass wire screen used in the papermaking mold. It originally measured 15 by 17.5 inches. Opposite, the pioneer all-metal press, invented about 1800 by Lord Stanhope of England, paved the way for all modern presswork based on the increased efficiencies of mass production. While retaining the shape of Gutenberg's wooden presses of the 1450s, Stanhope increased strength by the use of cast-iron and compound levers, enabling printers to make larger impressions more easily and quickly than ever before.

binding of a quarto, and only near the top of the binding edge of an octavo. Any disruption of these certainties indicates that someone—the author, the printer, a later owner of the book—removed or added a leaf.

This chapter has dealt mainly with letterpress printing, in which individual pieces of inked type were brought in contact with paper. This was the most common form of printing until the 19th century. Today, letterpress has largely been replaced by offset and rotogravure printing on large, power-driven presses that often are fed by great rolls of paper rather than individual sheets.

When type is set for offset printing, the resulting copy, called repro, is then assembled and pasted down on a board just as it will appear on the printed page. The finished board, called a mechanical, is photographed and the negatives are combined with any color and black-and-white illustrations. All are assembled or stripped into forms according to the imposition of the book. One piece of film is required for each color to be printed: if a book is to be black and white, only one piece of film (for the black) is needed for each form; but for one with color illustrations, four pieces of film in black, magenta, yellow, and cyan must be made for each form.

The negatives are used to etch a light-sensitive printing plate. Wherever the light strikes the photosensitive plate (that is, wherever it can pass through the clear areas of the negative), it etches an image onto the plate. These lightly etched areas will accept ink and are equivalent to the inked types of the letterpress. On the press, the plates—thin metal sheets wrapped around rotating cylinders—transfer their inked images to a rubber roller, which "offsets" them to the paper.

In rotogravure printing, cylindrical plates are engraved (again photographically) with the images to be printed and are bathed in ink. A wiper blade then squeegees away all the ink except that which remains in the engraved channels of the plate. A good way to distinguish the three printing processes is to compare their printing surfaces: in letterpress, raised; in offset, flat; in rotogravure, recessed. In letterpress, paper and type make contact; in offset and rotogravure, they never do.

There is something deeply satisfying about printing. Its literalness is its strength. The press does only what you tell it to do, and it does it with leaden precision. Today this exactness can be appreciated fully by a much wider audience than ever

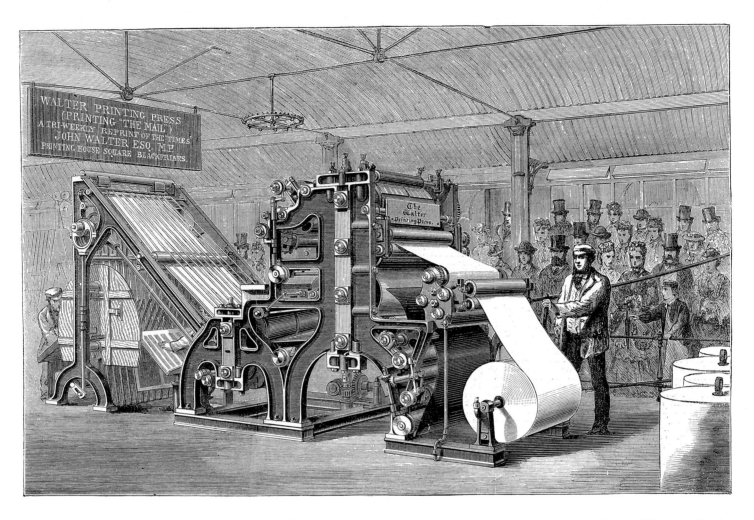

before, because computers are just as precise, just as stubborn. They are both wonderful machines.

Regularity and stability are what English painter and writer Leonard Woolf was seeking in 1917 when he considered printing as a healthful distraction for his wife, writer Virginia Woolf, who was teetering on the edge of breakdown. On March 23 of that year, the pair walked into the Excelsior Printing Supply Company in London and bought a small handpress and type for £19, 5s, and 6d.

"By following the directions in the pamphlet," Leonard said, "we found we could pretty soon set the type, lock it up in the chase, ink the rollers, and machine a fairly legible printed page." After one month, they had produced a pamphlet containing two of Virginia's stories. Their fourth production, in May 1919, was a 250-copy edition of *Poems* by their friend T. S. Eliot.

Leonard, Virginia, and countless others before and after them have discovered that printing is soothing not because it is mindless, but because it demands such a high level of concentration that everything but the book at hand—and the idea it's trying to communicate—fades into the corners of the mind and the print shop.

And when the printing is done, the book is a thing in itself—not an imitation of anything else. It's a child nourished on love and independence that can go forth and make something happen.

Forsaking the flat-bed presses of yore in favor of rotary designs, modern printers achieve sizzling speeds of tens of thousands of impressions an hour on endless sheets. The big rolls of paper, called webs, were first fitted to the British Walter press, as opposite, after 1869. This web press, however, needed to be shut down to change rolls. Today's web machines, such as the Compacta s60 used to print your Smith-sonian Book of Books (see computerized console below), change webs on the fly, splicing paper from a full roll to the old, nearly empty roll just before it runs out.

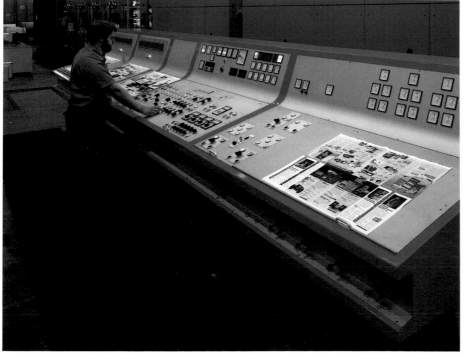

To Print or Not to Print?

◖ FOR SHAKESPEARE,
THAT WAS THE QUESTION

An engraving of William Shakespeare graces the title page of the first printed edition of his collected works. Published in 1623, seven years after Shakespeare's death, and known as the First Folio, the volume contained 36 plays, including the first printed versions of Macbeth, The Tempest, As You Like It, *and 15 others.*

Shakespeare loved books. In *Romeo and Juliet,* in an extended metaphor, Lady Capulet compares Juliet's lover, Paris, to a rare and captivating volume:

Read o'er the volume of young Paris'
*   face,*
And find delight writ there with beauty's
*   pen.*
Examine every married lineament,
And see how one another lends content,
And what obscured in this fair volume lies
Find written in the margent of his eyes.
This precious book of love, this unbound
*   lover,*
To beautify him, only lacks a cover.
The fish lives in the sea, and 'tis much
*   pride*
For fair without the fair within to hide.
That book in many's eyes doth share the
*   glory*
That in golden clasps locks in the golden
*   story.*
So shall you share all that he doth possess,
By having him making yourself no less.

Despite these and numerous other references to books, however, Shakespeare seemed to show little regard for the business of printing, which had been around for more than a century. Consider what his character Jack Cade says in *Henry VI, Part 2:*

Thou hast most traitorously corrupted the youth of the realm in erecting a grammar school. And whereas before, our forefathers had no other books but the score and the tally, thou hast caused printing to be used, and, contrary to the King, his crown, and dignity, thou hast built a papermill.

Shakespeare was an actor and a playwright, and a partner in a successful theatrical company. The stage was his world. Printed versions of a play? Perhaps they were beneath his dignity. In any case, plays were for acting, not reading. It's puzzling: the greatest writer of all time saw none of his plays through the press. Instead, he stood by as pirated editions of his works appeared throughout his life. Only in 1623, seven years after his death, did his friends and colleagues publish his collected plays. And even this book, known as the First Folio and considered the foremost volume in literary history, omits at least two of his plays and contains thousands of errors.

At the time, London had not yet attained the standard of printing set a century earlier by Venetian and other pressmen. Finely printed books were never the goal of the London printers and publishers. What they wanted were profits, and so they turned out pamphlets on the sensational, broadside ballads on the unspeakable, and hair-raising tracts on sinners and a vengeful God. These serviceable, legible books reaped financial benefits for printers, publishers, and booksellers, but offered little in the way of aesthetics for poets and aristocrats.

Change came slowly to that world. Almost a century and a half after the invention of printing, the technology was still distrusted. It was regarded as clumsy and unattractive. And, compared with the best calligraphic manuscripts, it was. So poets continued to circulate their songs in manuscript rather than plain print.

It appears, though, that young Shakespeare (1564–1616) did descend to the level of print for his two long narrative poems, *Venus and Adonis* (1593) and *The Rape of Lucrece* (1594).

Mr. WILLIAM
SHAKESPEARES

COMEDIES,
HISTORIES, &
TRAGEDIES.

Publiſhed according to the True Originall Copies.

Martin Droeshout sculpsit London.

LONDON
Printed by Iſaac Iaggard, and Ed. Blount. 1623.

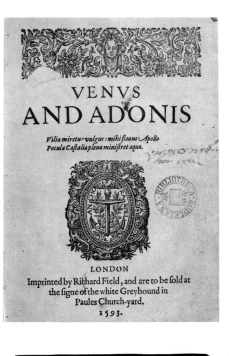

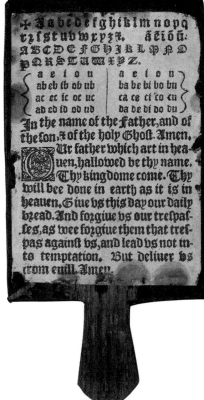

This may have been because the printer was Richard Field, who, like Shakespeare, had grown up in Stratford-upon-Avon and then moved to London to try his luck in the big city.

In contrast to most of the products of Elizabethan printing, these slim volumes of poetry are relatively free of printers' or compositors' errors, which suggests that Shakespeare himself may have had a hand in the proofreading. *Venus* has a few errors, all of them trivial, but the 1593 edition of the poem survives in only one known copy; without others to compare it to, we can't look for on-press corrections.

It's a different matter with *Lucrece:* 11 copies of its 1594 edition survive, and in them we can note corrections that were made during the printing run. Again there are very few errors; perhaps Shakespeare indeed was hovering about the press. One "correction," however, is worse than the original mistake, and that gives some scholars considerable pause regarding Shakespeare's actual role in the poem's printing.

Here's the rub: in some copies of *Lucrece,* line 50 reads, "When at Colatium this false lord arived. . . . " While that form was still being printed, someone unlocked the chase to correct the misspelled "arived," and at the same time took the liberty of changing the spelling of "Colatium," an ancient city 10 miles east of Rome, to what was then considered the more correct—but also pedantic— "Colatia." The trouble is this person forgot to change the spelling of the same word in line four. Would Shakespeare have made that change? Could

he have made that mistake? If the answer is "no" on either count, then perhaps Shakespeare never set foot in Field's shop at all.

And if this last is so, it may mean that the two poems were printed the same way in which his plays first were: they were pirated. There were a number of ways to do this. A printer could "borrow" or pay someone to sneak off with the acting company's prompt copy, the copy held by the prompter during a performance. Apparently this happened with the 1599 edition of *Romeo and Juliet*—the case of a telltale printer's error. The error occurs in Act IV, in which a stage direction ought to read "Enter Peter." Instead, the direction in this version reads, "Enter Will Kempe." Will Kempe was the famous comedian of Shakespeare's playhouse company, and so the compositor was simply copying what he held before him— a handwritten manuscript that named a specific actor rather than a character.

Editions of Shakespeare's works are referred to by their printed format. Plays, for example, are in quarto form, which means they are printed on single sheets of paper that are folded twice, yielding four leaves to each gathering in the book. The 1599 edition of *Romeo and Juliet* is called Q2 because there was an earlier pirated quarto of this play in 1597. That copy, known as Q1, is very corrupt, lacking some 700 lines that are in Q2.

Oddly, Q2 mimics Q1 in printing much of the Nurse's dialogue from Act I in italics, for no apparent reason. It also prints two contradictory versions of the lines Romeo speaks over Juliet's body, lines Shake-

OCTO. X.

When as the witherd leaf doth fall
And wan-hewd Autumne doth apall
And with fowle tanny spots desgrace
The beautie off the faire yeares face
Their maye as in glas be seene
Thy lyfe, ô wordling! Some tymes greene,
And sometymes faded and forlorne
As yow no fruict nor leafe had borne

The calligraphy of Esther Inglis, above, was admired by Queen Elizabeth I herself. Most literature in 17th-century England was published in manuscript.

Opposite (top), this 1593 title page of Shakespeare's Venus and Adonis is from the last known complete copy of this poem's first printing. Opposite (bottom), hornbooks such as this introduced young Elizabethans to the alphabet, the Lord's Prayer, and other examples of the printed word.

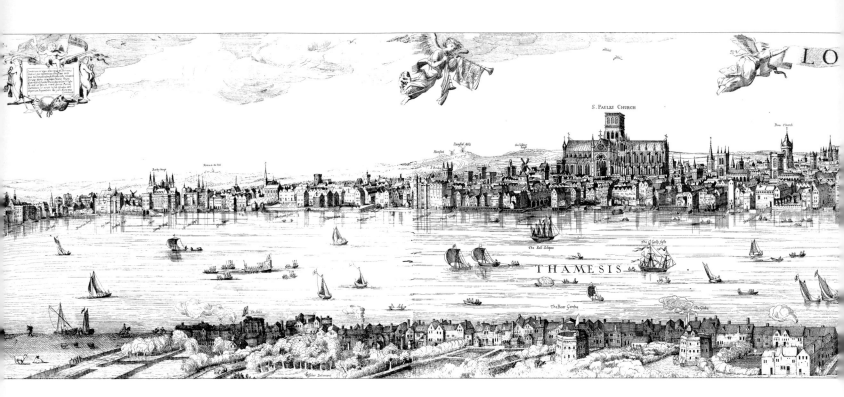

The Globe

A 1616 engraving of a panoramic view of London, top, includes such familiar landmarks as London Bridge, St. Paul's Cathedral, the Southwark gaming district, and, at lower left, Shakespeare's Globe Theater, depicted in a detail above. In fact, the Globe had burned down during a performance of Henry VIII *in 1613.*

speare may have been revising at the time. Was the compositor's text of Q2 actually Shakespeare's autograph manuscript? It's tantalizing, because no plays or poetry in Shakespeare's handwriting have ever been found, apart from three controversial manuscript pages from the play *The Book of Sir Thomas More,* said to be in his hand.

We should not be too hard on the printers of the time, however. The orthography of early modern English was itself unsettled; many words were spelled several ways. Shakespeare's autographs even show variant spellings of his own name. But in *Cymbeline,* it was a printer's error that resulted in the misspelling of the name of the character Innogen as "Imogen" and thus popularized this name.

Pilfering copy was not the only way to force reluctant authors into print. A publisher also could pay someone to attend several perfor-

mances of a play, memorize the dialogue to the best of his ability, and then dictate it to the printer. This is called memorial reconstruction, and it has been implicated in the printing of a number of plays, especially those that appear in the very corrupt quartos. One celebrated case is the dimly remembered soliloquy from the *Hamlet* published in 1603 and known as Q1:

To be, or not to be, I there's the point,
To Die, to sleepe, is that all? I all:
No, to sleepe, to dreame, I mary there it
*   goes,*
For in that dreame of death, when wee
*   awake,*
And borne before an everlasting Judge,
From whence no passenger ever retur'nd.

This is probably not so bad, considering the difficulty of the task. About 1930, pioneer bibliographer W. W. Greg tested the memorial-reconstruction theory by attending a

FLUVIUS

South Warke

new play in London and then racing home to copy out the dialogue without the benefit of notes. After a few tries, he found he could do as well as the *Hamlet* Q1, known as the "bad quarto."

Rather than depend on someone who was a complete stranger to the text, enterprising publishers also suborned actors into their game, a better idea that yielded at least some sensible readings. In *King Lear,* for example, the printer of the first quarto may have hired the two boy actors who played Goneril and Regan, since the dialogue for those two characters is nearly perfect, while the rest of the text is very corrupt.

The quartos were sold as paperbacks, which owners were free to have bound more substantially if they wished. The biggest investment for the publisher was the paper, rather than the press time or labor. No bookseller wanted to be stuck with

surplus quartos, so print runs were kept quite small, probably under 1,000 copies. The little books sold for sixpence apiece; today there are between one and twelve copies of each of these quartos, some of which, depending on the particular play, would fetch hundreds of thousands of dollars on the market.

In 1616, the year of Shakespeare's death, a folio edition of Ben Jonson's *Workes* was published in London. It included nine of his plays. Suddenly it must have seemed that the printing of plays could be both decorous and profitable. Seven years later several publishers and printers collaborated with Shakespeare's theatrical associates in the publication of a huge volume entitled *Mr. William Shakespeares Comedies, Histories, & Tragedies. Published according to the True Originall Copies.* We call this landmark work the First Folio, after the book's format: a single sheet folded only

This drawing of the Swan Theater, sketched in 1596, is the only surviving depiction of the interior of a 16th-century English playhouse. Three tiers of galleries surround the stage, where a play appears to be in progress. The theater could accommodate about 3,000 people.

A rare First Folio page from Anthony and Cleopatra, *with proofreader's marks intact.*

frequent interruptions for smaller or more remunerative jobs. Such lapses in concentration resulted in countless on-press corrections, and there were other production woes as well. None of these detracts from the greatness of the First Folio. Oddly enough, however, considering its stature, it is not a rare volume: from a first pressrun of about 750, some 230 complete First Folios survive. The lion's share of these are at the Folger Shakespeare Library in Washington, D.C. Our understanding of this celebrated book took a quantum leap in 1963 with the publication of *The Printing and Proof-reading of the First Folio of Shakespeare,* by Charlton Hinman, a work of monumental scholarship based on painstaking examinations of the Folger's First Folios. Hinman was looking for variants in punctuation and spelling that would betray the secrets of the printing house.

To help him, he used a machine developed for him by U.S. Navy engineer Arthur Johnson. Johnson adapted the machine—which came to be known as the Hinman Collator—from one he had built to assess bomb damage during World War II. His technique involved taking before-and-after photographs of a target and then rapidly projecting them one after another onto a screen, causing the altered areas to appear to blink. The device he built for Hinman worked similarly: when the same page from different folios was flashed onto a mirror again and again, a renegade punctuation mark or curious spelling wriggled while the rest of the page remained still.

Eventually, Hinman was able to

once, making it twice the size of a quarto. Scholars refer to the First Folio as F1 to distinguish it from later folio editions that appeared in 1632, 1663–1664, and 1685.

The printing of the First Folio was a massive task that took nearly two years to complete, in part because of deduce the precise order in which each of the plays had been set in type and printed. In fact, he placed in sequence not only the printing of the plays, but that of the quires, or 12-page groups of folio sheets, as well. Extensive examinations of the nature of the type—especially broken or worn pieces—enabled him to determine the number of type cases that had been in use in the printing shop. Turning his attention to spelling peculiarities, Hinman was able to identify the five compositors who set the book, one of whom had been an apprentice at the time. (Later studies would add four more First Folio compositors to Hinman's list.)

Hinman discovered that, perhaps as a time-saving feature, two different compositors sometimes would set type for two different pages in one form—that is, there would be two pages on the press at once. Such a scheme demanded a great deal of confidence in casting off, or predicting how much type will fit on a page. Trying to accommodate the text in advance was a challenging and constant problem, and errors in casting off were adjusted by crowding type, compressing text, and eliminating white space, or, conversely, by bloating the text to fill up the page. The result is text that is often uneven, at times appearing slipshod.

Recent discoveries by scholar Peter W. M. Blayney, curator of the Folger Shakespeare Library's 1991 exhibition on the First Folio, contributed significantly to what is known of this work. Among other key findings, Blayney found specific evidence of the haste in which printers switched from the First Folio

Ham. To be, or not to be, I there's the point,
To Die, to sleepe, is that all? I all:
No, to sleepe, to dreame, I mary there it goes,
For in that dreame of death, when wee awake,
And borne before an euerlasting Iudge,

Ham. To be, or not to be, that is the question,
Whether tis nobler in the minde to suffer
The slings and arrowes of outragious fortune,
Or to take Armes against a sea of troubles,
And by opposing, end them, to die to sleepe
No more, and by a sleepe, to say we end

to other jobs: on a single page of a copy of the folio appears the faint image of a page from another book, *The Theater of Honour.* It was transferred to the Shakespeare page from wet ink on the tympan of the press.

Is all this intense research much ado about nothing? Just how impor-

Top, a dancing Will Kempe, comedian in Shakespeare's company from 1587 to 1599. Above, the 1603 quarto version of Hamlet's soliloquy (top) garbles the supposedly truer 1604 version.

A replica of the Shakespeare Temple, above, built by preeminent 18th-century Shakespearean actor David Garrick at his home in Hampton, holds an 1825 set of the Bard's works and was said to have been presented to William IV as a coronation gift. Above (right), Fritz Weaver appears in the title role of King Lear, shown here comforting the Earl of Gloucester, played by Ted Van Griethuysen, in a 1991 production by the Shakespeare Theatre at the Folger in Washington, D.C. Opposite, Prospero rules the waves in a dramatic image from the title page of a 19th-century edition of The Tempest. *Written about 1611, this was Shakespeare's last comedy.*

tant is the First Folio? It contains the only versions we have of *Macbeth, The Tempest,* and 16 other plays. Without it, they would have been lost forever.

Still, because of Shakespeare's disdain for print, we can never be completely certain about the extent of his playwrighting. Consider *Love's Labour's Won,* surely the Loch Ness monster of bibliography: first sighted in a list of Shakespeare's comedies compiled in 1598, the play has never been found.

In the end, Shakespeare's regard for books is clear: his writings hold no fewer than 366 references to reading and books. We have Berowne and the bookmen of *Love's Labour's Lost* attempting, and failing so lovingly, to re-create a book culture; Lavinia, the pitiful daughter of *Titus Andronicus,* trying to turn the pages of Ovid with the bloody stumps that were once her hands; and the servant

in *Romeo and Juliet,* unable to decipher the Capulets' guest list, stopping Romeo and asking for help: "I pray, sir, can you read?" His innocent question sets the whole play in motion.

The Tempest offers perhaps the most powerful book reference of all: the heavy volume of "rough magic" that Prospero throws into the sea at the end of a grand and glorious career as wizard of his little island.

. . . I'll break my staff,
Bury it certain fathoms in the earth,
And deeper than did ever plummet sound
I'll drown my book.

Since *The Tempest* capped Shakespeare's career as playwright, it's tempting to consider Shakespeare and Prospero here as one and the same, each saying good-by not only to an island but also to the theater, and to us, the audience. What a splash that book has made.

CASSELL'S
ILLUSTRATED
SHAKESPEARE
THE
TEMPEST

By Its Cover

❧ THE ART OF THE BINDER

This gold-tooled binding on red Turkish leather was most likely crafted about 1675 in the large Westminster shop of William Nott, also known as Queen's Binder A.

The great diarist Samuel Pepys informs us that, just after midday on March 12, 1668/69, he went by coach to "Nott's, the famous book-binder, that bound for my Lord Chancellor's library; and here I did take occasion for curiosity to bespeak a book to be bound, only that I might have one of his binding."

Today, this book still gleams as brightly as it did when Nott returned it to Pepys's London library rooms overlooking the Thames. It's easy to imagine Pepys's response to the newly bound volume: he turns it slowly at arm's length, allowing the glints in the goldwork to flash in the afternoon sun; he luxuriates in the rich dialogue between leather and gilt; and he's bedazzled by the inter-laced design, vaguely reminiscent of Gothic tracery windows. But the new book is not just a feast for the eye. The crisp but pliant leather is perfect in his hand, and smells so new, so connected to the earth, so alive.

This sensual aspect of a book is both hazard and haven of the book-binder's art. You can't tell a book by its cover: a bad book—or a worthless one—can be well bound. Not that this was ever a problem for Pepys (1633–1703), the author of the most famous diary ever written and the creator of a fine 3,000-volume library, for which he designed the world's first glass-door bookcases. Pepys knew books.

In re-binding his collection, Pepys was taking part in a tradition as old as books themselves. The Egyptians used wooden cases, sometimes in the form of statues of the pharaoh, to hold papyrus rolls. Babylonian clay tablets were protected inside clay jars. After the invention of printing, it was just too big an investment for pub-lishers to bind all the copies they issued. Most were offered for sale in inexpensive vellum or even paper covers. Customers were then free to have them re-bound in the highest style their wallets could afford.

Books are bound in two stages. The first, called forwarding, involves holding the separate leaves together so they can be turned and read. From the earliest days, sewing these folded leaves together with thongs or thread has worked best. By punching two holes in the fold of a gathering and looping the thread from one gather-ing to the next, many gatherings, or signatures, can be held together as a book. If the loops are plaited together, the result is a chain stitch, which raises two welts across the book's spine. In time, it was thought better to attach the thread-loops to separate, heavier strings or thongs running across the spine. These thongs, called bands, could then firmly anchor the book to its cover. Bookbinders traditionally have nipped the leather book covers around those bands, making distinct, squarish panels along the spine for book labels.

Once the cover is attached, the second stage of bookbinding, called finishing, begins. And, whereas for-warding is all about protecting and preserving books, finishing deals with decoration. Two different tools with wheeled ends are used to decorate leather covers: the fillet, which applies a single or double line; and the roll, which impresses a fanciful

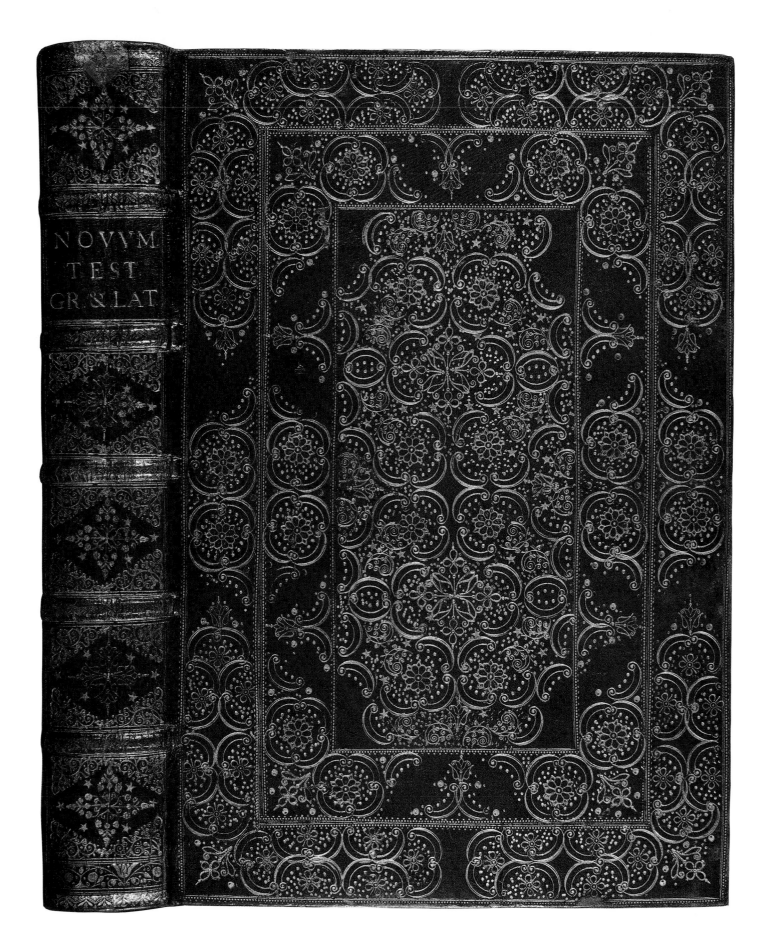

border or repeated ornament.

Whichever tool is to be used, it first must be heated on a charcoal stove. And bookbinders still gauge temperature in the time-honored way—by the sound of the sizzle produced by briefly touching a licked finger to the brass wheel. If the wheel is too hot it burns the leather; if too cool, it makes no impression. Rolls and fillets are used in two ways: in blind-tooling or blind-stamping, the indentation of the leather is the sole decoration; or, if a thin sheet of gold is inserted between the cover and the tool, the result is gilt decoration.

Over the years, wood, old manuscripts, pasteboard, and cardboard all have served as cover-board material to protect the fragile leaves within. Wood seems to have been the first great success. The classical world may have gotten the idea from the hardy little school book called a codex, whose wooden leaves were hollowed out and filled with wax that could be incised with a stylus.

Early on, while codices still were being made of papyrus, leather was either pasted over boards or stiffened with old manuscripts to protect books. In 1945, in Nag Hammadi, Egypt, a farmer accidentally uncovered a buried library of 12 Coptic codices that had been hidden away about the year 400. These are among the earliest books bound in leather that have ever been found. The hides are strengthened with discarded papyrus letters and documents, inserted scraps called cartonnage that provide added protection to the book and can help in dating the binding. The Nag Hammadi cartonnage dates

A 17th-century illustration, above, shows German bookbinders sewing and pounding the materials of their trade. Opposite (top), a conservator at Washington's Folger Shakespeare Library employs some of the same age-old techniques to stitch a restored 16th-century book. Opposite (center), a

Library of Congress binder uses a heated tool called a fillet, or pallet, to impress gold leaf onto the spine of a book. Opposite (bottom), a fore-edge painting on a volume of William Cowper's 1820 Poems portrays Great Berkhamstead, England, the poet's childhood home.

from 341 to 348, and some of the letters belonged to a man named Sansnos, who was in charge of a nearby monastery's cattle.

The Nag Hammadi find also displays a feature of Middle Eastern bindings that has been carried down to our times through Islam: running horizontally across the middle of the codex is part of the skin that covered the animal's spine. As the leather narrows near the animal's tail, that slender strip has been kept as a thong to close and secure the whole volume. It's possible the binder had in mind a similar thong that was used to close many Egyptian papyrus rolls. In any case, one of the distinctive features of the Islamic book to this day is a leather binding flap that wraps completely around the fore-edge, sealing out dust and heat.

The late Graham Pollard, a modern scholar of printing and binding, identified a crucial change in binding history with a shift in the color of leather. Most medieval bindings were of rough white leather. These were generally left untooled, because any such decoration would have been difficult to see. From 1150 to 1250, in Winchester, London, and Paris there was a brief period of interest in calf bindings, but the craze died out. Then, beginning about 1460, the making of bindings moved away from the use of colorless leather toward tanned, brown leather. "This change," said Pollard, "spread over northern Europe more rapidly than printing, though both started about the same time."

Bindings offer many clues to the life of the book. For part of the Middle Ages, for example, books

were packed in chests with their fore-edges facing down. Binders would leave a projecting tab—a little ear of leather—at the top and bottom of the spine so that even the heaviest of volumes could be easily removed.

Libraries, too, influenced the way books were bound. Islamic and other early libraries stored books flat on a shelf, so the title had to be written on the top edge or the tail of a book in order to be seen. In the West, the ecclesiastical habit of chaining books to lecterns meant that a book's back board had a large, hooped staple for attaching the chain. The staples were typically fastened to the boards with four nails; nail holes are a dead giveaway that a volume was once a chained book and has been re-bound.

In time, this style of chaining was abandoned in favor of a staple that projected from the foot of the book. This allowed books to be stored on shelves with their spines in and their fore-edges facing out. It also meant that the title had to appear on the fore-edge, and not on the spine.

From the beginning, the book-binder's trade was separate from the printer's. William Caxton used a man known to us only as "the Caxton binder." Where he lived or worked is lost to us, but a fine binding by him, dated 1483, is in the library of Durham Cathedral in England. Its dark leather is blind-tooled in diagonal double lines forming a repeating design called a diaper, stamped with fleurs-de-lis. Although his identity remains unproven, the Caxton binder may well have been one Jacobus Bokebynder, who leased space near Caxton's shop, although we know nothing of Bokebynder before 1495 and by 1510 he has dropped from sight entirely.

In fact, almost all the binders of English incunables are mysterious and are known to us mainly by their distinctive stamps—the "unicorn binder" of Cambridge and the "dragon binder" and the "fishtail binder" of Oxford. The latter used a curious stamp of a forked-tail fish that appears on 17 books between the years 1473 and 1499. He has been connected tentatively with the Oxford stationer Christopher Coke, but identifying early binders is tricky: they did not sign their work and their stamps and tools could have been borrowed or copied.

Despite their obscurity, these craftsmen started a tradition of fine work that continues today. T. J. Cobden-Sanderson (1840–1922), the partner of William Morris and Emery Walker in the Victorian revival of the arts of the book, was known for his simple, elegant bindings. Once confronted by a client who questioned the high cost of a volume with too little gold on it, Cobden-Sanderson replied, "I charge as much for my restraint as for my elaboration."

Restraint versus elaboration is a common way of classifying bookbinding. So-called "English" bindings are thought to be dignified, whereas "French" bindings are all flash. These nationalistic titles often are applied without regard for a binding's actual place of origin, but in fact there may be a shadow of truth behind them. The early French bindings of Jean Grolier and Thomas Mahieu, for example, both of whom lived in the 16th century, bear intricate designs of

interlaced scrolls, bars, bands, and ribbons, and were often gold-tooled and inlaid with variously colored leathers. Most French binders continued this trend toward over-elaboration, but in the late 17th century the French Jansenist bindings—named for Bishop Cornelius Jansen—began a move toward simplicity. The style featured a center motif that was repeated in the four corners; the rest of the cover remained plain.

If there was ever a middle ground

An 18th-century Moroccan book, opposite (top), displays the characteristic tail of Islamic bindings used to tie books shut. Opposite (bottom), a sampling of bindings from the Clementine Library, a collection of some 10,000 rare books that once belonged to Pope Clement XI (1649–1721) and now reside at the Catholic University of America. Below, a maze of designs and a jewel-studded gold cross cover the back of the ninth-century Lindau Gospels, *the first manuscript acquisition at New York's Pierpont Morgan Library.*

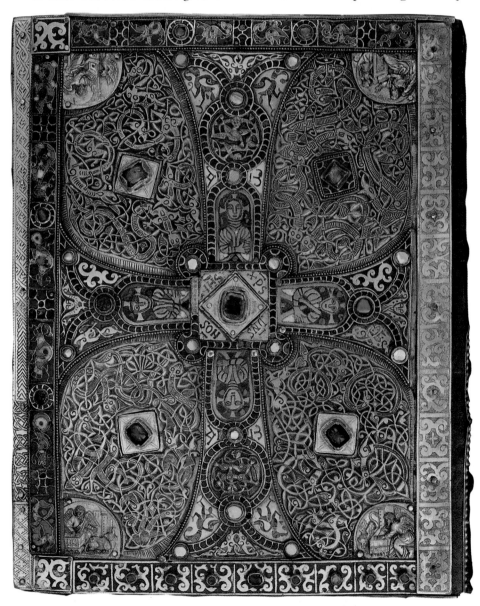

most delightful surprise is the fore-edge painting. These scenes, usually landscapes, sneak up from behind the gilded fore-edge; you have no idea the edge conceals a picture until you bend the pages slightly. A favorite is a two-volume 1820 edition of the poems of William Cowper (1731–1800). Its two fore-edges depict the villages around which his fragile life centered: Berkhamstead, his child-hood home; and Olney, the village where he tried to recapture the hap-piness of his youth. Cowper was the world's most domestic poet; these scenes are perfect for him.

The materials used over the years for binding vary widely. Medieval book covers in silver and gold, encrusted with jewels and ivory plaques, attract the lion's share of attention from art historians, but paper bindings crafted by the right hands can be stunning. Marbled paper has often been used as a covering material, and there are many fine bindings of floral papers in subtle colors, sometimes embossed with gold.

Poet Robert Southey (1774–1843) created an interest in fine cloth bindings by having books from his library covered in bright cotton patterns and calicoes. Southey jokingly referred to them as his "Cot-tonian" collection, a nod in the direc-tion of Sir Robert Cotton (1571–1631), whose library is the very soul of both English literature and the British Library. Southey knew what he was doing. His copy of poems by Walter Savage Landor lives on today in a yellow gingham check. Books do brighten a room.

They also illuminate, and that is

in binding, it was achieved in Venice, and specifically in a 1542 edition of Aristotle's *Nicomachean Ethics* that is now in the Clementine Library at the Catholic University of America in Washington, D.C. Its calf is lightly tanned, but it appears darker near the margins because of a series of blind-tooled fillets. The gilt work amounts to just an outer border of interwoven bands, an inner border of fleurons (flowers) and bands and, within a

chained oval, the short title ETICA AR. What really makes the volume outstanding are the tiny gold triangles that mark its five bands and the edges of its pages, striped in gold and silver.

Indeed, book edges did not long escape the attention of bookbinders, and today we know goffering as the art of impressing or indenting geo-metric or floral designs in the fore-edge, top, and tail of a book, usually after it has been gilded. Binding's

the impulse behind the best modern binding. Herman Melville's *Billy Budd, Sailor*—bound by Benjamin and Deborah Alterman in 1987—depicts Billy's last view of earth, the mast and yardarm on which he was sacrificed. A single, dangling sapphire represents Billy in his transformed state, as the sky above ricochets with delight at this tale of innocence victorious over death.

King Lear—bound by Philip Smith in 1967/68—gives us a monarch incarcerated in a tragedy of his own devising, the letters of his name constituting the bars of his cage. In its deepest sense, *Lear* is about binding, double-binding—"bind fast his corky arms"—and the imprisonment of self-deception. Even Lear's crowned head seems aflame, the perfect metaphor for a king who claimed to be " . . . bound Upon a wheel of fire."

King Lear peers from behind bars that spell out his name, opposite, on the feathered-leather cover designed for this Shakespearean tragedy in 1967 by Philip Smith. Artists Benjamin and Deborah Alterman revived a thousand-year-old tradition in crafting a precious-metals binding, above, in 1987 for Herman Melville's Billy Budd, Sailor. *A sapphire set in 14-karat gold recalls Billy's fate.*

Polidoro Virgilio de gli'Inuent. 1587

Flor. Medic. Venetiis 1491

HIER. CARD OPVS NOVV DE ALGEBR LIB. I.

IOL. PICVS MIRANDVLA HEPTAPLVS DE SEPTIFORM

DURER INSTITUT GEOMET. 1535

EUCLIDES GREGORII Gr: & Lat:

MATTHIOL DIOSCORID: 1544

ROB. FLVD. BVS PHILO MOSA

"THE INFINITE LIBRARY, TIMELESS AND INCORRUPTIBLE"

**S**AN MARINO, CALIFORNIA, IS A WELL-manicured, upper-class community a few miles south of the Rose Bowl in Pasadena. It has smog and traffic—but it also has treasures. They are housed in the Huntington Library, one of the world's great collections of rare literary and historical books and manuscripts. Here is a Gutenberg Bible; the Ellesmere Chaucer, the most important manuscript of *The Canterbury Tales;* the original manuscript of Benjamin Franklin's autobiography. And here also is a modest little quarto volume called *The Mirrovr of Maiestie: Or, The Badges of Honovr Conceitedly Emblazoned: With Emblems Annexed, Poetically Vnfolded,* printed in London in 1618. ❧ The places of Gutenberg, Chaucer, and Franklin in cultural history are well established, but many surprises still lurk in the Huntington's stacks. Consider the case of *The Mirrovr of Maiestie,* admittedly a minor book, and Shakespeare's *Hamlet.* In the play, the young prince makes a remark about his dead father. He had, the lad tells us, "An eye like Mars, to threaten and command" and "A station [stance] like the herald Mercury"—a potent combination. ❧ Roland M. Frye, an English professor emeritus from the University of Pennsylvania and a specialist in Shakespeare, had always taken these words of Shakespeare to be a typical classical allusion to the golden mean: moderation in all things. But then Frye came across *The Mirrovr of Maiestie,* a collection of illustrations and poems. ❧ Among the illustrations was the model of a perfect king, adorned on his right side with the arms and armor of Mars, on his left with the winged helmet and boots of Mercury. The implication was clear: in the ideal ruler, the aggressive, martial side should always be balanced by the thoughtful,

Preceding pages: Some of the priceless manuscripts in the collection of the Smithsonian's Dibner Library. Opposite, framed by marble columns, a patron of the Library of Congress sits in an alcove overlooking the Main Reading Room. More than 45,000 volumes housed in this room provide researchers with quick and easy access to reference material. The LC, as the Library of Congress is known to users, opened in 1800 in the Capitol building. It accepts about 7,000 new items every day. The art-noveau initial S at the head of the column on this page was designed by Frenchman Maurice Dufrène.

circumspect side. In fact, *Hamlet* shows us a prince of Denmark who spends most of his time trying to reconcile these two aspects of his own young personality.

The *Mirrovr* thus preserves the past like a message in a bottle. "Shakespeare's public," says Frye, "knew exactly what he meant by the Mercury-Mars combination. At least some of them may have seen the very illustration, or one like it."

Frye is representative of the 1,400-odd scholars from around the world who make the trek to San Marino each year seeking the answers to literary and historical questions. They are pilgrims to the Huntington, the greatest independent research institution in the United States. In a modern building with earthquake-proof shelves, the Huntington collection includes nearly 600,000 rare and reference books, among them 5,400 incunabula—that is, books from the

Railroad executive and avid collector of the rare books and art treasures that formed the nucleus of the Huntington Library, Henry E. Huntington stands before the San Marino, California, library's ornate doors in a 1925 photograph. The Vallard Atlas of 1547, the most famous manuscript atlas in the Huntington Library's collection, features this chart, opposite, showing the landing of French explorer Jacques Cartier in Canada. Another of the collection's rarities is the 1618 edition of The Mirrovr of Maiestie, a page of which appears above.

201

"cradle period" of printing, 1455 to 1501—and more than two million manuscripts, not to mention many other items.

This magnificent collection began coalescing in the deserts of southern California about the turn of the century under the direction of a wealthy railroad executive, Henry E. Huntington (1850–1927), who first came to California to help his uncle, Collis Huntington, run the Southern Pacific Railway. In 1902, Henry Huntington bought a 550-acre ranch in San Marino and built a mansion there in which to live comfortably among his books and art. Photographs show Huntington as an imposing, bald-domed figure in black, often peering at his beloved books. But the most amazing thing about the man was his taste for and devotion to scholarship. He collected only in depth and only in certain circumscribed fields. Not a little of everything, but the best in a few selected areas.

Although he had no college education, his literary decisions were seldom wide of the mark. He was an early buyer of first editions of H.G. Wells and Joseph Conrad, for example, well before their literary reputations were even remotely secure. He also had a very early collection of William Blake drawings, largely to support his interest in Blake's poetry. Huntington, it seems, was that rarest of species, the tycoon who actually read and loved the books he collected.

Thomas Carlyle once said that "the true university these days is a collection of books." All the great American book collectors, such as Huntington and his contemporaries Henry Clay Folger (1857–1930), creator of the Folger Shakespeare Library in Washington, D.C., and J. Pierpont Morgan (1837–1913), founder of New York's Pierpont Morgan Library, certainly would have agreed with that. All three libraries continue to this day to operate like small universities and attract not only fine books but also bright minds to think about them. Without the minds, the books lie fallow.

They are not wasted, however. A book will wait for you. Most of us have had the pleasure of reading today a book we bought years ago but somehow never got around to. From the very beginning, libraries have been based on that very principle: to preserve and protect information, data, receipts, poems, words, scripture—until they are needed again.

There is something grand and positive about the idea of a library. It suggests that there will be a future, and that the people who live in it will have the interest and skills to interpret and understand the past by what we bequeath them on our library shelves. But, of course, there has always been another reason to create libraries. Information is power.

The most ancient libraries were vast storehouses of clay tablets on practically every administrative, commercial, and military aspect of managing—and controlling—society. Archaeological research at the libraries of the ancient Near East, such as those at Nimrud, Nineveh, and Pergamum, have yielded some 400,000 clay tablets. Ninety percent of them deal with money, property, and taxes. These collections were kept in special palace rooms or in temples, and the clay tablets often were arranged on end, leaning against one another like books on a modern shelf.

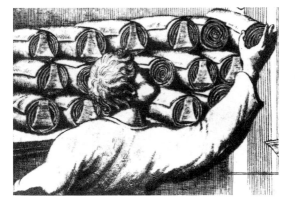

A cuneiform-covered stone bas-relief, opposite, portrays Assyrian king Ashurbanipal (668–627 B.C.), who assembled the great clay-tablet library at Nineveh. The preservation of such Mesopotamian epics as the Creation and Gilgamesh can be attributed to his unusually diverse collection. Above, a Roman bas-relief (c. A.D. 100) depicts a patron removing a scroll from the shelf or nest where it was kept. This is thought to be the only existing illustration of the way scrolls were stored in an ancient library. A label called an index *or* titulus *identified each scroll.*

In the world of the papyrus book, too, orderliness prevailed. In Egypt, the temple libraries at Philae and Edfu had niches for storing rolls. Individual rolls were identified by papyrus or parchment labels so the contents could be known without their being unrolled. Groups of rolls were stored in wooden chests or boxes, also identified by labels made of clay or faience, a hard-glazed pottery.

The Greeks also wrote on papyrus and had fine libraries. The sixth century B.C. tyrant Peisistratus created a library at Athens where he brought together the many corrupt versions of Homer's poetry into one approved text. Textual scholarship started here. The Athens library is famous not only for its literary gains but also for its losses. Herodotus tells us that the great Ptolemaic library at Alexandria, Egypt, borrowed a series of papyrus books from Athens to copy for its shelves; however, it then decided not to return the originals, apparently happy to forfeit the deposit it had sent to Athens to secure them.

The Alexandrian library was in fact a temple to the Nine Muses, the patrons of all the arts, and as such was the source of our word "museum." So the first museum was really a library. And what a library: it was said in the Middle Ages to have held 40,000 books, a huge total for any library up to modern times. Its longevity was remarkable as well, for it seems to have been in existence in the fifth century B.C. and was still important enough to have been burned by Christian fanatics late in the fourth century A.D.

Few Greek papyruses from the northern Mediterranean survived the ages; those that we have come from the dry sands of Egypt and the Middle East. What does survive is the Greek word for a papyrus roll, *biblion,* and the word for a container of rolls, the *bibliotheke.* The modern word for library in many tongues is thus derived from that Greek original. In English, the word library reflects the Latin word *liber,* which came to mean book.

The Biblioteca Capitolare in Verona, Italy, is probably the oldest library still in existence. Its collection of religious, literary, and historical manuscripts, including those of classical writers such as Pliny and Catullus, was started in the sixth century A.D. Library history in the Middle Ages is dominated by monastic and church collections, which were occasionally open to qualified outsiders. The 13th-century library at Sainte Chapelle in Paris was in fact a public library, but since the books were almost exclusively in Latin, it attracted a largely clerical clientele.

The world was changing, however. The Vatican Library, for example, certainly one of the greatest libraries of all time, is proof of the triumph of the humanism of the Renaissance. The library was founded during the reign of Pope Nicholas V (1447–1455). Earlier, Nicholas had traveled throughout Europe locating manuscripts and had advised Cosimo de Medici on what books he might include in an ideal library. When he came to develop his own papal collection, he knew what he wanted and where to find it.

As pope, Nicholas used revenues from the Jubilee pilgrimage to Rome in 1450 to build his library. The ploy was shocking, especially to his successor, Pope Calixtus III, since most of the volumes contained humanistic rather than devo-

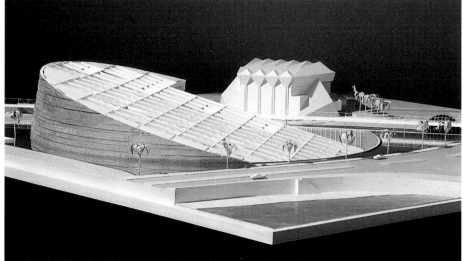

Australian artist Robert Ingpen's illustration of the Egyptian city of Alexandria, above, c. 270 B.C., features the famous lighthouse of Pharos, where scholars translated the first five books of the Hebrew Bible—the Septuagint— into Greek. During the reign of Ptolemy I Soter (305–283 B.C.), whose portrait appears on a Greek silver coin, opposite, both the lighthouse and the great Alexandrian library were built. Left, an architectural model of the new Bibliotheca Alexandrina, or Library of Alexandria, scheduled to open in 1995.

tional writings. The collection includes the greatest Virgil manuscript, the fourth-century Codex Vaticanus; a manuscript of Boethius in the Renaissance hand of Giovanni Boccaccio; and the poems of Michelangelo, in his hand.

Today, the Vatican Library holds 7,000 incunabula, some 60,000 important manuscripts, and 700,000 books. Oddly enough, this vast collection is still humanistic at its core. Although it could be turned from time to time to polemical and rhetorical outbursts—against scientists and other heretics during the Counter-Reformation, for example—it still persists as a storehouse of knowledge. And that is the source of its power.

Libraries are powerhouses. A reflection of that power is visible today in the most beautiful of library buildings, Michelangelo's Laurentian Library, built for the Medici family in Florence and completed in 1571. The stairs that lead up to the reading room appear curved and scroll-like underfoot. Scrolls blossom on the walls. Classical architectural motifs peer down on medieval chained books. In effect, the architect is handing down a caution. The heritage of the book is

The Salone Sistino in the Vatican Library, below, was built by Domenico Fontana in 1587–1589. Opposite, in a detail from Melozzo da Forli's fresco in the Vatican gallery, Italian humanist and historian Bartolomeo Sacchi, known as Platina, kneels before Pope Sixtus IV. Sixtus appointed Platina Vatican Librarian when the library opened in 1475.

TEMPLA DOMVM EXPOSITIS·VICOS·FORA·MOENIA·PONTES·
VIRGINEAM·TRIVII·QVOD·REPARARIS·AQVAM·
PRISCA·LICET·NAVTIS·STATVAS·DARE·COMMODA·PORTVS·
ET·VATICANVM·CINGERE·SIXTE·IVGVM·
PLVS·TAMEN·VRBS·DEBET·NAM·QVAE·SQVALORE·LATEBAT·
CERNITVR·IN·CELEBRI·BIBLIOTHECA·LOCO·

nothing to be trifled with, he says. Knowledge is power; the library is its home.

Certainly power was the chief artifact on display in the British Museum, founded in London in 1753. For along with its scholarship, it was an imperial showcase as well, displaying the geographical sway of British power from India to Egypt, China to Peru. Following the Alexandrian custom of keeping books and artifacts in a temple dedicated to the Muses, the British Library was part of the British Museum until 1973. Between 1993 and 1996, the library will be moving its collection—11 million volumes—to a modern building near the St. Pancras Railway Station, about a mile north of the British Museum.

At its foundation, the library drew on several important collections, but none more important than that of Sir Robert Cotton (1571–1631), who amassed 958 manuscripts, attracting such scholars as Ben Jonson, Sir Francis Bacon, and Sir Walter Raleigh. The collection was passed on to the nation by Cotton's grandson in 1700.

Cotton had arranged his books in 14 bookcases topped by busts of the 12 Roman emperors and of Cleopatra and Faustina, wife of Marcus Aurelius. Each book was known by its shelf mark. For instance, a book called Cotton Nero A.x. would be found in the Nero case, shelf A, the 10th book in the row. Today the Cottonian nomenclature is still used; Cotton Nero A.x. is the unique manuscript of *Sir Gawain and the Green Knight.*

The history of English literature would be dimmer indeed without these volumes. In fact, it is a test of a student's mettle that he or she can recognize the greats by their Cottonian shelf marks: Cotton Tiberius B.i., Old English poetry; Cotton Nero D.iv., the *Lindisfarne Gospels;* Cotton Otho A.vi., Boethius; and the most important of them all, Cotton Vitellius A.xv., Beowulf.

An etching of the British Museum Library's Reading Room, opposite, appeared in the May 1857 Illustrated London News *shortly after the room opened. It has since achieved world renown for the richness and diversity of its reference collection. Above is a caricature of playwright and critic George Bernard Shaw, one of many celebrated scholars and writers to have used the Reading Room. Some of Shaw's works were bequeathed to the British Museum. Left, a rendering of the Humanities Reading Room in the new British Library, which is scheduled to open in 1996.*

The *Beowulf* codex, written down in the 11th century, is an example of the harrowing adventures some books must have survived. In 1731, fire attacked the Cotton collection, destroying more than a hundred books and damaging many others. We have an eyewitness account of books being thrown out of windows to save them. Although *Beowulf* was not consumed by the flames, its parchment was fatally desiccated by the heat and began to crumble.

Fortunately, an Icelandic scholar named Grímur Jónsson Thorkelin came to London in 1786 and either made or commissioned two copies of *Beowulf*. Ironically, Thorkelin was preparing to publish his edition of the poem in Copenhagen in 1807 when the British Royal Navy bombarded the city, destroying Thorkelin's house and his manuscript. Fortunately, he had donated his two copies of the poem to the Royal Library of Copenhagen, which survived the British assault on the city. Although he despaired at the loss of his manuscript, a Danish nobleman talked him into preparing a new edition for publication. Meanwhile, back in the British Museum, the original *Beowulf* became more and more illegible with each passing year. Today, the manuscript has been stabilized against further deterioration, but Thorkelin's second edition, eventually published in 1815, remains the basic guide to passages that can no longer be read.

In the United States, the hunger for books and libraries was strong from the very beginning. The French politician and writer Alexis de Tocqueville, traveling in the United States in the 1830s, found that the standard reading kit for a backwoods pioneer was "a Bible, the first six books of Milton, and two of Shakespeare's plays." The frontier American, he observed, was "a highly civilized being, who consents for a time to inhabit the backwoods, and who penetrates into the wilds of the New World with the Bible, an axe, and some newspapers."

For the ancestors of these rugged readers, Benjamin Franklin and others had created the Library Company of Philadelphia, incorporated in 1742, which clearly had a democratic impulse. Wrote Franklin in his *Autobiography:* "Such libraries had made common tradesmen and farmers as intelligent as gentlemen elsewhere and had contributed to the ability of Americans to defend their privileges."

"Defend their books," Franklin might well have said, because the first Library of Congress was burned in the 1814 sack of Washington by British troops. It was generously replaced by Thomas Jefferson, with a sale of 6,487 books, his entire library from Monticello. The price was $23,950, which included Jefferson's specially designed pine boxes that did double duty as shipping cartons and bookshelves.

Ten wagonloads shifted the book boxes from Virginia to the nation's capital. "There is, in fact, no subject," said Jefferson, "to which a member of Congress may not have occasion to refer." For ease of reference, he even sent along his personal library-classification system, based on Sir Francis Bacon's tripartite system of memory, reason, and imagination, augmented by 44 more categories. Jefferson's system was used until the 1930s.

According to Charles Goodrum, author and longtime coordinator of research for the Congressional Research Service, the Library of Congress "is the largest collection of stored knowledge in the world ... the world's greatest encyclopedia of everything known by Western man to date." With 15 million volumes, almost 40 million manuscripts, and 54 million other items, such as maps, musical recordings, prints, photos, movies, and videotapes in its collections, to say nothing of the 7,000 *daily* additions to its shelves, it is hard to see how the Library of Congress will ever be eclipsed.

Except in the surreal world of the imagination. The Argentine writer Jorge Luis Borges once conjured up an infinite library as large as the universe itself. It appears in his story "The Library of Babel" (1945) and covers not only the past but the future of humankind.

This library has everything that has ever been written or will ever be written, including "the true story of your death," but there is no librarian. You must search in there alone, for that is the ultimate quest of life itself. "I suspect," says Borges's narrator, "that the human species—the unique species—is about to be extinguished, but the Library will endure: illuminated, solitary, infinite, perfectly motionless, equipped with precious volumes, useless, incorruptible, secret."

THE
SWISS FAMILY ROBINSON;
OR, ADVENTURES
OF A FATHER AND FOUR SONS

NEW YORK

Many of our nation's bibliographic treasures are preserved within the collections
of the Smithsonian Institution's museums.
The National Museum of American
History holds the only complete set of
The American School Library (1839),
opposite, a traveling frontier library. The
Daily Express Children's Annual
(1933), left, pops up at the Smithsonian's
Cooper-Hewitt Museum in New York.
Below, Jacob Lawrence celebrates a great
institution in The Library (1960), from
the collection of the National Museum
of American Art.

HERALDS OF SCIENCE

¶ BOOKS THAT CHANGED
THE WORLD

*A demonstration of a human dissection
provides a fitting subject for the frontispiece of Andreas Vesalius's 1543
classic* De humani corporis fabrica
(On the Fabric of the Human Body).
*Vesalius's book, the first to offer an
inside look at the human body based on
dissection, revolutionized the study of
human anatomy and surgery.*

Scientific revolutions have always been a matter of books. Consider the year 1542–43. The heliocentric concept of the heavens had its sunrise in Copernicus's *De revolutionibus orbium coelestium (On the Revolutions of the Celestial Orbs),* printed in Nuremberg. From Basel came Leonhard Fuchs's *De historia stirpium (On the History of Plants),* the book that made botany a science, with illustrations of more than 500 plants, including the American pumpkin and maize, and, from the Old World, a medicinal plant, the foxglove. That same year, the print shops of Basel also gave us the first look inside the human body based on dissection, Andreas Vesalius's *De humani corporis fabrica (On the Fabric of the Human Body).*

In the case of these books, type and paper work together to keep the eye moving, the mind engaged. These are not reference books; they were meant to be read, their line of inquiry closely followed. Revolutionary, subversive ideas must be expressed carefully: the goal is persuasion as much as enlightenment. In a perfectly rational world, new ideas could be accepted on their own merits. But when new ideas must first supplant old ones that prop up an entrenched scientific, ecclesiastical, medical, academic, economic, and legal establishment, rhetoric and persuasion are as important as an accurate portrayal of nature itself.

All three books are illustrated with woodcuts that not only adorn the text but clarify and extend the meaning of the words. The solar system of Copernicus is a confident, perfectly circular diagram not to be trifled with:

"sol" in the center, the moon and "terra" on the third circle out, and the outermost sphere of the fixed stars last. What could be more obvious? It is difficult for us today to recapture what all the fuss was about, until we realize this: if the sun did circle around the Earth, as had been previously believed, the heavens would appear just the same. Fuchs's plants are realistically portrayed but also are seen as ideal, a kind of burgeoning perfection under the control of man and his newfound powers of observation. And in Vesalius's schematic of the secondary muscular system, man himself parades through a landscape of sublime classical ruins. A brave new world is at hand.

Scientific illustration made all the difference. It changed the way the mass of mankind saw. In 1610, Galileo published *Sidereus nuncius magna (The Great Starry Messenger),* an account of the Copernican heavens made with the help of his telescope. The book announced nine major celestial discoveries, including the moons of Jupiter, the stars in the Milky Way, and the craters and valleys in the face of the moon. It made him famous throughout Europe.

Sidereus featured the moon as seen through a lens—a rough, pitted orb. That illustration, that book, and that man made quite an impression on a young John Milton when he visited Galileo in August 1638. When Milton came to write his own masterpiece, *Paradise Lost* (1667), Galileo's drawings reappeared in the poetry, transmuted from the realm of science into art. The scene is the flaming shore of Hell, on which a conquered but unvanquished Satan

ANDREAE VESALII
BRVXELLENSIS, SCHOLAE
medicorum Patauinæ profeſſoris, de
Humani corporis fabrica
Libri ſeptem.

CVM CAESAREAE
Maieſt. Galliarum Regis, ac Senatus Veneti gra-
tia & priuilegio, ut in diplomatis eorundem continetur.

BASILEAE.

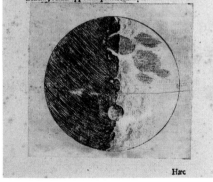

strides, his shield dented and pitted from the fray:

. . . his ponderous shield,
Ethereal temper, massy, large, and round,
Behind him cast; the broad circumference
Hung on his shoulders like the moon,
  whose orb
Through optic glass the Tuscan artist views
At evening, from the top of Fesole,

Or in Valdarno, to descry new lands,
Rivers, or mountains, in her spotty globe.

(Book I, 285–291)

The "Tuscan artist" is Galileo himself, the "optic glass" his telescope, "Fesole" the hilltop town northeast of Florence, and "Valdarno" the valley of the Arno River, which flows past Florence. In Milton's hands,

science becomes more than just test tubes and calculators; it's a new way of seeing.

Today, the books of Copernicus, Fuchs, Vesalius, Galileo, and other scientific pioneers all have come to rest at the Dibner Library of the History of Science and Technology, part of the Smithsonian Institution. This 17,000-volume collection is

216

Primus

Præfatione aut ptolemei ad litterã exprimere libuit:tum propter crebras in ea sentẽtias scitu dignissimas:tum propter auctoritatẽ Ptolemei:quo etiam imitatio nostra fidelior redderet. Nunc ad sciẽtiã chordarũ feliciter descẽdamus

Propositio Prima.

Ata circuli diametro : latera decagoni : hexagoni : pentagoni : tetragoni : atq̃ trianguli isopleurorũ eidem circulo inscriptorũ reperire.

Sit semicirculus.a.b.g.supra diametrum.a d.g.z centrum.d.erectus. Protrohã.d.b.perpendicularem super.a.g.per.11.primi euclidis. lineamq̃.d.g.diuidam per duo æqualia super puncto.e.z ducam linea.e.b.huic æqualem faciam.e.z.productaq̃.b.z.dico.z.d. esse æquale lateri decagoni:z.b.z.æquale lateri penthagoni. Quod sic ostendam:Quia g.d.diuiditur in duo æqua super.e.z addita est ei in longum.d.z.ergo per sextam secundi/quadrangulum quod fit ex.g.z.in.d.z.cum quadrato.d.e.æquũ est quadrato lineæ.e.z.sed.e.z.est æqualis.c.b.z per penultimã primi quadratum.e.b.equũ est duobus quadratis.b.d.z.d.e.quod igitur fit ex.g.z.in.z.d cum quadrato.d.e.æquale erit duobus quadratis.b.d.z.d.e.ablato comuni quadrato.d.e.erit quod fit ex.g.z.in.z.d.æquale quadrato.b.d.ideo etiã cõ le quadrato.d.g.ergo per secundã parte.16.sexti.g.z.ad.d.g.proportio fiet sicut.d.g.ad.z.d.proportio/ideo per principium sexti linea.z.g.est diuisa in puncto.d.secundum proportionẽ habentem medium z duo extrema.sed maior eius portio scz.d.g.est latus hexagoni per correlarium.16.quarti.ideo per quersam none tredicimi minor eius portio scz.d.z.est latus decagoni:quod est primũ Et quoniã per penultimã primi quadratũ.b.z.est æquale duobus quadratis.b.d.z.d.z.z.b.d.est latus hexagoni:z.d.z.latus decagoni.ideo per conuersam decime tredicimi.b.z.crit latus penthagoni : quod est secũdũ. Quz si duxeris lineam.a.b.constabit ipsam ex sexta quarti esse latus quadrati circulo inscriptibile/sed z per octaua tredicimi manifestũ est latus trigoni potentialiter triplum esse lateri hexagoni seu semidiametro.Qualicunq̃ igitur diuisione diameter diuisa fuerit:in eadem constabit eius medietas scz latus hexagoni : cuius quadratum z medietatis quadratum sunt quadratũ lineæ z.e.ideo.z.e.nota.a qua ablata.d.c.remanebit.z.d.nota:chorda decime partis circuli. Sed z huius quadratũ cum quadrato lateris hexagoni sunt quadratũ lateris penthagoni.ideo chorda quinte partis circuli nota fiet.Quadratum vo lateris tetragoni duplum est quadrato lateris hexagoni:z quadratũ lateris trigoni triplũ eidem quadrato lateris hexagoni : ideo vtrũq̃ eorum notum fiet.

Propositio ij.

Ata alicuius arcus chorda:nota fiet chorda arcus residui de semicirculo.

Patet ex.30.tertij angulum quem continent tales chorde rectum esse.ideo per penultimã primi quadratũ diametri circuli æquũ erit quadratis duobus ipsarum chordarum:igitur zc. Sic ex latere decagoni inuenies chordam arcus.144.graduũ based on books assembled over 50 years by the Connecticut engineer and inventor Bern Dibner (1897–1988).

In 1955, Dibner published *Heralds of Science,* an annotated bibliography of what he considered the 200 most important printed documents in the history of science up to the early 20th century. The book covers astronomy through zoology and ranges from Herald of Science (or Herald) No. 1, a 1496 translation of Ptolemy's *Almagest* printed in Venice, possibly the first book of pure science ever printed, to Herald No. 200, August Weismann's 1885 identification of the so-called germ plasm (or gene) as the transmitter of heredity. Scholars and booksellers the world over still refer to these seminal volumes by their Herald numbers.

Tracing the evolution of scientific ideas through books is like watching a relay race. Take electricity, for example. In 1751, Ben Franklin published *Experiments and Observations on Electricity, Made at Philadelphia in America* (Herald 57), in which he described his invention of the lightning rod and deduced that electricity flowed in positive and negative charges—terms that he introduced. With this book, Franklin elevated electricity from a carnival sideshow act to a science.

Then, in 1791, what Bern Dibner termed the "most remarkable document in the history of mankind" was printed. At Bologna, professor of anatomy Luigi Galvani saw that a dead frog's leg muscle would twitch when its nerves were touched simultaneously by the two different metals of his scalpel. What he called "animal electricity" resulted from his accidental creation of a primitive battery. In effect, the frog's muscle had become the world's first electrometer.

Galvani printed only 12 copies of his 58-page pamphlet *De viribus electricitatis in motu musculari* (Herald 59), but he sent one—now in the Dibner library—to his colleague Alessandro Volta, a professor of physics at the University of Pavia. Based on Galvani's frog experiment, Volta made the first battery out of silver and zinc and called it a "voltaic pile." The old static electricity of the carnival magi-

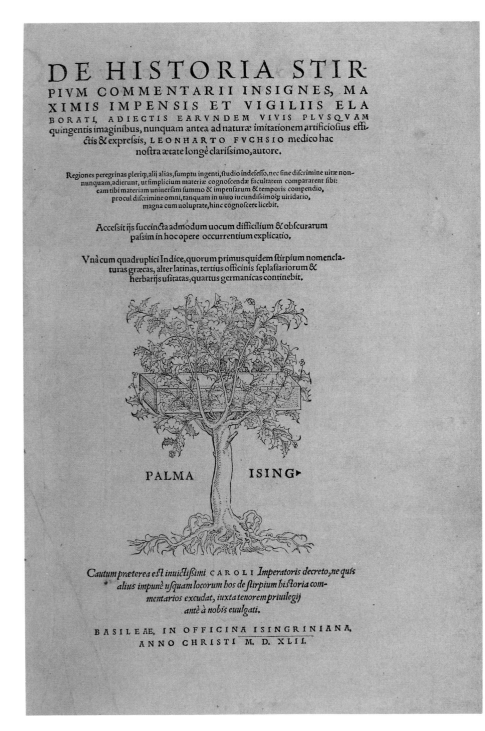

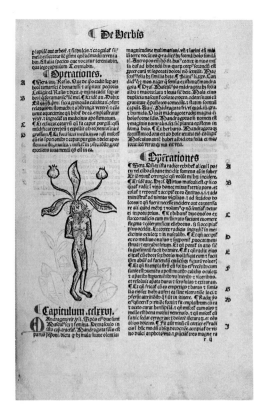

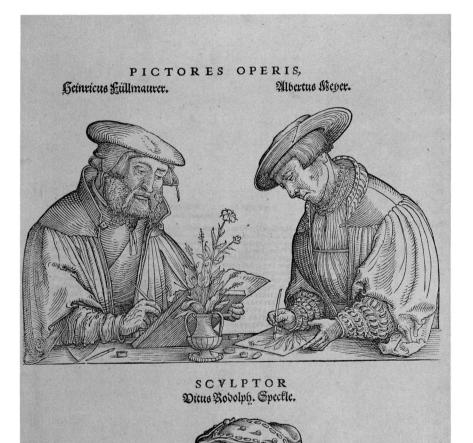

Leonhard Fuchs's 1542 De historia stirpium (On the History of Plants), whose title page is seen opposite, elevated botany to a science. Fuchs, for whom the plant genus *Fuchsia* is named, based his work on extensive scientific observations, and was assisted in his ambitious endeavor by artists Heinrich Füllmaurer, below left, and Albrecht Meyer, below right, and engraver Vitus Speckle, bottom. At left (top), a mandrake as depicted in Jacob Meydenbach's 1491 Hortus sanitatis, *and (bottom) as shown in Fuchs's masterpiece.*

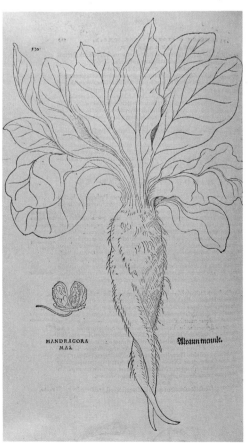

In dissecting frog and lamb legs, above, Italian anatomist Luigi Galvani noted muscular convulsions that he mistakenly attributed to "animal electricity." He published his findings in 1791 in the pamphlet De viribus electricitatis in motu musculari. *Further investigation of his work by countryman Alessandro Volta revealed that it was the contact of dissimilar metals that had caused the convulsive movements. Volta went on to develop the first battery—variations of his "voltaic pile" appear opposite—and to usher in the age of electricity.*

cians could now be supplemented by a constant electrical source available to experimenters. Volta's results were published in the *Transactions* of London's Royal Society in 1800 under the title *On the Electricity Excited by the Mere Contact of Conducting Substances of Different Kinds* (Herald 60).

During a lecture in 1820, Danish professor Hans Christian Oersted chanced to lay a conducting wire over a magnetic compass. The needle immediately swerved. Oersted's results, published in four pages of Latin on July 21 as *Experimenta circa effectum conflictus electrici in acum magneticam,* or "Experi-

ments on the Effect of a Current of Electricity on the Magnetic Needle" (Herald 61), established the link between electricity and magnetism.

In 1831 another remarkable incident: working in London, Michael Faraday had been trying for 10 years to reverse the Oersted experiment, reasoning that if electricity caused magnetism then magnetism should generate electricity. Nothing seemed to work. After 10 days of feverish activity in November, Faraday went off to the Brighton seashore for a rest. The short trip from London to the coast must have crystallized his thoughts, for just after he arrived he outlined—in four pages—the principles of electromagnetic induction. These were read to the Royal Society on November 24, 1831, and published among Faraday's *Experimental Researches in Electricity* (Herald 64).

The 80 years between Franklin's experiment in 1751 and Faraday's principles of electromagnetic induction in 1831 had seen the articulation of the main ideas that underlie 20th-century electronics, all published in a series of small, illustrated books and pamphlets.

Restraint, efficiency, close attention to nature—these characteristics dominate the history of great science. They also apply to the prose often found in the musings of scientists. Even as they confront monumental puzzles their talk is modest and questioning. Here, for example, is a quote from a letter from Charles Darwin, voyaging with H.M.S. *Beagle,* to his professor of botany back at Cambridge, J. S. Henslow. Darwin wrote from Rio de Janeiro, Brazil, on May 18, 1832: "It is exceedingly interesting to observe the difference of genera & species from those which I know; it is however much less than I expected. . . . I have just returned from a walk, & as a specimen how little insects are known—Noterus, according to Dic. Class. consists solely of three European species. I, in one haul of the net, took five distinct species." And this from Montevideo, Uruguay, on November 24, 1832: "As for one little toad, I hope it may be new, that it may be christened 'diabolicus.' Milton must allude to this very individual, when he talks of 'squat like a toad.'"

The *Beagle* voyage afforded Darwin

large doses of time when there was little else to do but classify his samples and read and brood over the three volumes of Charles Lyell's just published *Principles of Geology, Being an Attempt to Explain the Former Changes of the Earth's Surface, by Reference to Causes Now in Operation* (1830; Herald 96). Lyell's impertinent notion was that the world was created not with a

bang but with a slow, pot-boiling disregard for the passage of time. So when Darwin was faced with his collection of South American fossils, he noticed and questioned the telltale resemblances between extinct and living species—between the extinct *Megatherium,* or giant sloth, and one of the much smaller species of sloth he collected, for example, or between the

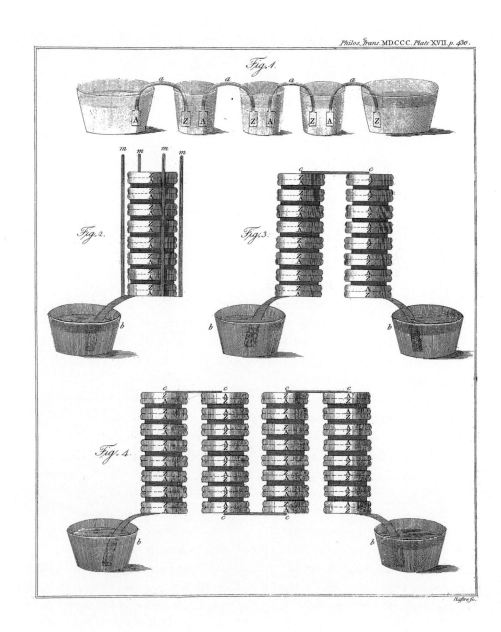

differing from the Progne purpurea of both Americas, only in being rather duller coloured, smaller, and slenderer, is considered by Mr. Gould as specifically distinct. Fifthly, there are three species of mocking-thrush—a form highly characteristic of America. The remaining land-birds form a most singular group of finches, related to each other in the structure of their beaks, short tails, form of body, and plumage: there are thirteen species, which Mr. Gould has divided into four sub-groups. All these species are peculiar to this archipelago; and so is the whole group, with the exception of one species of the sub-group Cactornis, lately brought from Bow island, in the Low Archipelago. Of Cactornis, the two species may be often seen climbing about the flowers of the great cactus-trees; but all the other species of this group of finches, mingled together in flocks, feed on the dry and sterile ground of the lower districts. The males of all, or certainly of the greater number, are jet black; and the females (with perhaps one or two exceptions) are brown. The most curious fact is the perfect gradation in the size of the beaks in the different species of Geospiza, from one as

1. Geospiza magnirostris. 2. Geospiza fortis.
3. Geospiza parvula.   4. Certhidea olivacea.

large as that of a hawfinch to that of a chaffinch, and (if Mr. Gould is right in including his sub-group, Certhidea, in the main

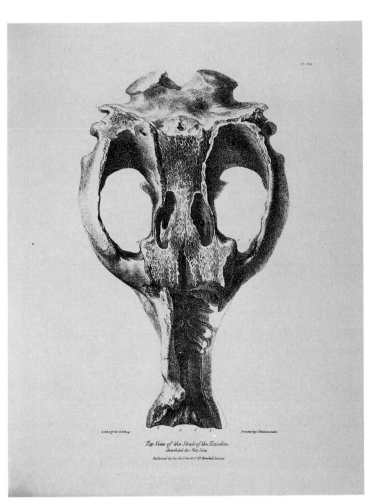

Top View of the Skull of the Toxodon
One third the Nat. Size.

extinct, rhinoceros-sized *Scelidotherium* and the armadillo. As he wrote in his notebook, "This wonderful relationship in the same continent between the dead and the living will, I do not doubt, hereafter throw more light on the appearance of living beings on earth and their disappearance from it."

For all the food for thought Darwin found in Lyell's pages, the concept of evolution developed slowly. The *Beagle* returned to England in 1836; three years later, the *Journal of Researches in the Geology and Natural History of the Various Countries Visited by H.M.S Beagle* appeared and became a best-seller— as a travel book, not as science.

It was not until 1859 that *On the Origin of Species by Means of Natural Selection* (Herald 199) was published, and even then largely because Alfred Russel Wallace, who had been working in the Malay Archipelago, was about to print a similar theory. Darwin clearly expected trouble. As he wrote to a colleague, "As an honest man I must tell you that I have come to the heterodox conclusion that there are no such things as independently created species—that species are only strongly defined varieties. I know that this will make you despise me."

The great complaint about science in the time between Aristotle and the Middle Ages was that scholars turned to books rather than to nature for answers. To understand bees, for instance, medieval scholars would read what the "authorities" said about bees instead of watching a hive. As a result, passages like the following were being written as late as 1579:

"Aristotle thinketh that in greate windes the Bees carry little stones in their mouthes to peyse [balance] their bodies, leste they bee carryed away or kept from their hives, unto whiche they desire to returne with the fruites of their labour."

In 1620 all this changed when Sir Francis Bacon's *Instauratio Magna,* or *The Great Renewal* (Herald 80), was published in London. Its title page depicts the ship of human intelligence slipping away from the old classical fetters, which are represented by two

Mammalia Pl. 4

Desmodus D'Orbignyi.

Tuscan columns. Flowers bloom promisingly on shore while dolphins and whales play in the ship's wake, the seascape a canvas of possibility. Inside is a philosophy that modernized the world through the use of the scientific method, which replaced library research with observation and experiment.

It is surprising that the scientific method took so long to appear, especially since the ancient origins of writing and books had to do with a more efficient way of collecting and comparing data. Memory wasn't enough, and observation had to come first. This is true whether we're talking of Mayan calendars or Babylonian bookkeeping.

Memory leads to mistakes; only in manuscript or book is there a modicum of safety. In 1789, the first published naturalist and bird-watcher, Gilbert White, remarked that "the bane of our science is the comparing of one animal to the other by memory." He knew books were the key.

Provocative ideas from Franklin to Faraday, from Lyell to Darwin, and from Newton to Einstein are passed on in books and then must be tested on the forge of intelligence and experiment. Nineteenth-century biologist T. H. Huxley called this "the great tragedy of Science—the slaying of a beautiful hypothesis by an ugly fact." The old order passeth away.

In 1839 Charles Darwin published his Journal of Researches in the Geology and Natural History of the Various Countries Visited by H.M.S. Beagle, *an account of his now legendary five-year, around-the-world voyage. In it he included the drawing, opposite (left), of four of the 14 finches he observed on the Galapagos Islands. The differentiations among these birds, now known as Darwin's finches, intrigued Darwin and caused him to ponder their origin. Drawings of a skull of the extinct* Toxodon platensis, *opposite (right), and of a bat appear in his* Zoology of the Voyage of H.M.S. Beagle.

THE BEST OF THE PAST

❦ A MEDIEVAL REVIVAL
IN THE ARTS OF THE BOOK

Printing and socialism—not exactly a matched set. Yet in Victorian England, the two combined to produce some of the finest books ever printed. What is more important, they revitalized the art of the book.

The genius behind all this was visionary poet William Morris (1834–1896), remembered today not only as a great writer (his collected works run to 24 volumes) but also as a designer who produced hugely popular wallpapers and tapestries. Twin threads formed the warp and woof of all Morris's work: a love for the Middle Ages and the arts it produced, and a profound sense that only in crafts and craftsmanship could the modern world be saved from what he regarded as the pit of industrialization.

In the mind of William Morris, Satanic mills were a blot on the landscape and psyche of Victorian England. Even book printing had succumbed: the emphasis was on high-speed presses, not fine presswork. Books were widely available but cheap and ugly.

Morris and other writers and artists of his time found refuge and inspiration in the works of art critic John Ruskin (1819–1900), who preached a form of socialism based on a return to medieval values in both life and art. Medieval themes resurfaced in poetry (Tennyson's, for example) and in the arts, especially in the work of the Pre-Raphaelite Brotherhood, who held that everything from Raphael on—even the late Renaissance— was corrupt.

In 1891, at his home in Hammersmith along the banks of the Thames in West London, Morris founded the Kelmscott Press. Here he printed books that drew on the best of the past—the fine calligraphy and decorative borders of medieval manuscripts, and the startling woodcuts and typography of early printing. The medieval book, Morris believed, like the medieval cathedral, was a product of a society in balance, rather than of individuals. In the building of a cathedral, groups of artisans and craftsmen— scribes and illuminators, architects and stonecutters—had worked together to perfect their crafts and glorify their God. The Kelmscott Press aimed to produce little "cathedrals" to reunite art and craft.

The crown jewel of Morris's printing career was his monumental edition of *The Works of Geoffrey Chaucer,* published in a large folio format in 1896, just months before 62-year-old Morris himself would die. The book is thoroughly medieval; borders, initial letters, fleurons, and large woodcuts contend on the pages. The medium is print, but the whiff of the 14th-century scribe is in the air. And that's just as it should be: Chaucer, after all, died in 1400.

The Kelmscott Press *Chaucer* was printed on two presses—in a run of 425 copies on paper, 13 on vellum— and took 23 months to complete. The text is complemented by 87 woodcuts based on drawings by Edward Burne-Jones, the Pre-Raphaelite painter and Morris's lifelong friend. Twenty-six large initial words as well as the border foliage and type ornaments were engraved from designs drawn by Morris himself. (In total, Morris is said to have completed 644 designs for Kelmscott Press books.) No detail was

William Morris stands fifth from the right, middle row, in this photograph of the Socialist League of Hammersmith, above. Passionate in all his interests, Morris spent more than 500 hours in four months learning how to weave. His friend Edward Burne-Jones depicted him at his loom in the cartoon opposite.

too small: The *Chaucer* was printed on heavy linen paper handmade for this edition. Special inks, in red as well as black, were ordered from the chemists.

Designing the Kelmscott types consumed Morris's attention. Over the years, three great faces emerged. The first, called the Golden type, was a roman face based on the work of Nicolaus Jenson in Venice in the 1470s; the face was cut for Morris

by Edward P. Prince in 1890.

The second face, Troy, was ready in 1891; it was a gothic face based on the best types of the early German printers. A bulky face, it was more a good idea than a work of art. The first book produced by the Kelmscott Press, *The Story of the Glittering Plain* (1891), used it to counterbalance 23 dark woodcuts by Walter Crane and a great many initial letters by Morris. Still, the face is too heavy to be read

looked leaden. The lighter Chaucer face still counterbalances all the woodcuts on the page.

To the modern eye, the best of the Kelmscott books are those set in the Golden type. This is not just a matter of our preferring a roman face—the kind we are used to reading—to the gothic faces. These volumes have much less decoration on the page and appear far less cluttered. Initial letters and a few type ornaments usually suffice. The Golden books are thus closer to the standards set by the Venetian printers than the gothic books are to the medieval scribe.

Morris came to typography through calligraphy. He worked hard to understand and reproduce the medieval book calligraphy styles. That background served him well when he began to design his own faces, based on large photographic blowups of letter forms from early printing, especially those of Jenson. It is instructive to see Morris's minute directions—in a rapid but clear italic hand—to Edward P. Prince, who was cutting the lowercase h for the Golden type. After drawing a corrected version of the letterform, Morris adds: "Note the different shape of white in corrected letter . . . seriffs [sic] perhaps a little too fat . . . this flattened curve to be noted and followed . . . a tendency to make everything a little too rigid & square is noticeable." God is in the details.

In 1891, not long after those notes were written, Morris remarked to the *Pall Mall Gazette:* "Even the books of our best authors are spoiled by the type. Look at Mr. Ruskin's works. They are about the worst printed and ugliest-looking books in

with pleasure, unless you happen to be reading to a large audience from a rostrum. The face looks stentorian.

But Morris wrote *Glittering Plain* as a medieval romance, as if for reading aloud in the court of a mighty lord. In that imagined context, the face works perfectly. Actually, it was Morris's own past that caused him to make the Troy face so bold. In 1865, he had planned to print an edition of his long poem *The Earthly Paradise,* illustrated

with woodcuts by Burne-Jones. He soon discovered, however, that no Victorian type could stand up to the heavy ink of the illustrations. The edition was scuttled, but Morris always remembered that lesson.

The third Kelmscott face, the *Chaucer* type, was a smaller (12 point) version of the Troy (18 point). It was needed because the big Kelmscott Chaucer was going to be set in two columns; in Troy, it would have

The library at Kelmscott House, below, photographed in 1896, reflects Morris's long and scholarly interest in the history of books. A 13th-century book of Psalms known as the Windmill Psalter *rests on the bookstand in the foreground. Opposite, Morris's stated aims in founding Kelmscott Press, which basically were to put Victorian printing back in touch with its roots.*

the language." Such an admission must have been hard for Morris. He had out-Ruskined Ruskin, and was determined that later generations would be freed from mean-spirited typography.

In the seven years of its existence, the Kelmscott Press printed 52 works (in 66 volumes) in editions of about 300 copies each. The press restored printing to what its founder thought of as its rightful place among the arts, snatching it from the jaws of industry. It launched the craft-printing movement that extends to our day.

Ultimately, of course, Morris and his poetry and printing failed to change society itself. In the best of all possible worlds, a well-ordered society would have good art and typography. Morris reckoned that, no matter how society turned out, he could ensure that it had nice books.

Only the marketplace defeated him. Morris's printing, like his tapestries and stained glass, was far too expensive for Everyman. The paper copies of the *Chaucer* cost £20 each; vellum, 120 guineas—equivalent to about $1,000 today. Morris himself acknowledged this problem, declaring "if we were all Socialists things would

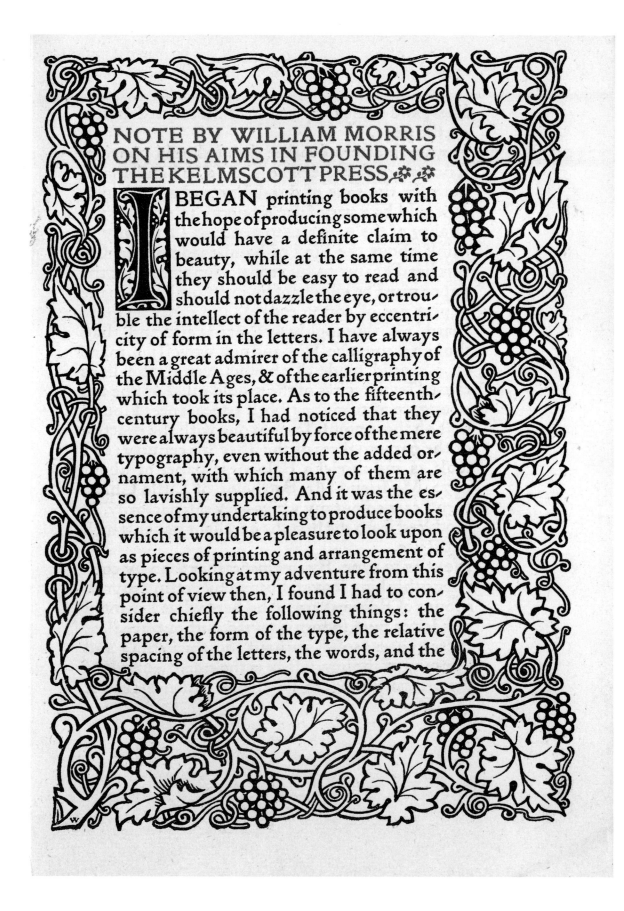

NOTE BY WILLIAM MORRIS
ON HIS AIMS IN FOUNDING
THE KELMSCOTT PRESS ❦ ❦

I BEGAN printing books with
the hope of producing some which
would have a definite claim to
beauty, while at the same time
they should be easy to read and
should not dazzle the eye, or trouble the intellect of the reader by eccentri-
city of form in the letters. I have always
been a great admirer of the calligraphy of
the Middle Ages, & of the earlier printing
which took its place. As to the fifteenth-
century books, I had noticed that they
were always beautiful by force of the mere
typography, even without the added ornament, with which many of them are
so lavishly supplied. And it was the essence of my undertaking to produce books
which it would be a pleasure to look upon
as pieces of printing and arrangement of
type. Looking at my adventure from this
point of view then, I found I had to consider chiefly the following things: the
paper, the form of the type, the relative
spacing of the letters, the words, and the

Morris's Hammersmith neighbor Emery Walker, above, lent his expertise in technical printing to the Kelmscott Press. In fact, it was Walker's 1888 lecture on type design that inspired Morris to take up printing. Walker continued to advise and encourage, and, after Morris's death in 1896, to carry on Morris's aesthetic principles. The press room at Kelmscott, above (right), would have been familiar to Gutenberg, although the toggle-action press, an Albion, is made of iron rather than wood. Walker introduced medievalist Morris to such advances as electrotypes, opposite, shown paired with woodblock prints to demonstrate image quality.

be different. We should have a public library at each street corner, where everybody might see and read all the best books, printed in the best and most beautiful type."

Morris's other failure had to do with his doubts about his commitment to medievalism. In championing the printing press, he felt he had betrayed the ideals of the Middle Ages: "Pleased as I am with my printing, when I saw two men at work on the press yesterday, with their sticky printers' ink, I couldn't help lamenting the simplicity of the scribe and his desk, and his black ink and blue ink and red ink, and I almost felt ashamed of my press after all."

Surely this was an excess of modesty, for the Kelmscott books do exist, a huge body of fine printing. When the *Chaucer* was complete, Burne-Jones insisted, the sumptuous volume would be "a pocket cathedral." "[O]r at least a parish church," writes modern critic William S. Peterson, "constructed of sound

materials and inspired by the Ruskinian vision of craftsmanship as an act of worship. Lending order to the printed page is, for Morris, ultimately one way of lending meaning to human existence."

If Morris had worked alone, his Kelmscott achievement would have died with him in 1896. But he bequeathed a passion for fine craftsmanship in books to two colleagues—Emery Walker, an engraver and typographic expert, and T. J. Cobden-Sanderson, a bookbinder.

Actually, it was Walker (1851–1933) who instigated Morris's first serious forays into type design. Walker was a Hammersmith neighbor of Morris who befriended the Morris family in the early 1880s. In 1888, Walker gave a seminal illustrated lecture on the history of type design. Oscar Wilde attended the lecture and reported: "He pointed out the intimate connection between printing and handwriting—as long as the latter was good the printers had a living model to go by, but when it decayed printing decayed also." William Morris was in that audience and was hooked.

To Walker belongs no small share of the Kelmscott success. Many of Morris's printing ideas were idealistic and impractical; he preferred design to production. In fact, Morris had planned to have others print his books, but with Walker at his side he had the confidence to design the type for them and print them himself. Walker knew the problems and pitfalls of the print shop, and supervised the production of every Kelmscott book.

More important, Walker helped Morris overcome his doctrinaire resistance to the role of photography in printing. The Kelmscott woodcuts, for example, were carved from photographic images of designs projected on the wood surface. Walker also proved to Morris's satisfaction that intricate initial letters could be printed just as clearly from electrotypes as from woodblocks.

T. J. Cobden-Sanderson (1840–1922), like Morris, was a newcomer to printing. He began bookbinding at age 42 after a career as a lawyer. It was a suggestion from Morris's wife that got him apprenticed to the craft; by 1884 he had his own shop, and in 1893 he opened the Doves Bindery in Hammersmith, where he was known chiefly as Morris's binder.

After the close of the Kelmscott Press in 1897, Walker and Cobden-Sanderson joined forces, turning the Doves Bindery into the Doves Press. There they carried on Morris's craft and design principles with more concern for the book as an object to be read than as a work of art. Their

books focus on typography and layout, with a minimum of decoration, often a sole red capital designed by Cobden-Sanderson. And the books are all of uniform size, a small, readable quarto in an elegant Doves binding.

Perhaps the most distinguishing feature of these books is their typeface, designed by Walker and again (like the Golden type) based on a Venetian face by Nicolaus Jenson (that of his 1476 Pliny). Called the Doves type, it has hardly been superseded even today.

After the production of some 20 volumes, a rift between the two caused Walker to bow out of the operation. Cobden-Sanderson directed the Doves Press alone between 1909 and its close in 1916. On August 31, 1917, for reasons we may never fully understand, an old and bitter Cobden-Sanderson walked out on Hammersmith Bridge and consigned the Doves type to the bed of the Thames.

Sydney Cockerell, Morris's secretary and a historian of printing, said that without Walker there would have been no Kelmscott Press—to which we may add, no small-press movement in the 20th century, either. Although he was knighted in 1930, the silent and competent Walker was outfaced on the stage of printing history by both Morris and Cobden-Sanderson. In fact, both men knew little of the printing press until they joined forces with Walker. But they both knew how to write, which is why they appear so often in story of craft printing. Cobden-Sanderson articulated the movement's unofficial creed in 1901, in an essay called "The

Ideal Book, or The Book Beautiful":

"The Book Beautiful is a composite thing . . . made beautiful by the beauty of each of its parts—its literary content, its material or materials, its writing or printing, its illumination or illustration, its binding and decoration—in subordination to the whole which they collectively constitute."

In the same way, Morris, Walker, and Cobden-Sanderson—The Printers of Hammersmith Reach—together constituted a critical mass more powerful than any of them probably realized. In *The Earthly Paradise*, Morris had advised:

Forget six counties overhung with smoke,
Forget the snorting steam and piston stroke,
Forget the spreading of the hideous town;
Think rather of the pack-horse on the
　　down,
And dream of London, small and white
　　and clean,
The clear Thames bordered by its gardens
　　green. . . .

They—the three of them—had done it. Within the covers of books they had re-created a green and pleasant land not seen on Earth for 500 years. Truly, they were good and faithful craftsmen.

The masterpiece of the Kelmscott Press, The Works of Geoffrey Chaucer (1896), opposite, rests before a cabinet custom-built to hold it. Morris designed the woodblock for an initial word in The Canterbury Tales, *below (left), as well as the blind-tooled binding below. The roman type designed by Emery Walker, bottom (left), was believed lost when the Doves Press closed in 1916, but this specimen was discovered after the bombing of Hammersmith during World War II.*

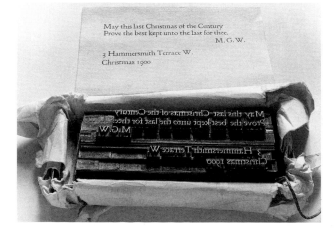

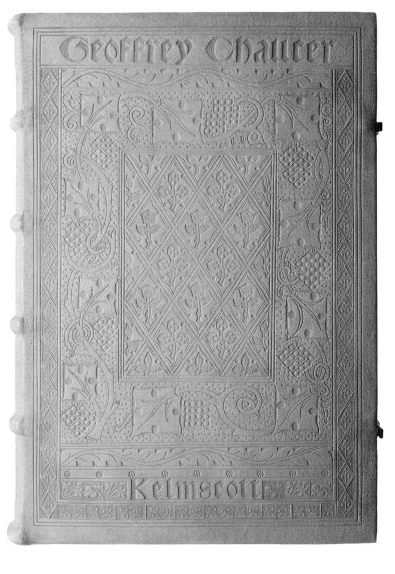

A PICTURE'S WORTH....

EADING IS AN ACT OF WIT. We think when we read, grapple with ideas and wrestle them down. But the best of books also engage our imagination. The illustrator can be crucial in this. When he or she captures our imagination, we soar. ❡ Some illustrators have done their work so well it's hard to think of certain books without them. Who today can recall Dante's *Inferno* without the wood engravings of Gustave Doré (1832–1883)? What would *Alice's Adventures in Wonderland* be without the pictures of John Tenniel (1820–1914), or Oscar Wilde's *Salomé* without those of Aubrey Beardsley (1872–1898)? ❡ Other illustrators have made marks on both literary and art history by illustrating their own books. William Blake is a notable example: his *Songs of Experience* (1794) contains not only one of the most famous poems of all time, "The Tyger," but also the unforgettable illustration in which it's embedded. Blake was following the pioneering engraver Albrecht Dürer (1471–1528), who, in 1498, brought out the *Apocalypse,* for which he was artist, printer, and publisher. ❡ Historically, the distinction between illustrator and artist has been a fine one. American illustrator N. C. Wyeth (1882–1945) suffered depression because he felt he was dismissed as a mere illustrator instead of the artist he in fact was. And yet who today can imagine *Treasure Island* without Wyeth? ❡ In the end, the illustrator's job is to intensify our reading, nothing less. His is an interpretive art, as if he's standing by our reading lamp pleading, "See, see!" He has been there a very long time. ❡ In fact, the technology of reproducing illustrations from an image carved in wood preceded the

"The Forest," opposite, from the opening of the 1861 French illustrated version of Dante's Divine Comedy, *displays the elegant craftsmanship of artist Gustave Doré's carefully chosen engravers. Considered the 19th century's most successful illustrator, Doré supplied drawings for works as diverse as the* Bible *and* Don Quixote. *Dante, however, was always his favorite. The initial R at left was sketched by 16th-century German master Hans Holbein and cut in woodblock by Hans Lützelburger.*

A late-15th-century Albrecht Dürer woodblock of the holy family, above, and an impression of it, above (right), illustrate the way printing reverses an image. The "Hand as the Mirror of Salvation," opposite, is a hand-colored woodcut crafted in 1466.

invention of printing from movable type by more than 800 years. Early Chinese printing as well as the printing of fabrics and playing cards in Europe were also proven technologies by the time of Gutenberg. With the introduction of the letterpress, all that remained was to ensure that the woodblock was "type-high"—the same height as the printing surface of the type—and words and pictures could be inked and printed at the same time.

In 1480, William Caxton, the first English printer, began using woodcut illustrations in his books to increase both interest and sales. Not surprisingly, he based his woodcuts on the art that appeared in manuscript versions of the works he was reprinting. The success of these woodcuts was so immediate that after about 1510 a book without woodcuts was a rarity, and printers who produced a text-only edition often found they had to go back to press to bring out an illustrated version of a new book.

Since woodcuts could be used over and over, just like pieces of movable type, there was a great deal of traffic in them among printers. Woodcuts were traded between England and the Continent and even between book genres, so that a cut originally made to illustrate a saint's life could be recycled in an English ro-

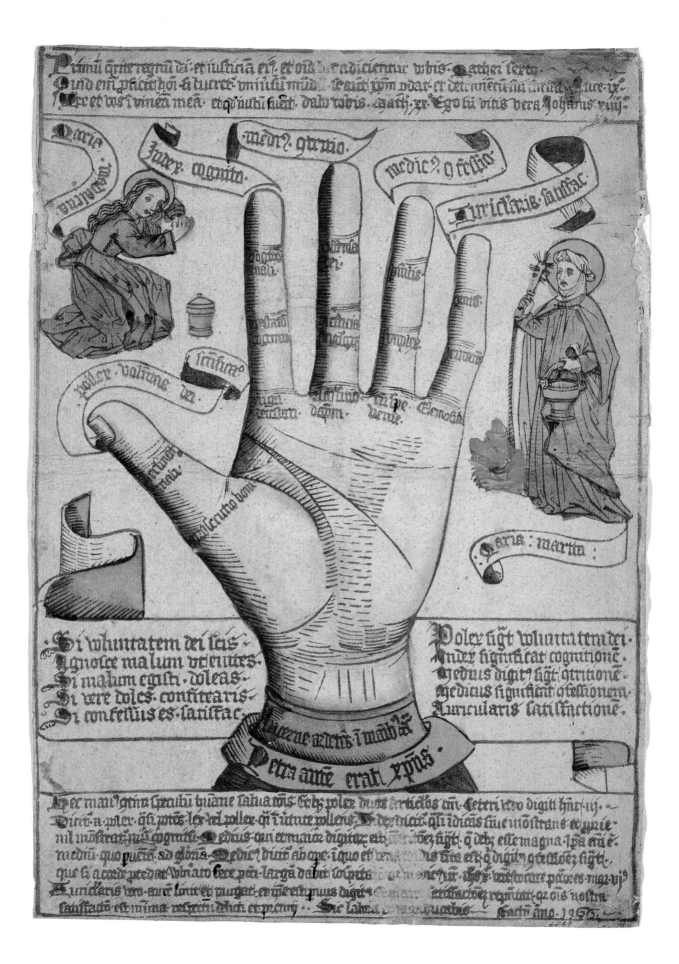

mance. Unfortunately, however, Henry VIII declared a ban on the use of old, Romish religious books; after 1535 printers stopped using existing woodcuts and made few new ones to take their place.

Still, according to a census by bibliographer Edward Hodnett, English printers used a total of 2,514 different woodcuts in the years between 1480 and 1535. Although the comparatively few lines and the lack of shading on the figures point up the deficiencies of these early woodcuts, the best of them both enhanced and dramatized the text.

Over the centuries, methods of printing illustrations changed frequently in a quest to improve the image on the page. Early woodcuts were crudely cut in soft, large-grain woods that could not hold fine details for long under the constant pounding of the press. Harder and finer grains of wood were tried until, in time, boxwood was recognized as the best medium for capturing minute details and the tiny crosshatched patterns used for shading.

In working with boxwood, a technique called wood engraving, the illustrator first would make a preliminary drawing. This would then be redrawn or traced on the cross-grained end of a piece of boxwood that was as high as a piece of type. That drawing would guide the engraver as he cut the image into the wood. Since boxwood trunks are seldom more than seven inches in diameter, large engravings are rare. Those that were made were fashioned from several blocks of wood bolted together, and the seams between blocks in these large prints show to this day.

Both woodcuts and wood engravings are relief illustrations. As with type itself, the background is removed and only the image receives ink and transfers it to paper. With intaglio, another method of engraving, the image is cut into the surface of a copper or steel plate. The whole plate is inked and wiped clean; when paper is squeezed against it in a rolling press, whatever ink remains in the lines and pits and nooks and crannies of the plate will print the image.

A plate can also be engraved by etching. The plate first is sealed in wax, into which an image is drawn with an etching needle. Then the plate is dipped in acid, which eats into the metal wherever it's not protected by wax. When the wax is removed, only the etched area of the plate will hold ink.

The great advantage of copperplate engravings is that they can be easily changed or corrected by burnishing areas flat and re-engraving them with a tool called a burin. The engraving of Shakespeare by Martin Droeshout on the title page of the First Folio (see page 181), for example, changed continually as more and more crosshatching was added to reduce the impression that Shakespeare's disembodied head was floating above his shoulders.

For mezzotint engravings, the entire plate is roughed with a tool called a rocker. Burnishers or scrapers then are used to smooth pits from the areas that are to be free of ink. The image on the resulting print often appears in various tones of gray and black. With aquatints, a plate is etched or engraved with a design and then covered with powdered resin and heated so that the resin adheres. With continued etching, the resin leaves a granular finish on the metal that produces different ink tones on the final image.

"The Four Horsemen," opposite, one of the Apocalypse *series of woodcuts designed in 1498 by German Albrecht Dürer, represents the young artist's first independent work. His engraving of the dancing peasant couple, above, dated 1514, displays his unique emblem, which incorporates his initials. Dürer's 16th-century shop perfected both the woodcut and the engraving.*

Some of the different stages in the process of intaglio illustration and the tools associated with them appear in this 1748 hand-colored drawing, above, which also depicts (at left) the artist receiving inspiration from his muse. At center, a crouching figure etches a copperplate in an acid bath, while in the background another worker heats a plate preparatory to making an aquatint. The early-18th-century English engraving, opposite (above left), discovered at Oxford University's Bodleian Library, was instru-mental in the 20th-century reconstruction of Williamsburg, Virginia's Colonial build-ings. In the mid-17th century, Maria Sibylla Merian sailed from Amsterdam to Surinam, in northeastern South America, to pursue her interest in tropical butterflies. One of the first artists to combine art and science, she painted such tropical treasures as this flowering Surinam banana plant, opposite (above right). The great scientific classifier Linnaeus referred to her pioneering work Metamorphosis Insectorum Suri-namensium *more than 100 times in preparing his 1758 edition of* Systema Naturae. *Opposite, American naturalist John James Audubon painted the original for this hand-colored aquatint of an American avocet in 1836 for his magnum opus* The Birds of North America. *London engraver Robert Havell produced 435 plates for the four-volume work between 1827 and 1838. Engraved from Audubon's originals, the outlines of the images were powdered with resin to create shading.*

"The Tyger," above, was written, illustrated, etched, and painted by visionary William Blake for his 1794 Songs of Experience. *Blake's etching process united word and image in relief on the plate. Blake and his wife, Catherine Sophia Boucher, individually watercolored most of his works, including* Europe: a Prophecy *(c. 1794), right. Artist Marc Chagall etched this illustration of "The Raven and the Fox," opposite, for a 1952 edition of La Fontaine's* Fables.

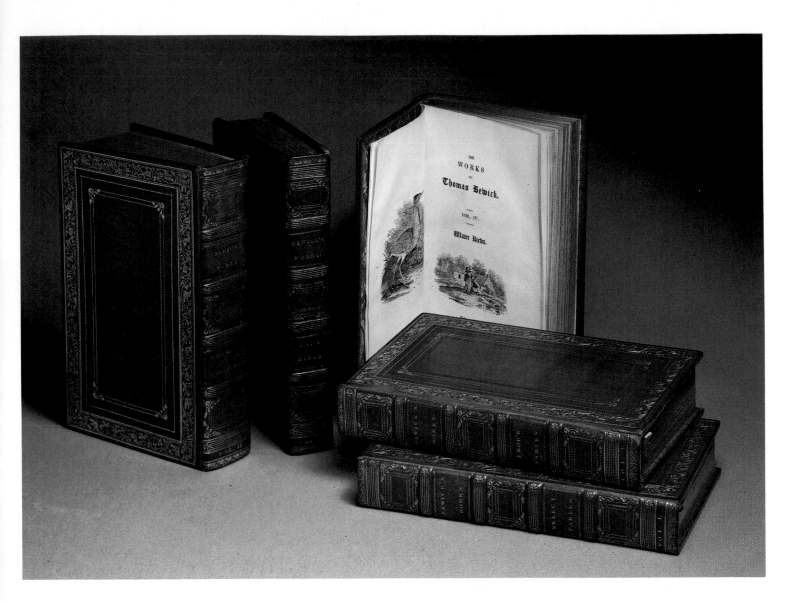

The collected works of Englishman Thomas Bewick span 28 years and feature thousands of intricate wood engravings. Bewick produced two classics of natural history: The General History of Quadrupeds *(1790) and* History of British Birds *(1797–1804).*

Lithography, from the Greek *lithos*, or stone, and *graphos,* writing, offers a third way of printing illustrations. In this case, the image is neither cut in relief nor incised but is drawn directly on a flat lithographic slate with either pencil or crayon. When the stone is drenched with water, ink will adhere only to those greasy areas that define the drawing; the water will reject the oil-based ink everywhere else.

Lithography was developed in the late 1790s by Aloysius Senefelder, who lived near the great slate quarries at Sölnhofen in southern Germany. Looking for an inexpensive way to print his plays, he turned to the cheap, plentiful stone material, which at first he thought had to be etched. He soon invented a special press that was sturdy enough to handle the lithographic stones and began turning out not just illustrations but entire books. His experiment was a great success for the printing of music books, books on Oriental or African languages, and other volumes—such as those of math and chemistry—whose abundance of symbols would have required the making of thousands of specialized type pieces for printing on a letterpress.

In England between 1823 and 1828, Thomas Young, the physicist and Egyptologist who came so close to deciphering the Rosetta Stone, published a series of lithographic volumes entitled *Hieroglyphics, Collected by the Egyptian Society*. His nemesis, French archaeologist Jean-François Champollion, followed Young in printing as well as Egyptology; his lithographed *Grammaire égyptiénne* was published posthumously between 1836 and 1841.

Wood engraving was regularly used to illustrate books from the late 18th to the late 19th centuries. One of the finest engravers, British illustrator Thomas Bewick (1753–1828), was such a pioneering observer of nature that he is known as much for introducing a taste for natural history to the public as he is for his art. His first book, *The General History of Quadrupeds* (1790), was an immediate hit and ran through eight editions over the next 34 years. Bewick also produced volumes on land and water birds and on Aesop's fables, and began a work on British fishes that was never completed.

As a child, Bewick filled every available space on his school slates and scrap papers with finely detailed sketches. A friend was to recall: "There were three windows in the front room, the ledges and shutters whereof he had pencilled all over with funny characters.... I have seen him draw a striking likeness on his thumb-nail, in one moment; wipe it off with his tongue, and instantly draw another."

Although he worked within the artistic confines of the boxwood block, Bewick gave the viewer much more than just the animal under study. Finely detailed leaves, rocks, and logs round out each scene, and people, too, enliven his backdrops. His illustration of a shepherd's dog, for example, includes the dog's Scottish master in bonnet and plaid.

There is also social criticism. In one view, two blind fiddlers are led about by a young boy who holds out a hat for alms. As they approach the walls of a great estate, a sign warns, "Steel traps—Spring guns." But the child cannot read, nor—as Bewick's art suggests—would his innocence allow him to comprehend the mean spirit behind those words.

Almost 40 years after Bewick's death, Victorian novelist Charles Kingsley wrote of one of the artist's bird books: "When [the] book on birds first came out, my father, then a young hunting squire in the New Forest, Hampshire, saw the book in London, & bought at once the beautiful old copy which was the text book of my boyhood. He was a sportsman & field-naturalist, loved the book, & carried it with him up & down, in days when no scientific knowledge could be got ... he was laughed at in the New Forest for having 'bought a book about dicky birds'—till his fellow squires, borrowing the book of him—agreed that it was the most clever book they had ever seen, & a revelation to them." Dicky birds, indeed.

Not unlike Bewick, Frenchman J. J. Grandville (1803–1847) worked with wood engraving on boxwood, was a close observer of natural history, and was appalled by injustice. But Grandville set out to change society with his pen, becoming a savage cartoonist and satirist and working on the political humor sheets *La Silhouette* and *La Caricature*. After the government repressions of 1835, how-

Thomas Bewick's illustration of a shepherd's dog (top), a wood engraving from his Quadrupeds, *includes the dog's Scottish master in bonnet and plaid and even sheep in its background. The barn owl (center) and the two blind fiddlers were intended only as decorations for the bottom of a page but also are minutely detailed.*

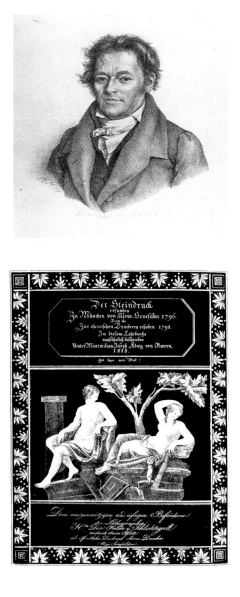

A lithographed plate, above, of a scene recalling the classical era introduces an 1818 manual on the then newly invented printing process of lithography. Above (top), a 19th-century lithographic portrait of Aloysius Senefelder, the Bavarian inventor of lithography and author of the 1818 manual. Developed in 1796, the lithographic or "chemical-printing" process relies on the different properties of grease and water to produce print on stone. French artists have dominated the medium almost since the beginning: above, Eugène Delacroix's portrayal of Mephistopheles for an 1827 printing of Goethe's Faust; opposite, Odilon Redon's Profil de lumière (Profile of light), 1886.

In the fantastic world of French satirist J. J. Grandville, sharks and sawfish instruct ravens and rats on the finer points of surgery, above, and fish use such lures as jewels, awards, and money, opposite, to catch people. Grandville produced 3,000 such bizarre drawings between 1827 and 1847 for lithographed book illustrations. Overleaf: American artist N. C. Wyeth created a series of large oil paintings for Charles Scribner's 1911 edition of Robert Louis Stevenson's Treasure Island. *Although Wyeth completed some of them in a single day, masterpieces such as "Israel Hands" (left) and "Blind Pew" have become an enduring and integral part of the story for generations of readers.*

ever, it was clear that newspapers could no longer support him. Political cartoons had become too dangerous.

In desperation, Grandville turned to books, and over the next 20 years he turned out 3,000 illustrations—an average of about one every two and a half days. Such industry can bring fame and adoration, but it may also kill: Grandville died at the age of 43.

But between 1840 and 1842, the volume that ensured Grandville's fame, *Scènes de la vie privée et publique des animaux (Scenes of the Private and Public Life of the Animals),* was published in 100 installments. In *Scènes,* Grandville finally had a chance to showcase all the elements that had characterized his earlier career. His depictions of animals revealed his intimate knowledge of natural history and the insights gained from a lifetime of observing that curious, plodding primate *Homo sapiens.*

The framework of the book is simplicity itself. The animals in the Paris zoo revolt. And why not? The humans of France had overthrown their masters several times in those days—and were to do so again before mid-century. The revolutionaries elect Grandville as an honorary animal and enlist him to record their republic.

Change fills the air. In one tale, the ravens open a medical school, convinced that they can do better than their former veterinarians. Grandville's look inside their surgery unit depicts a shark and a sawfish as teachers, and rats, scavenger beetles, ravens, and buzzards as students, while in the back room an army of ants cleans the bones of an ex-patient. A look of pure terror fills the one dying eye of the dog-patient, who, after all, had entered the hospital with only a sprained paw.

In 1844, Grandville's most famous work, *Un Autre Monde (Another World),* appeared. Detailing the excursions of three travelers who reconsider the modern world from three points of view—from under the seas, from the sky (by balloon), and from new rovings about the land—it offers up truly another world: the fish go fishing for humans with jewelry, champagne, money, gold, and high-fashion accessories as bait; a dog walks his master; aristocrats stay home, their place in the public eye usurped by their walking sticks, hats, boots, and boot trees. The book trade also is satirized, as literature is ground off a roller at the publisher's shop and marketed in chunks like so much pork sausage.

Grandville's influence was widespread. Lewis Carroll, for example, and his illustrator, John Tenniel, drew on Grandville's ideas for the battle of the playing cards and for the mock turtle, whose crying calf's head is almost identical to the Grandville original. And there are echoes of Grandville still to be seen today, from Walt Disney to Gary Larson.

Jumping to another time and another place, a 20th-century illustrator steeped in the history of printing is Milton Glaser. He has designed successful magazines, such as *New York,* and several typefaces—Baby Fat and Baby Teeth—and is known for his way of illustrating a story with one basic picture that changes slowly from page to page as the reader becomes more involved with the narrative. It's an effective way to show time passing.

Glaser often relies solely on black-and-white designs—a bow in the direction of the woodcut. When he does add color, it is usually in a flat pattern of one ink. This is no allusion to Matisse or to the Japanese print. Instead, it's a concession to the printer who must reproduce his work in one or two press-runs, without the fuss and expense of four-color work. The illustrator today must know not only typography and design but also how to live with the economics of modern printing.

One of Glaser's most famous illustrations was for a magazine article on the Russian ballet impresario Diaghilev and his dancer, Nijinski. Glaser shows us a straightforward Diaghilev in top hat and sea-otter coat. As for the dancer, only his legs appear as he bounds out of the top of the frame. The rest of Nijinski's body must be extrapolated from his shadow on the floor.

The Victoria and Albert Museum in London holds a leaf from an illuminated Psalter made in Canterbury about the year 1140. In its depiction of the Ascension, the panel shows Christ's feet only. The rest of his holy body—like Milton Glaser's Nijinski—is bounding out of the frame, leaving the upturned faces of his astonished apostles below. The arc that connects medieval Canterbury and modern New York is clear in both pictures. The illustrator's enthusiastic response to the story is what lifts a tale—and us the readers—off the page. And that is any illustrator's ultimate goal.

Dancer Vaslav Nijinski leaps off the page, right, as impresario Sergey Diaghilev looks on, in a watercolor illustration for Audience *magazine by 20th-century graphic artist Milton Glaser. Printmaker and sculptor Leonard Baskin returned to the art of the woodcut to create his 1967* Icarus, *above. Opposite, the great white whale breaches, as depicted in a wood engraving by artist and master illustrator Rockwell Kent. This print was one of 280 images drawn by Kent for a 1930 Lakeside Press edition of Herman Melville's classic,* Moby Dick.

"No teeth, no teeth, no teeth!" The speaker is Mr. Jackson, a toad and an uninvited visitor down the yards and yards of soft sandy passages that are the underground home of Mrs. Tittlemouse. People are always dropping in on her, and they're ever so much trouble to clean up after. Mr. Jackson, for one, drips. When she offers him some savory cherrystones, his toad-mouth gapes and he points out—three times—what is rather obvious: he has no teeth.

The characters are from *The Tale of Mrs. Tittlemouse* (1910), one of Beatrix Potter's best. Potter (1866–1943) lived a long and productive life turning out 46 children's books that have been reprinted around the world. Her trademark is a startling combination of delicate watercolors and a prose style that features some big words set in short sentences and very short paragraphs.

The first page of her early story *The Tailor of Gloucester* (1902–03), for example, contains no fewer than five words for types of cloth—taffeta, satin, pompadour, lutestring (watered silk), and padusoy (Padua silk). What we all learned from Potter is that children, even very small ones, will absorb the tough bits as long as they are charmed along by the narrative flow. The big words give a taste of the adult world they know they all must someday face.

Oh, how young listeners squirm with excitement at the prospect of adventures and scares in the great outside world: the nice gentleman "with sandy whiskers" who offers to help Jemima line her nest with feathers he has stashed in his fox-den (*The Tale of Jemima Puddle-Duck,* 1908). Or, Peter Rabbit's mother, who abruptly announces: ". . . don't go into Mr. McGregor's garden: your Father had an accident there; he was put in a pie by Mrs. McGregor" (*The Tale of Peter Rabbit,* 1901–02).

The process by which books for children achieve classic status stands in refreshing contrast to that of adult books. Kids don't respond to literary trends. Potter or Maurice Sendak or Dr. Seuss are only as good as their next book. To succeed with kids, a book must simply hold their attention, delight them, teach them something they can use, give them a hairsbreadth escape once in a while, and show them something of the adult world, the thing they're most interested in anyway.

The first children's books concentrated on teaching. Johann Amos Comenius (1592–1670) is credited with publishing *Orbis sensualium pictus (The Visible World in Pictures),* the first illustrated book for children, printed in Nuremberg in 1658. It featured 150 woodcuts depicting birds and other animals, jobs and morality, games and law, war and magic, and the text listed the Latin words for everything in the pictures.

Spelling books, primers, ABCs, and books of morality—including tiny "thumb" Bibles—constituted the bulk of children's reading in the 17th and 18th centuries. This is true for both England and America. The Colonial Williamsburg library holds a well-worn 1789 book, *Entertaining Fables for the Instruction of Children,* whose frontispiece cautions:

Observe this book, here fix thine eyes,
The mother to her darling cries,

MOTHER GOOSE AND COMPANY

❦ BOOKS FOR THE YOUNG—AND THE YOUNG AT HEART

A charming original watercolor from Peter Rabbit *celebrates Beatrix Potter's love and knowledge of nature. Her classic story, composed originally as a picture-letter to a child, was first published—in black and white and at her expense—in 1901.*

(224)

CX.

Prudence.   *Prudentia.*

Prudence, 1.
looketh upon all things
as a Serpent, 2.
and doeth,
speaketh, or thinketh
nothing in vain.

She looks backward, 3
as into a looking-glass, 4
to things past;
and seeth before her, 5.
as with a Perspective-
glass, 7.
things to come,
as the end; 6.
and so she perceiveth

Prudentia, 1.
omnia circumspectat,
ut *Serpens,* 2.
nihilq; agit,
loquitur, & cogitat
in caſſum.
Respicit, 3.
tanquam in *Speculum,* 4.
ad *Præterita;*
& *Prospicit,* 5.

tanquam *Telescopio,* 7.
Futura
seu *Finem:* 6.
atq; ita perspicit

what

256

This little BOOK *will make thee wise.*
Thou here as in a glass wilt find,
The faithful image of the mind,
From hence thou'lt learn betimes to know
Those proper duties thou shalt owe
To God, to man, to friend, to foe.

Clearly, this is the sort of advertisement that appealed to parents, not children. Yet the fact is that throughout the Middle Ages and the Renaissance, children were considered to be small adults. They were dressed as adults and were expected to behave like them—as much as possible, anyway—and both their play and their books sought to inculcate socially desirable conduct.

We now realize that children are much smarter than we ever thought. They size up social realities and family dynamics instantly, and are fully capable of diving beneath the surface reality of a tale to bring up a usable pearl of wisdom. Consider the simple nursery rhyme:

Pussy cat, pussy cat, where have you
    been?
I've been up to London to look at the
    queen.
Pussy cat, pussy cat, what did you there?
I frightened a little mouse under her chair.

Even the smallest child can understand this. Adults see it as merely quaint. Yet it also carries a serious message: if you're going to do the same thing in London as you did at home, why bother? Pussycat might just as well have saved her train fare. The rhyme was published in *Songs for the Nursery* in 1805, but probably circulated orally for centuries before that, handed down from generation to generation.

To French poet Charles Perrault (1628–1703) goes credit for mining the oral literature of the nursery. His

The lessons of Prudence are not lost in this woodcut, opposite, from a 1685 English translation of Johann Amos Comenius's Orbis sensualium pictus (1658), the first picture book for children. Today the tradition continues, only in a less didactic, more entertaining style: below, O is for ostrich in Bert Kitchen's 1984 Animal Alphabet.

The world of fantasy has long been the special domain of children's literature and the illustrations that accompany it. Water fairies disport among the water lilies, above, in one of a set of pictures by Richard Doyle that inspired verses by Irish poet William Allingham. Pictures and text were united in 1870 for the publication of In Fairyland: A Series of Pictures from the Elf-World. Opposite, one of Arthur Rackham's exquisite watercolors from "The Old Woman in the Wood" in the 1917 edition of the Grimm brothers' Little Brother and Little Sister. Rackham worked his magic in dozens of children's classics in the early 20th century.

Contes de ma mere l'Oye (1697), or Mother Goose's Tales (1729), showed that children's tales were worthy of serious study.

The brothers Grimm, Jacob (1785–1863) and Wilhelm (1786–1859), are credited with founding the modern science of folklore, chiefly in a multi-volume edition of folktales called Kinder-und Hausmarchen (Nursery and Household Tales, 1812–1822), known in English as Grimm's Fairy Tales. Though their academic interests were in linguistics, they came to that work mainly through collecting fairy tales, which they said reflected our simple, primordial past—a past that can be revisited in children's stories.

Because of the popularity of books like Perrault's, publishers began to consider a regular trade in entertaining, illustrated books for children. The London publishing firm of John Newbery (1713–1767) turned out some 400 titles specifically for children up through 1815, including The History of Little Goody Two-Shoes (1765), the story of the education and travels of an orphan girl. It is said to be the first long piece of fiction just for children.

Since 1922, the (John) Newbery Medal has been awarded annually for the "most distinguished contribution to American literature for children." The first prize-winner was Hendrik van Loon's The Story of Mankind. The Caldecott Medal, by contrast, has been awarded each year since 1938 to the best American picture book for children. The medal honors Randolph Caldecott (1846–1886), the celebrated Victorian illustrator whose A Frog He Would A-Wooing Go (1883) became a best seller. The book deeply impressed a young Beatrix Potter, who was especially influenced by Caldecott's portrayal of dressed-up animals.

The ultimate children's story, of course, is Hamlet, a cautionary tale about what can go wrong if you run away from home (to university) and return to discover your parents utterly changed. It's amazing how much adult literature seems to be about this kind of choice. From The Odyssey to Paradise Lost, they all suggest "There's no place like home."

For a child, there are really only

Young Alice Liddell, above, was the muse for whom Oxford deacon Charles Dodgson, better known as Lewis Carroll, created Alice's Adventures in Wonderland *(1865). Artist John Tenniel worked with Dodgson to create indelible images for this classic, such as the Queen of Hearts and her entourage with Alice, above right.*

two choices, after all: to stay or to go. Childhood itself is a time of trying out strategies for life. Shall I be aggressive or passive, independent or domestic, good or bad? And, whichever I choose, will someone still love me? Approve of me? The best of children's literature deals with the consequences of these tough choices. *Alice's Adventures in Wonderland, Pinocchio, The Wind in the Willows, Winnie-the-Pooh*—all are about getting away from home.

Even Graham Greene, when he came to write his first children's story, *The Little Train* (1946), made it about

the struggle for independence that every creature must go through, even if it is a locomotive.

The Reverend Charles Dodgson (1832–1898) taught mathematics at Christ Church, Oxford, and was a family friend of Dean H. G. Liddell of the college, himself a great bookman and co-author of Liddell and Scott's *Greek-English Lexicon* (a book still in print). As an 1864 Christmas present for Liddell's young daughter, Alice, Dodgson presented her with a manuscript of stories he had been inventing for her over the past two years. The book, illustrated by his own hand, was entitled *Alice's Adventures Underground.*

Dodgson financed the book's publication himself, adopting the pen name Lewis Carroll and employing the *Punch* cartoonist John Tenniel to redo his drawings. Although printing was complete in June 1865, Tenniel was disappointed with the way his art was reproduced, and the entire 2,000-copy edition was suppressed. (It was altered and later distributed in America.) By Christmas 1865, reprinting was complete and the world at large at last was treated to *Alice's Adventures in Wonderland,* Carroll's final choice for a title.

Alice's voyage of discovery takes her to many strange places, but in every case she learns about herself and home. In 1927, the novelist Hugh Walpole sized up *Alice's* impact: "I have never seen anywhere sufficient emphasis laid upon the greatest of its powers, namely, the extraordinary resemblance of the figures in it to a child's everyday relations. A child of six or seven sees its elders as 'trees walking.' . . . These resemblances did not strike me as in any way odd; it simply was that the people in *Alice* behaved more normally and more reasonably than the people at home."

The next great runaway child came from the imagination of Carlo Collodi, the nom de plume of Carlo Lorenzini (1826–1890), a journalist who turned to writing for children. Between 1881 and 1883 he wrote installments of "La Storia di un Burratino" ("The Story of a Puppet") for a children's journal. Its opening illustration showed Pinocchio as the pathetic single-string kind of puppet that's held in one hand while

the string is pulled from below. By the time of the book version, *Avventure di Pinocchio* (1883), the puppet had acquired the Mazzanti illustration— the boy with the wooden peg nose— that is still used.

Like the *Alice* books, Kenneth Grahame's *Wind in the Willows* (1908) and A. A. Milne's *Winnie-the-Pooh* (1926) were written with a particular child in mind, the respective authors' sons—Alastair "Mouse" Grahame and Christopher "Robin" Milne. The wonderful line drawings by Ernest H. Shepard played a large part in the

Christopher Robin on an outing with Winnie-the-Pooh and Piglet, above. Ernest Shepard rendered the drawings for A. A. Milne's Pooh stories, including this one, originally published in The House at Pooh Corner *(1926), and hand-colored them 30 years later. Overleaf: "Let the wild rumpus start," declares Max, King of the Wild Things, in Maurice Sendak's perennial favorite and Caldecott-award-winning* Where the Wild Things Are *(1963).*

success of both books: Mole lost, cold, and afraid on his ill-advised venture into the Wild Wood; or Christopher Robin, Pooh, and Piglet, masters of all they survey.

Today, after the pioneering work of Maurice Sendak and the late Dr. Seuss (Theodor Seuss Geisel), the world open to children through books seems limitless. And advances continue to be made, not only in illustration but also in language. Dr. Seuss certainly expanded these new horizons with a half-century of publishing hilarious books that celebrate the wackiness of words. His stock in trade was confidence in language and life. The character in his recent book

Oh, the Places You'll Go! (1990) is very much in the tradition of Alice, Pinocchio, Mole, and Christopher Robin. The book is a guidebook to life's pitfalls, but directed at the whole family—new college graduates as well as children and parents.

In the Annunziata Church in Florence is Andrea del Sarto's fresco "The Virgin of the Sack," a Holy Family scene in which Mary holds the wriggling babe while Joseph reads to them both. (It's an anachronism, because Joseph reads from a codex, which had not been invented yet, instead of a scroll.)

I long to know what children's book it is.

Today children's books abound, with engaging stories and illustrations for all. In Chris Van Allsburg's Just a Dream *(1990), opposite, dreams of the future stir the slumber of a boy. Above, a small person faces down a potentially big problem in* Oh, the Places You'll Go!, *a 1990 offering by the late, great Dr. Seuss.*

El sueño de la razon produce monstruos.

EVERY WORD
FOR EVERYMAN

HE MOST IMPORTANT BOOK ever written? Certainly there's no shortage of candidates—the Bible, Newton's *Principia mathematica*, Einstein's 1905 paper outlining the theory of relativity, or almost any play by Shakespeare. All these, and many more, have their adherents; each is a significant, influential, historic work. ❡ But there is another book, which first appeared in 1828, written in North America, that ranks with all of the above. *An American Dictionary of the English Language* was a two-volume celebration of the United States' intellectual independence from Europe. It quickly became the foremost dictionary in the English-speaking world. ❡ Its author was Connecticut writer Noah Webster (1758–1843), who had achieved fame with the 1783 publication of what eventually was titled the *Elementary Spelling Book*. Popularly called "the blue-backed speller," it went on to sell 100 million copies up through the 20th century—while standardizing American spelling. ❡ In 1806, Webster published his first dictionary, the *Compendious Dictionary of the English Language,* which established once and for all that i and j and u and v were separate letters, no longer interchangeable. Such spelling was to be the American Way. More important, Webster challenged the supposed superiority of British English over North American English, and so introduced many Americanisms (tomahawk, snowshoe, and livestock, to name a few) to the world at large. But this was just the beginning. ❡ Webster's 70,000-word *Dictionary* of 1828 was his triumph. It was scholarly and dependable, making the dictionary a common sight in households and offices and on the desk of every

Dream-like banner of the Enlightenment, Francisco Goya's 18th-century aquatint El sueño de la razon produce monstruos, or The sleep of reason produces monsters, opposite, conjures up the "human errors and vices, follies and blunders" that must be met head on with reason and truth. Logic and the scientific method could banish the superstition and ignorance prominent in Europe since the beginning of the Middle Ages. Books made knowledge cumulative. Printing made books more accessible. Left, a decorated initial T from a 20th-century booklet celebrating the Old Face Roman types designed more than 200 years earlier by English typefounder William Caslon.

The founding father of American spelling, Noah Webster, opposite (right), published his An American Dictionary of the English Language, *opposite, in 1828, standardizing spelling and pronunciation in the United States. His copy of Samuel Johnson's famous 1799* Dictionary, *right, reveals annotations that Webster incorporated into his own work.*

W

writer. Webster put words in our mouths. It is not too much to say that this book had more influence on writing of every kind than any other literary innovation of the century: the fountain pen, which allowed writers to write anywhere; the gaslight, which allowed them to scribble all night without going blind; and the typewriter, which allowed their work to be read rather than deciphered. But the greatest success of Webster's *Dictionary* was that it gave ordinary people a voice. With the dictionary, everyone had the confidence to write.

Webster revised the *Dictionary* in 1840, and its descendants are still published today. The word "Webster's" was possibly the first of that class of proper nouns or trade names that have become generic—like aspirin or Frigidaire in our time. A "Webster's" refers to a dictionary, no matter who compiled it.

Webster's *Dictionary* is a product of the Enlightenment, an 18th-century move-

ment dedicated to the proposition that the world operates according to orderly and rational processes whose governing principles are as open to inspection as the mechanism of a clock. The Enlightenment's stock-in-trade was confidence—intellectual, economic, scientific, artistic. There was simply no problem facing humans that would not submit to hard work, solid thinking, and good books. This intellectual milieu created a generation of polymaths such as Benjamin Franklin and Thomas Jefferson, whose scholarly and bookish interests were boundless.

The confidence of the Enlightenment gave rise to two historic literary enterprises well before Webster published his dictionary. In England, Samuel Johnson's *A Dictionary of the English Language* (1755) was hailed as an intellectual achievement that earned its author an honorary doctorate from Trinity College Dublin. In France, the publication of *L'Encyclopédie* (1751–1772) demonstrated

A number of the best and the brightest of France's 18th-century minds gathered, below, after 1745 to work on Denis Diderot's Encyclopédie, ou Dictionnaire raisonné. *A comprehensive survey of the Enlightenment, the project blossomed into 28 volumes by 1772. Philosopher Denis Diderot, whose portrait appears opposite, undertook the exhaustive task of overseeing and editing the* Encyclopédie. *Opposite (below), the first page of volume one of the* Encyclopédie *appears with one of the work's illustrations, which offers instructions for raising silk worms.*

its editor's certainty that all mysteries under the sun would eventually yield up their secrets to rational investigation. The works are united in that they are "democratic" documents that acted to transfer the power of knowledge from a small, scribal elite to anyone who could read. Revolutions depend on such books.

Edited for 20 years by philosopher Denis Diderot (1713–1784), *L'Encyclopédie* was published in 28 volumes with seven volumes of supplement—17,000 folio pages in double columns—and contained not only major contributions by Voltaire and Jean-Jacques Rousseau but also illustrations of such clarity and thoroughness that they are still our major source of information on 18th-century industry and life. Without them, our understanding of Europe (and America) in the period would be greatly diminished. Simply put, the books are a monument. More important, they were a financial success as well: a rational world, after all, would recognize quality and pay for it. The book earned a profit of 300 percent on a one-million-livre investment.

Across the Channel, Johnson's *Dictionary* made him a superstar. To be sure,

there had been dictionaries before his. The difference is that, while these were compiled, Johnson's was *written*. In London's salons and coffeehouses, Johnson (1709–1784) was lionized, his frequent rude outbursts of superiority and condescension tolerated and encouraged, and he became the subject of the first great literary biography, written by his young friend and confidant, James Boswell (1740–1795). *The Life of Samuel Johnson* appeared in 1791 and quickly ran through several editions. Among other matters, it established the dominant position of books in 18th-century culture.

Boswell's description of Johnson reading is unforgettable: "Before dinner Dr. Johnson seized upon Mr. Charles Sheridan's *Account of the late Revolution in Sweden,* and seemed to read it ravenously, as if he devoured it, which was to all appearance his method of studying. 'He knows how to read better than any one,' said Mrs. Knowles; 'he gets at the substance of a book directly; he tears out the heart of it.' He kept it wrapped in the table-cloth in his lap during the time of dinner, from an avidity to have one entertainment in readiness, when he should

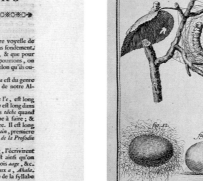

Œconomie Rustique. Vers a Soye.

have finished another; resembling (if I may use so coarse a simile) a dog who holds a bone in his paws in reserve, while he eats something else which has been thrown to him."

Johnson lived solely by his wits, by writing, and found it a very hard life. He was constantly under pressure to produce for hungry presses and publishers. The printer's messenger was always at his door waiting for more copy. His novella *Rasselas* had to be written rapidly in January 1759 to raise money for his mother's funeral. He once remarked, "No man but a blockhead ever wrote, except for money."

But for all his protestations, when it came to his *Dictionary,* Johnson couldn't stop writing. The book's definitions often reflect Johnson's biases and his ironical humor. Oats were "a grain, which in England is generally given to horses, but in Scotland supports the people." In a self-effacing vein, he defined a dictionary-maker, a lexicographer, as "a harmless drudge, that busies himself in tracing the original, and detailing the significance of words." He even gave us the world of the hack writer in his entry for "Grub Street": "The name of a street in London, much inhabited by writers of small histories, dictionaries, and temporary poems; whence any mean production is called Grub Street."

The glory of the book is that it is also a compendium of English literature, reprinting fine examples of words from the masters, often Shakespeare or Sir Francis Bacon. Johnson sought to "intersperse with verdure and flowers the dusty desarts of baren philology." Said Thomas Carlyle in the 19th century: "Had Johnson left nothing but his *Dictionary*, one might have traced there a great intellect, a genuine man." Noah Webster, despite his assertion of independence from things English in his own books, nevertheless seems to have followed Johnson closely for about a third of the words in his 1828 book.

By the middle of the 19th century, dictionaries were regarded as more than

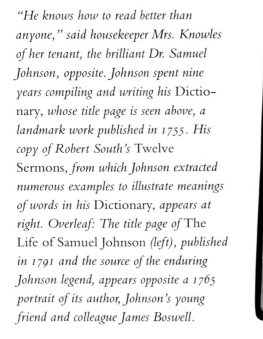

"He knows how to read better than anyone," said housekeeper Mrs. Knowles of her tenant, the brilliant Dr. Samuel Johnson, opposite. Johnson spent nine years compiling and writing his Dictionary, *whose title page is seen above, a landmark work published in 1755. His copy of Robert South's* Twelve Sermons, *from which Johnson extracted numerous examples to illustrate meanings of words in his* Dictionary, *appears at right. Overleaf: The title page of* The Life of Samuel Johnson *(left), published in 1791 and the source of the enduring Johnson legend, appears opposite a 1765 portrait of its author, Johnson's young friend and colleague James Boswell.*

THE
LIFE
OF
SAMUEL JOHNSON, LL.D.

COMPREHENDING

AN ACCOUNT OF HIS STUDIES
AND NUMEROUS WORKS,

IN CHRONOLOGICAL ORDER;

A SERIES OF HIS EPISTOLARY CORRESPONDENCE
AND CONVERSATIONS WITH MANY EMINENT PERSONS;

AND

VARIOUS ORIGINAL PIECES OF HIS COMPOSITION,
NEVER BEFORE PUBLISHED.

THE WHOLE EXHIBITING A VIEW OF LITERATURE AND LITERARY MEN
IN GREAT-BRITAIN, FOR NEAR HALF A CENTURY,
DURING WHICH HE FLOURISHED.

IN TWO VOLUMES.

BY JAMES BOSWELL, Esq.

———— *Quò fit ut* OMNIS
Votiva pateat veluti defcripta tabella
VITA SENIS.————   HORAT.

VOLUME THE FIRST.

LONDON:
PRINTED BY HENRY BALDWIN,
FOR CHARLES DILLY, IN THE POULTRY.
M DCC XCI.

mere conveniences: they were essential, especially to the fledgling sciences of etymology and philology, folklore and linguistics. Taking a hint from the historical citations in both Johnson and Webster, the Victorian era embarked on its own great historical enterprise—the *Oxford English Dictionary*.

On January 18, 1884, from the Clarendon Press, Oxford, appeared the first volume of a work that has become an indispensable tool for writers and wordsmiths, scholars, critics and the congenitally curious for more than a century. The volume's title page proclaimed it as *A New English Dictionary on Historical Principles,* of which this was to be the first part, covering "A. through Ant-." The "Historical Principles" noted in the title are what aroused so much interest in the work and what keep it alive today.

Each word is not only described in all of its meanings but also presented in its original context with a line or two for poetry, a phrase or sentence for prose. Further, the listing for each sense is continued, through time, from the

Mastermind and editor of the Oxford English Dictionary, *or OED, perhaps the greatest dictionary ever published, James Murray labors in his Scriptorium, built in the back garden of his house at Oxford. Murray spearheaded more than half of the OED's 44-year production effort; he died with entries through T completed in 1915.*

first appearance of the word in English to the close of the 19th century.

The dictionary begins, for example, with the first time the letter "A" is used as a word. It appeared around the year 1340, in a poem that suggests you can determine a newborn's sex by the sound of its first cry:

> If it be man it says a!a!,
> That the first letter is the name of
> our forme-fader Adam.
> And if the child a woman be,
> When it is born it says e!e!
> E. is the first letter and the head
> of the name of Eve. . . .

And so the dictionary is off to a riveting start, reflecting an ancient custom obviously promulgated by nervous fathers outside the birthing chambers. The

OED editor James Murray wrote to prominent English physicist Silvanus Thompson concerning the word "dynamo" in July 1902. In 1900 Mark Twain paid a visit to the Scriptorium, and Murray corresponded with other writers as well, including George Eliot and Robert Louis Stevenson.

Almoin

1523 Fitzherbert, Boke of Surv. g. xii, And all these tenaunts maye holde their landes by diverse tenures, customes, and servyces: as by homage, fealtie, escuage, socage, knyght servyce, graunt sergentie, petyte sergentie, franke almeyne, homage auncetrell. 1602 Fulbecke, Lec. Part Par. g. 11, A thing given in frankalmoigne remaineth laye fee. 1657 Reeve, Gods Plea, 237, Do ye hold allb things in Frank-almoigne, and yet will ye not know your own Benefactour? 1765-74 Blackstone, Comm. I. 156, William the Conqueror thought fit proper to change the spiritual tenure of frank almoign or free alms under which the bishops held their lands ... into the feodal or norman tenure by barony.

A definition for inclusion in the Oxford English Dictionary *appears here in James Murray's hand. Completed in 1928, the dictionary listed 414,825 words and numbered six pages for every one in Noah Webster's* Dictionary.

entry continues with entries for other significant uses for "A"—Chaucer in 1386, Samuel Butler in 1678, and Tennyson in 1842.

The need for such a dictionary had been seriously discussed since 1857, when the work was first sponsored by Britain's emerging Philological Society and its early director, F. J. Furnivall. But a task of this scale needed a full-time editor and, by degrees, the job was turned over to a 42-year-old schoolmaster, James A. H. Murray, in 1879. Murray directed the project until his death in 1915. Still, the *Oxford English Dictionary,* or OED, as it is known today, was not completed until April 1928, when the last section, "Wise" through "Wyzen," was printed (the easier installment, "XYZ," had been completed in October 1921.) A catchall supplementary volume for words missed the first time around appeared in 1933.

The continuity alone is impressive—54 years of production and 44 years of continuous publication. It is rumored that one of the Oxford University Press compositors set nothing else in type for the whole of his working life. Murray himself gave 38 years of labor to the dictionary and was knighted for his trouble—and achievement—in 1908.

One reason the OED is so valuable to us today is that so much unalloyed hard work went into its production. Under the direction of the indefatigable Murray and his editorial staff at Oxford, a corps of readers from around the globe undertook to read the entire body of English literature, as well as legal and historical documents, private papers, tracts, and other ephemera. Five million such excerpts were collected on thin slips of paper that constantly poured in upon the staff; about 1.8 million such quotations appear in print. The result is a 12-volume work of 15,487 oversize pages, nearly half of them written by Murray.

The great advantage of the OED, of course, is that it shows, dramatically, how some words have been transformed from their former meanings. "Pedagogue," for example, originally meant a type of Roman slave who accompanied patrician youths on their walks to school each day. The OED derives the word from the Greek roots meaning "child-leader." The original pedagogues were in no sense leaders or tutors, but merely escorts who drilled the children as they walked and who often sat in on the day's classes in an attempt to improve themselves.

Such men often became moralistic, platitudinous bores. In the OED entries, you can see the early use of the word connoting contempt and hostility (1735: "Cow'd by the ruling Rod, and haughty Frowns of the Pedagogues severe"). With the passage of time, this sense became so watered down that some educators actually sought to have education renamed "pedagogy."

A particularly attractive word category is represented by onomatopoetic words, those that imitate actual sounds. Such words had early appearances: mum (1377), buzz (1530), ding-dong (about 1560), to name a few. Consider bow-wow, which was not used to stand for the dog itself—only its bark—until around 1800 when it appeared in a poem by William Cowper about a good bird dog gone bad:

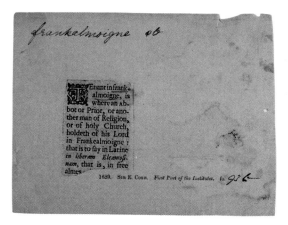

The quotation slip for the word Frank-almoigne, *from Sir Edward Coke's 1629* First Part of the Institutes, *is but one of some five to six million such slips compiled for the OED.*

> *Sir, when I flew to seize the bird*
> *In spite of your command,*
> *A louder voice than yours I heard,*
> *And harder to withstand . . .*
>
> *Well knowing him a sacred thing,*
> *Not destined to my tooth,*
> *I only kiss'd his ruffled wing*
> *And lick'd the feathers smooth.*
>
> *Let my obedience then excuse*
> *my disobedience now,*
> *Nor some reproof yourself refuse*
> *From your aggrieved bow-wow. . . .*

In the face of this wealth of detail, the OED's editors were aware their work would be closely followed by future dictionaries. And it has been. But to put off the slavish imitators, the editors, it is rumored, concocted a single spurious word, complete with false etymology and meanings. It lies somewhere in those 15,487 pages to this day, a lexicographic time bomb waiting to catch a thief.

In the end, an encyclopedia and three dictionaries in a little over a century amount to much more than just four successful publication projects. They speak well of society. These enterprises were produced for and by a reading and contemplative public newly dependent on books. Books had come of age—and would reign unchallenged until the arrival of radio and television.

THE BOOK BUSINESS

❦ "AH, YOU PUBLISHING
SCOUNDREL!"

A satisfied customer leaves a London bookshop in this 1828 colored-pencil drawing by Georg Scharf. The introduction of powered machinery in the 19th century revolutionized printing and dramatically lowered costs. Books became affordable for almost anyone who wanted them.

"Seven copies," he thought, "have been sold. Seven is a mystical number, and the omen is good. Let me find the seven purchasers of my seven copies, and they shall be the seven golden candlesticks with which I will illuminate the world."

Fat chance. The speaker is Scythrop Glowry, long-winded writer and protagonist of Thomas Love Peacock's hilarious novel *Nightmare Abbey* (1818). Scythrop has been driven to this fit of optimism by a letter from his publisher announcing that a mere seven copies of his tedious book have moved and demanding cash for the printer.

Like Scythrop, we forget that the book trade is just that, a trade. We keep telling ourselves it's about beauty and truth, when all the evidence shouts that it's about self-help and cellulite.

Books are products. Like any other product, they are subject to fashion and are sometimes sold for qualities that have nothing to do with their contents. Books do furnish a room, we learned from Virginia Woolf. And so today you can buy wallpaper that masquerades as bookshelf after bookshelf of fine volumes.

Not that this hasn't been going on for a long time. In 18th-century Russia, during the reign of Catherine the Great, any courtier who desired a visit from the Empress was expected to have a library. A certain Mr. Klostermann, unofficial "librarian to the imperial court," made a fortune selling books at 50 to 100 rubles "per yard." In reality, the books were mostly fine bindings filled with wastepaper.

Wastepaper aside, the book trade at the close of the 20th century seems surprisingly robust. In the United States alone, 135,000 new titles were published in 1991. Obviously, with numbers that large, more than a few deserve to be sold by the yard. But in the land of MTV and the indoor shopping mall, it's a wonder that any books are sold at all.

In a mall bookstore such as Waldenbooks, the shelf life of a typical paperback is six weeks to three months. Such stores make money on high-volume sales and rapid turnover of titles, often offering best-sellers at significant discounts to attract customers. They usually don't carry many older or slower-selling titles. At first, industry observers thought that the proliferation of such chain bookstores would doom the mom-and-pop store, the locally owned shop with a cat and a comfy chair where you could browse and set a spell. The local bookstore was a place where the salespeople actually read and loved books and could trade recommendations with you.

Contrary to expectations, the local bookstore has not been plowed under by the chains. Instead, a new generation of bookstores that cater to book lovers has emerged. Such places feature a huge inventory, plenty of alcoves to get lost in, and shelves bursting with favorites selected by customers and staff. The Tattered Cover Book Store, for instance, fills four floors of an old warehouse in downtown Denver. It has chairs and tables that encourage reading—and possibly note-taking as well. There is even a chain—Borders Book Shops—growing throughout the

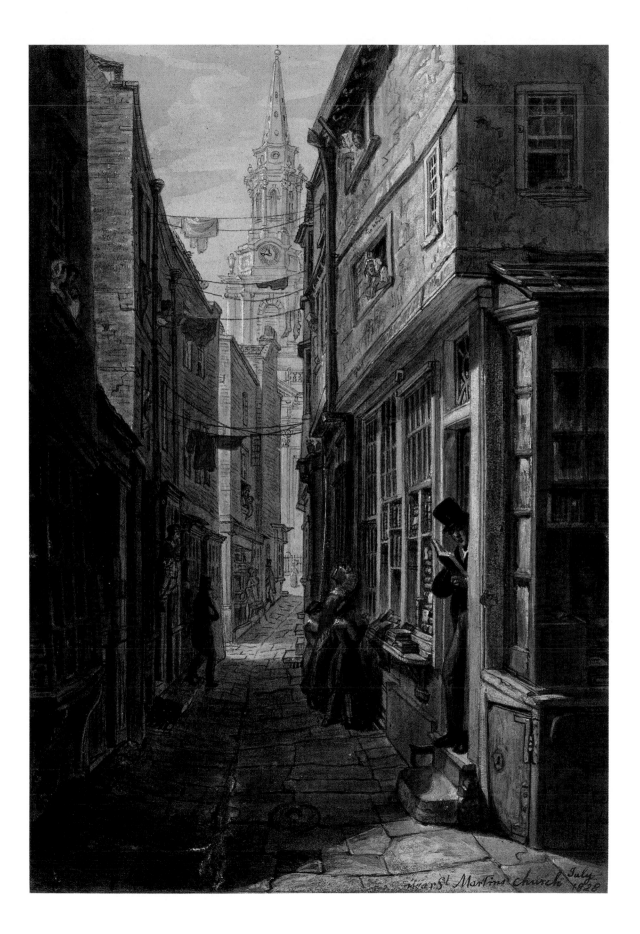

near St Martins church July 1838

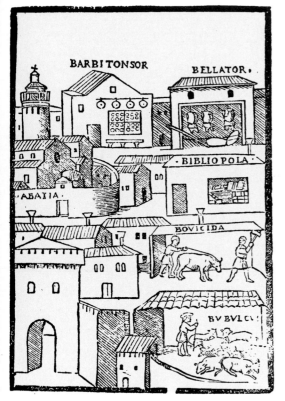

The world of books
is the most
remarkable creation of man.
Nothing else that he builds ever lasts.
Monuments fall; nations perish;
civilizations grow old and die out;
and, after an era of darkness,
new races build others.
But in the world of books
are volumes that have seen this happen
again and again,
and yet live on, still young, still as fresh
as the day they were written,
still telling men's hearts of the hearts
of men centuries dead. CLARENCE DAY

A Venetian woodcut, above, from 1533 contains the earliest known depiction of a European bookshop, labeled here a "bibliopola." Above (right), calligrapher Hermann Zapf penned this tribute to a book by Clarence Day as part of a broadside for the 1973 Frankfurt Book Fair. Originally a medieval trade fair, the Frankfurt Book Fair, shown opposite in a 1984 photograph, first offered Gutenberg Bibles for sale in 1455. It soon became the premier annual gathering for Europe's book trade.

Midwest, South, and East whose stock includes not only the best sellers but the back-listed classics and serious books from the university presses.

The experience of Borders and the Tattered Cover—stores that have as much the ambiance of libraries as dynamic sales centers—shows that there are enough book lovers out there to sustain these new wrinkles on the old bookshop. But how will we all—book lovers, bookstores, publishers—deal with the book of the future? Perhaps with something called publishing-on-demand.

"My biggest headache is inventory," says James McGrath Morris,

president of Seven Locks Press in Washington, D.C. "When I publish a book, I have to babysit 4,000 copies in inventory until the 2,000 out on the street are sold.

"Publishing-on-demand will solve that. You'll go into a bookstore and you'll be able to browse through covers and descriptions of books. If you choose a title that's not a current hot seller, the store will locate it using a computer WYSIWYG system ['What You See Is What You Get,' pronounced 'wizzeewig']. If you want to buy one, they'll push a button, tell you to come back in 20 minutes, and—through high-speed copying

and binding—you'll have your copy. Stores will still have hard copies of the most popular books, but the arcane ones would only be on the computer."

Inventory management has always been a perilous guessing game. The Third Folio of Shakespeare, for example, printed in 1663–1664, is today much rarer than the folios of 1623, 1632, and 1685. The reason, we suspect, is that the publisher's stock was consumed in the Great Fire of London, 1666. No WYSIWYG then.

Or Data Discman, either. This is the book of the future from Sony. A little larger than the Sony Walkman,

it has a flip-up liquid-crystal display screen and a keypad for taking electronic notes. Insert a little disc containing, say, an encyclopedia, and you can have nearly all the world's accumulated knowledge at your fingertips.

Electronic publishing is certainly with us today. There are learned journals that circulate on floppy discs and can be read only on computer screens. Chadwyck-Healey, Inc., of Alexandria, Virginia, and Cambridge, England, is publishing the entire corpus of English poetry—every line written by 1,350 poets from A.D. 600 to 1900—on CD-ROM (Compact

Disc—Read Only Memory). It's a staggering concept, meaning that, with the combination of a computer and a compact-disc player, you'll be able to browse through the history of English poetry instantly and in the comfort of your own home.

In practically no time, literature in every language will be on CD-ROM. Even today the *Oxford English Dictionary* is available in electronic form, and Chadwyck-Healey has available on disc all issues of the *Guardian* newspaper since 1990 (one disc per year). The company also offers on CD-ROM the *Patrologia Latina,* virtually everything important written in

Latin between A.D. 200 and 1216. Originally printed in 221 volumes, it now takes up a few plastic discs.

But are these books? No one will read Tertullian (A.D. 150) for pleasure on a data screen, nor can Fido fetch your *Guardian* disc. Instead, these—and the Data Discman—are reference tools, just the thing for looking up how many times the word "asparagus" was used near the word "necktie" in a poem printed in Scotland between 1815 and 1848.

The trade in rare books is also changing rapidly. Few antiquarian book dealers still maintain shops where customers may browse. Instead, they do most of their business in regional book fairs all over the world, where they rent booths to display their titles.

Eric Korn, a dealer and writer for the London *Times Literary Supplement,* travels this international circuit. He notes: "Volumes that between 1485 and 1990 moved only from the second to the third shelf of a monastic library in Swabia now clock up lunar distances in a year. Some of my own bad buys have crossed the Atlantic so often they have earned free beach holidays in the Bahamas."

Computers are transforming the used-book market. Dealers are turning to "database" firms that list the holdings of countless other dealers, junkmen, and attics, and their computers match book requests with books. The database itself is a sort of subliterate, bookless middleman.

This is fine if you have a particular volume in mind, but what if you want to browse? All these computers and data screens prevent you from seeing books as books, living things that whisper to you as you pass them on the shelf. Poking around in bookstores and libraries (and their now endan-

gered card catalogues) has always been an exercise in serendipity. Lists and WYSIWIGS will never replace the thrill of the accidental discovery of a gem right next to the book you were looking for.

The British Library has acknowledged as much, declaring that in the future the "amount of paper that is stored annually will not diminish, although the amount of information stored digitally increases every year." The traditional book, in other words, is alive and well.

Certainly books have weathered such attacks in the past. Radio, movies, television, and videotape were all expected to eradicate books. Even the lowly comic book, which began in 1822 with Jemmy Catnach's *Life in London; Or, The Sprees of Tom, Jerry, and Logick,* was regarded as a repository of bad art, bad grammar, and bad printing. Surely Data Discman won't be the end of civilization.

The book as we know it is pushing its 2,000th birthday, and is unlikely to be supplanted soon by technology. The best of today's CD-ROMs mainly help us to find more and better things in books. Oddly enough, a very big

Academics meet for a book auction at Oxford in this 1747 painting, below (left). Englishman Samuel Russel began regular book auctions at Covent Garden in 1744. Russel was joined in the late-18th century by John Sotheby, first of three generations of Sotheby auctioneers. Below, the title page of the second part of a rare two-volume set, printed from 1605 to 1615, of Miguel de Cervantes' El ingenioso hidalgo don Quixote de la Mancha, *which sold for $1.65 million at a 1989 auction at Sotheby's New York.*

An 1860 American bookseller's broadsheet advertises for Harriet Beecher Stowe's anti-slavery novel Uncle Tom's Cabin, *first published in 1851. Thousands of copies of this book sold to a nation on the brink of civil war over issues related to slavery.*

threat comes from book lovers themselves. Books are being stolen in record numbers.

In 1990, a thief named Stephen Blumberg shocked the book world when authorities found 11,000 rare books stolen from 327 libraries around the country in his Ottumwa, Iowa, house. He did not, apparently, take the books for profit or resale. He just wanted to be near them. For all that he was still a crook, a crook who loved books.

Over the years bibliocrooks have been busy. The chained book of the medieval library was no metaphor; it was to prevent theft. According to a 13th-century book of instructions by Humbert of Romans (1194–1277), the primary job of a Dominican librarian was to keep books secure. As early as the 18th century, bogus Shakespeare First Folios were being sold as originals.

Scholars Arthur Freeman and Janet Ing Freeman recently proved that a consortium of 80 rare-book dealers in England rigged the celebrated Ruxley Lodge auction in 1919. A total of 13,000 books were on the block, and the dealers agreed among themselves not to bid up the prices against one another. After the sale, they met in secret, put the books back on the block, got their money back, and rebid for the books of most interest to their customers. The income from this closed auction was shared by the participants. In the end, the books sold for £20,000, in contrast to the mere £3,714 fetched by the original auction.

Publishing itself is not free from skulduggery. "Now Barabbas was a publisher," observed Lord Byron, not entirely in jest, referring to the criminal released by the Romans in lieu of Christ. There is even a class of novels that exposes the high-stakes world in which the literary remains of dead writers—from letters to laundry lists—are published. In these books, the scholar-publishers are, of course, venal, self-deceiving, hollow men.

Such books include William Golding's *The Paper Men* (1984): "We knew nothing about people. . . . We knew about paper, that was all." And Michael Innes's *The Guardians* (1955): "Almost the first thing Quail had learned about Tandon was that he possessed virtually no personal life." Both Innes and Golding, however, depend heavily on Henry James's *The Aspern Papers* (1888), which contains one of the great lines in all literature: "'Ah, you publishing scoundrel!'" This is followed shortly by:

'She had an idea that when people want to publish they're capable—' And she paused, blushing.
'Of violating a tomb?'

If a publishing archaeologist were to violate a tomb today, he would do well to start with the last and final resting place of James Edwards (1757–1816), bookseller and bibliographer who traveled throughout Europe buying and selling books.

In 1786, the great Bedford Missal, now in the British Library, was in his hands. Books made Edwards so rich and famous that when he came to die he decreed that his bookshelves furnish the wood for his coffin. He lies there to this day, in the little church of St. Mary Harrow-on-the-Hill, permanently on the shelf, but definitely out of circulation.

American book dealer Frank Shay, above at center, stands by as his traveling bookshop, Parnassus on Wheels, *is christened in 1928. The increasingly rare antique bookshop, such as the one at left, photographed in Venice in 1979, may be replaced by computer data bases and mail-order sales in the years to come.*

B efore the Industrial Revolution, it is said, nothing was ever thrown away. Everything was recycled: clothes, rags, bones, even urine. And books. Paper volumes were used as kindling. If the books were of vellum or parchment, the leaves had a way of earning, like Lazarus, a new life. Whole lots of discarded or mistakenly devalued manuscripts—often from defunct medieval monasteries—were bought in the past by bookbinders and book dealers, who used them to stiffen and strengthen the spines of newer books. Old bindings, then, can hide even older wonders.

The collections at Yale University's Beinecke Rare Book and Manuscript Library, for example, include a stout 14th-century Psalter roughly sewn into wooden boards. In the backing of the volume is an 11th-century leaf that features an excerpt from the first chapter of St. Mark, written in a Kentish script.

Also at the Beinecke is a leaf from a book that was copied at the monastery of St. Silvester at Nonantola, in northern Italy. An example of the distinctive style of calligraphy developed at the St. Silvester scriptorium, the leaf was wrapped around an account book that had belonged to 16th-century Florentine silk merchant Tommaso Spinelli. It is of heavy parchment, which must have made it especially attractive as binding material, and reproduces text from St. Paul's Epistle to the Philippians, written in an elegant ninth-century script. It may have come from the abbey's large lectionary Bible.

Over the centuries, binding scraps have been very helpful to literary historians, who have found countless examples of Anglo-Saxon writing and 56 copies of one sheet from William Caxton's 15th-century London print shop. The late Dorothy M. Schullian, who once worked at the National Library of Medicine in Bethesda, Maryland, made a second career out of rediscovering such gems. She did so by soaking old and worn-out bindings in her bathtub to loosen the glue. Gradually, the old books and manuscripts would offer up their secrets. Over the years, her "bathtub collection," as it came to be known, grew to include many wonders, such as parchment membranes covered with deep black Latin, many pages of printers' waste, and some sheets of uncut playing cards found in a 1555 report on the plague printed in Germany.

At Oxford and Cambridge the heyday of the recycling of leaves and other fragments of older books occurred in the 16th century. At that time, the sudden availability of new and more reliable Renaissance editions of the classics was rendering the medieval versions of those texts obsolete. The change was associated with the burgeoning of print at the universities and with advances in Greek and Latin scholarship. London binders, by contrast, working without benefit of a university's scrap heap, seldom reused manuscript in this way.

It's impossible to overestimate the value of such things found in books. One of the treasures of the British Library is a dramatic vellum page from a 42-line Bible printed in Mainz by Fust and Schoeffer in 1455. Illuminated by an English artist, it contains the end of St. Paul's letter to the Gala-

OLD LEAVES, NEW LIVES

❦ LOST AND FOUND BETWEEN THE COVERS

New life for an old leaf: A Renaissance choir-book manuscript, opposite, was used to cover the binding of a 1481 edition of Questiones super tota philosophia naturali *by Joannes de Magistris. Once cut up for scrap, early binding materials now are highly valued by bibliographic scholars.*

The symmetrical damage done by book-worms to a Hebrew manuscript, above, reveals how the pages were folded as part of a book. Such insects are particularly threatening to libraries, which go to great lengths to prevent or combat infestations. Opposite, a page from a Gutenberg Bible printed in Mainz, Germany, in 1455. Rediscovered in a 17th-century book, it is now at the British Library.

tians and the start of Ephesians. Somehow the leaf came to rest in a 17th-century book, where it was discovered by shoemaker and antiquary John Bagford (1651–1716). So far no other leaves from this Bible have been found, but chances are they're out there somewhere.

And it's not just manuscript leaves that turn up unexpectedly in books; it's often the other kind of leaves—from trees and other plants—or perhaps a flower, the long forgotten memento of an afternoon idyll in some distant woodland. Librarians and rare-book dealers regularly find such items, as well as shamrocks, butterflies, and feathers, all gently and

deliberately pressed into old books.

At the Folger Shakespeare Library, a 1615 pamphlet printed in Paris for Louis XIII has a perfectly preserved specimen of a crane fly. The long-legged insect is *in* the paper, not on it; you can see it right through the sheet. It's a 377-year-old bibliofossil.

Perhaps the greatest literary bug tale, however, belongs to Sir William Osler (1849–1919), Oxford's Regius Professor of Medicine, who once found a live worm in a 1730 French book newly acquired from a Parisian dealer. Osler sent the little wriggler to the British Museum of Natural History to be drawn by artist Horace Knight, and he then wrote a famous

The 1675 copper-engraved English tobacco label, above, is an example of the kind of work printers produced by jobbing, taking on small jobs vital to their business. Above (right), a wood-engraved funeral invitation, printed in 18th-century London. Trade cards, tickets, wrappers, posters, and other printed ephemera have become increasingly important as social and cultural vignettes.

paper on bookworms for the *Bodleian Quarterly Record*. He identified the pest as the larval stage of the beetle *Anobium hirtum,* which is a species not native to England but rather to central and southern France. The same bookworm, it turns out, was found in libraries in the French-speaking parts of Louisiana in 1895.

And there is more. Governor Francis Nicholson, the Englishman who laid out the street schemes for both Annapolis, Maryland, and Williamsburg, Virginia, reported back to his superiors in London on July 1, 1699, that the Virginia Colony's papers should be kept in strongboxes under lock and key so as to protect them "from being destroyed by some small Insects which we have in the Country." It is likely he was referring to *Anobium domesticum,* which belongs to a family of British bookworms that has become so common here you'd think it came over on the *Mayflower!*

Bugs do persist, and rare-book libraries go to great lengths to prevent infestations and protect their volumes. The Beinecke library acquired an industrial flash-freezer to deal with an infestation of deathwatch beetle, another member of the *Anobium* genus. And the Huntington Library in San Marino, California, fumigates its books in a small gas chamber.

Aside from insects, all sorts of other things turn up in books, too, often revealing small details or vignettes of everyday life in the recent past. Someone left a poem entitled "O.U. Hoover" on a small yellow card in a volume during the Depression. The first stanza reads,

My Tuesdays are meatless,
My Wednesdays are wheatless,
I'm getting more eatless each day,
My home it is heatless,
My bed it is sheetless,
They are all sent to the Y.M.C.A.

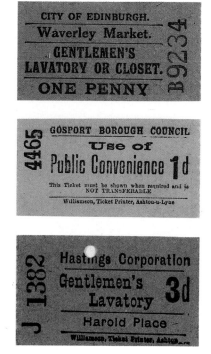

Other items that come to light hold messages that are far more cryptic. One such piece, a telegram dated June 19, 1882, was sent from South Boston to Clinton, Massachusetts, a distance of 25 miles. In it, one J. Sutherland demands of the Rev. R. J. Patterson in 10 stentorian words, "Send me my derrick at once or answer why not." A secret message? A code? We may never know.

Notes scribbled on the flyleaves and other pages of books are often trivial or puzzling, although sometimes they can become the stuff of history. Consider this reference from a Sarum book of hours: "This vi day of Aprill 1580 at __ of the clocke in the afternoone [there was] an earthequake in London and all about yt." This is certainly the quake to which the nurse in *Romeo and Juliet* alludes—"'Tis since the earthquake now eleven years"—in figuring Juliet's exact age. Such an eyewitness account can assist scholars in dating the play.

Leaves, feathers, insects, telegrams, notes, drawings—an almost endless array of things turns up in books. But some of the most numerous artifacts to be found are cards, broadsides, notices, and other printed ephemera—the word "ephemera" signifying, perhaps ironically in this case, something not intended or expected to last. In the early days of the printing press, taking on such small printing jobs, or jobbing, helped keep printers in business. Even Caxton and Gutenberg financed large book projects by turning out ephemeral but lucrative indulgences. Downtime is still anathema for printers; they keep the presses running at all costs.

The study of printed ephemera has a long pedigree. John Bagford, the cobbler who found the Mainz Bible leaf in the 17th century, amassed a major collection of such material that now rests in the British Museum. John Johnson (1882–1956), a former Egyp-

More ephemera: an engraver, above (left), heats a plate on an engraved 1685 printers' dinner invitation; a bookmaker's ticket, above (center), dates to the early 20th century in England, where betting remains legal; and above, public rest-room tickets from Oxford's John Johnson collection display various typographic styles of 1905.

tologist who became printer at Oxford University Press, bequeathed his huge collection of ephemera to that university's Bodleian Library. And, in 1962, British type designer John Lewis published *Printed Ephemera*, a study of printed matter ranging from menus to handbills, tickets to soap labels, and invitations to trade cards. His work demonstrates how vital such items are to cultural history.

To illustrate the importance of printed ephemera in depicting various developments in typography and design, Lewis included two auction notices—one from 1815, the other from 1827—by the same Dorset jobber. The 1815 notice is striking in its somber typography, and Lewis comments that it would have looked virtually the same had it been printed 200 years earlier. The 1827 notice, however, is embellished by several of the then newly invented fat faces and shaded letters.

Throughout the centuries, all kinds of ephemera have materialized unexpectedly between the covers of books. And the tables have been turned as well. Frontier historian J. Frank Dobie was fond of the story of pioneer rancher Charlie Goodnight and his scouts, who once uncovered some pages of Edward Gibbon's *Decline and Fall of the Roman Empire* in the lining of a Comanche shield. Out there on the Great Plains, hunkered down around the dying embers of a campfire, Charlie and his men must have passed around those leaves, amazed by the marble Rome of Tiberius and Caligula nearly 1,900 years earlier. How the centuries must have been compressed under the heavens that night.

In 1967, the Smithsonian acquired New York bookseller Isadore Warshaw's collection of more than a million pieces of printed business memorabilia from the late 19th and early 20th centuries. Featured here from the Smithsonian's collection are clockwise from upper left, the cover of the

Alneer Brothers seed catalogue from 1895; a clown promoting Quaker Oats, "the world's cereal," in an 1894 trade card; Columbia driving a tiger and riding farm machinery from the J. W. Stoddard Company; and, below, some advice from Carter's Little Nerve Pills.

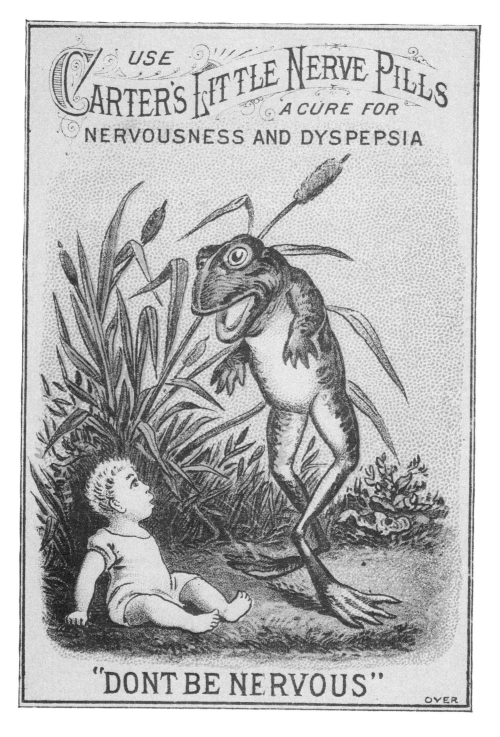

LAST WORDS

XPLICIT." MEDIEVAL SCRIBES wrote this single word at the end of every book. But "the end" in the modern sense was the last thing on their minds. Instead, *Explicit* was something far more hopeful: "It has been unfolded." The word survived into the world of the codex from the days of parchment and papyrus rolls. Then, *Explicitus est liber* meant literally that the fat roll of words once in your right hand had gradually moved over onto the dowel on your left: "The book is unrolled." ❡ The unrolling or unfolding of knowledge is a powerful act because it shifts responsibility from writer to reader. There are universes of meaning locked up in the words of every tablet, roll, codex, and book. But every reader must dive into that alphabetical-lexicographical-typographical-historical maelstrom on his own and come up with an understanding of the text that makes sense to him or her. ❡ Great books endure because they help us interpret our lives. It's a personal quest, this grappling with the world and ourselves, and we need all the help we can get. The fact that there are people who came before us and wrote so much down in books is consoling. We stand on their shoulders. ❡ And when we do, miracles happen. Books do more than define the world when they offer it up in words. They give the world existence in a way that can be passed around from brain to brain, examined, explored. Books help us to understand, to see. ❡ But all the wisdom and inspiration in books would be lost to us without the transcendental process we call reading. Kurt Vonnegut once said that reading was an Occidental form of Oriental meditation. Anyone who has tried to interrupt a deep reader knows

Preceding pages: A Cemetery Garden is a book by American artist Robbin Ami Silverberg with pages of handmade paper cut and painted in the forms of plants, creatures, and stones of a graveyard garden. Opposite, Rosamond Purcell, also an American artist, created this collage, which she called Keep This Book Clean, *using discarded parts of books old and new. The initial capital E at the head of the column originally illuminated the opening page of Cicero's* Epistolae ad familiares, *printed in Venice in 1469 by Johannes de Spira.*

LA CRITIQUE. (A.D.)

Il n'y a point d'Ouvrage si accompli qui ne fondît tout entier au milieu de la critique si son
auteur voulait en croire tous les censeurs qui ôtent chacun l'endroit qui leur plaît le moins (La Bruyère)

Books and the powerful ideas they convey often inspire critics to transports of agitation and rage, as depicted in an 1839 French cartoon, The critic confronts the work of art, *right. Books also provide priceless moments of serenity and reflection, captured here in German artist Albrecht Dürer's 1506* Study of Two Pairs of Hands with Books, *opposite.*

the grip of the book. You might as well try to distract a monk at prayer. In that other-world, the power of the book is released.

The elucidating, illuminating power of books gives us pleasure. People say that books please us with their beauty—crisp type on creamy paper, dazzling bindings. But that is not enough. It's the heat from a critical mass of ideas inside a book that we warm to. The library of English poet Leigh Hunt (1784–1859), for example, was large and handsome, but he loved it because it spoke to him and provoked him: "I entrench myself in my books equally against sorrow and the weather.... When I speak of being in contact with my books, I mean it literally. I like to lean my head against them.... give me a small, snug place, almost entirely walled in with books."

Hunt owes a great deal to diarist Samuel Pepys (1633–1703), who also liked to surround himself with books, so much so that he designed the first domestic bookshelves to organize his overflowing collection. On August 24, 1666, Pepys installed his shelves and then "fell in to the finishing of my new closett [study] ... and setting up my books, and as much as we could do, to my most extraordinary satisfaction."

Pepys's 12 bookcases are preserved today at Magdelene College, Cambridge. They still look good, but what is more important, they helped him organize his thinking and writing. For Pepys, bookshelves meant an end to chaos.

Books did not always enjoy this level of respect. In the early days of print-

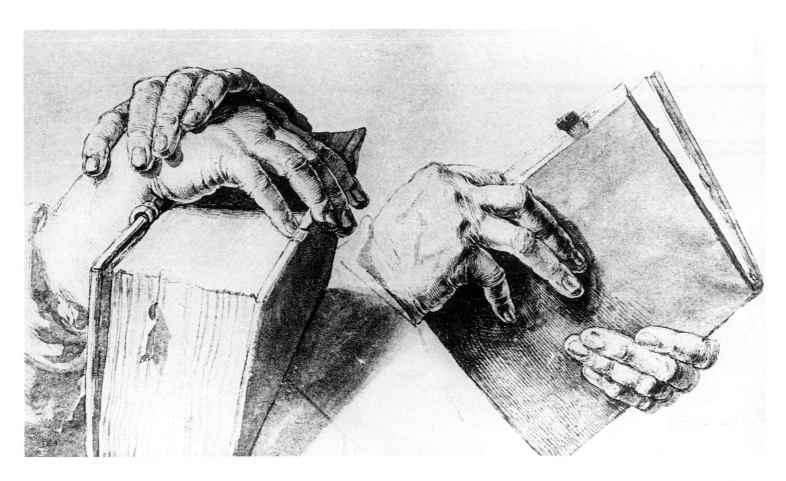

ing, books multiplied so rapidly that there was a danger they were causing more confusion than they eliminated. As Spanish playwright Lope de Vega's 1619 play *Fuente Ovejuna* put it:

> *So many books—so much confusion!*
> *All around us an ocean of print*
> *And most of it covered in froth....*
> *All the most famous men of Europe*
> *Rushed into print, but once they were published*
> *Their ignorance was obvious to all....*

In fact, despite these criticisms, the truly obvious thing about books is that if they are any good at all they always disturb the peace. Think of the great books of Euclid and Galileo, Molière and Shelley, Harriet Beecher Stowe and Upton Sinclair. They all raised the dust.

That is why books are the first victims of the thought-police in every totalitarian state. Books are bellwethers; they burn before people do. Usually the attack on books begins so quietly and is so easy to parody that we don't take it seriously until it's too late—as in this passage from Sheridan's *The Rivals* (1775): "Madam, a circulating library in a town is an evergreen tree of diabolical knowledge! It blossoms throughout the year!—And depend on it, Mrs. Malaprop, that they who are so fond of handling the leaves, will long for the fruit at last."

A good book is intellectually provocative, but it can also move us emotionally. There is, after all, a nonrational part of us that cannot be explained fully but that nevertheless has its priorities. Books speak to head and heart, as in this passage from Siegfried Sassoon's "The Child at the Window":

> For you must learn, beyond bewildering years,
> How little things beloved and held are best.
> The windows of the world are blurred with tears,
> And troubles come like cloud-banks from the west.
> Remember this, some afternoon in spring,
> When your own child looks down and makes your sad heart sing.

There is a very real kind of alchemy here, conjuring up future and past, weighing hope against experience. Words like these demand respect, and so do

Books appeal both to reason and to sentiment. Right, the first page of the oldest textbook of geometry—and logic: Preclarissimus liber elementorum Euclides … in artem geometriae, *or* Elements of Geometry, *by Euclid, published in Venice in 1482 and the first of more than a thousand editions of Euclid's* Elements. *Opposite, American artist Childe Hassam's watercolor* The Garden in its Glory *was painted in 1892 for Celia Thaxter's book* An Island Garden.

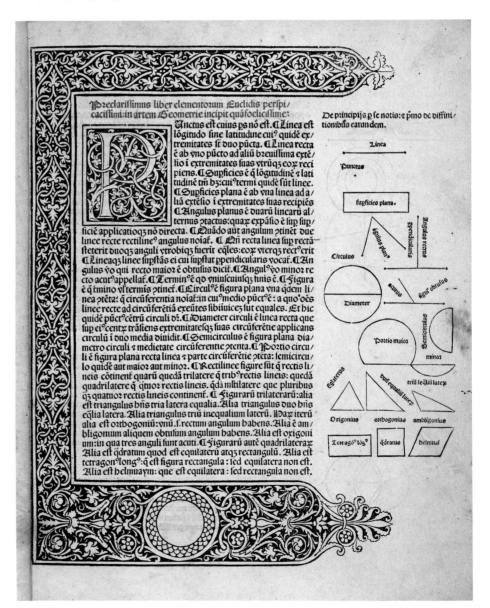

THE MARK ON THE WALL

By

VIRGINIA WOOLF

Perhaps it was the middle of January in the present year that I first looked up and saw the mark on the wall. In order to fix a date it is necessary to remember what one saw. So now I think of the fire: the steady film of yellow light upon the page of my book; the three chrysanthemums in the round glass bowl on the mantelpiece. Yes, it must have been the winter time, and we had just finished our tea, for I remember that I was smoking a cigarette when I looked up and saw the mark on the wall for the first time. I looked up through the smoke of my cigarette and my eye lodged for a moment upon the burning coals, and that old fancy of the crimson flag flapping from the castle tower came into my mind, and I thought of the cavalcade of red knights riding up the side of the black rock. Rather to my relief the sight of the mark interrupted the fancy, for it is an old fancy, an automatic

Enduring works of fiction are usually those that distill the very essence of human experience, illustrated opposite by Fritz Eichenberg's powerful wood engraving (1943–1946) for an edition of Emily Brontë's great novel Wuthering Heights, *originally published in 1847. Occasionally writers seek creative fulfillment beyond writing, when they print and publish their works and those of others. Through their own Hogarth Press, British writer Virginia Woolf and her husband, Leonard, published* The Mark on the Wall, *left, in a hand-printed book titled* Two Stories *(1917). Among other books published by Hogarth was T. S. Eliot's poem* The Waste Land.

the books that hold them. A holy communion exists between reader and book.

If that is so, then the place where books come from might be considered a temple, a sacred precinct. With just such a thought in mind, printing historian Beatrice Warde (1900–1969) composed the following notice in 1932. Set in Gill Sans typeface, it turned up on printers' walls everywhere:

This is a printing office,
Crossroads of civilization,

Transmitters from past to future, books and their images are timeless. American artist Ben Shahn reached back to Aramaic, the ancient language of Jews and Christians, to caption his 1950 serigraph Head of Lion: *"Where there's a book, there's no sword."*

Refuge of all the Arts
Against the ravages of time.
Armoury of the fearless truth
Against whispering rumor.
Incessant trumpet of trade.
From this place words may fly abroad
Not to perish on waves of sound,
Not to vary with the writer's hand,
But fixed in time,
Having been verified in proof.
Friend, you stand on sacred ground:
This is a printing office.

Warde might have added that books are timeless. They will wait for us on the shelves of libraries as surely as a clay tablet buried in the Middle East, or the *Diamond Sutra* in the Caves of the Thousand Buddhas, or a Dead Sea Scroll in Qumran. There is no "sell-by" date on any book, for every volume can tell the future something about us.

The link between time and books is universally acknowledged. In Milan there is an Italian Renaissance clock fabricated in the form of an incorruptible book of gold. "Words move ...," wrote T. S. Eliot, "Only in time; but that which is only living/Can only die." The sepulchre of Eleanor of Aquitaine (1122–1204) in Fontevrault Abbey, France, is capped by a life-size effigy of the queen reading a book, presumably for eternity.

Perhaps Eleanor shared a vision with Virginia Woolf (1882–1941), who saw the world as a timeless artwork in which "we are the words, we are the thing itself." For her, books made it all worthwhile: "I have sometimes dreamt ... that when the Day of Judgment dawns ... the Almighty will turn to Peter and will say, not without a certain envy when he sees us coming with our books under our arms, 'Look, these need no reward. We have nothing to give them here. They have loved reading.'"

You are what you read. EXPLICIT.

Let us hope that there will always be children as deeply absorbed in their books as were these French children of 1929, frozen in mid-page by photographer André Kertész.

ACKNOWL-EDGMENTS

❦ DEDICATION:
TO MEG DALEY OLMERT,
LA MIGLIOR FABBRO

Michael Olmert is a frequent contributor to Smithsonian *magazine. His articles have appeared also in* Archaeology, Sports Illustrated, Horticulture, *the* Chaucer Review, *and the* Times Literary Supplement *(London), among others. He has written the official guidebook to Colonial Williamsburg as well as television documentaries for the* Smithsonian World *series and the National Geographic Society. He holds a Ph.D. in English from the University of Maryland, where he teaches Shakespeare. He lives in Washington, D.C., with his wife, Meg, a television producer.*

As a child, I often saw my father, Kenneth R. Olmert, lost in books; ever since then, I've been trying to figure out what it was all about. This book is the result.

Thanks also to three great teachers of bibliography: Franklin D. Cooley, of the University of Maryland, and Bernard M. Wagner and Franklin B. Williams, Jr., of Georgetown University.

Many people contributed to this book, but special thanks go to: Jane Carr, Julian Conway, T. S. Pattie, Graham Shaw, and Frances Wood of the British Library; Christa Sammons and Robert G. Babcock of Yale University's Beinecke Library; Yale University Printer Roland A. Hoover; John E. Ingram, Carl Lounsbury, Willie Parker, Bruce Plumley, and Peter Stinely of the Colonial Williamsburg Foundation; James Mosley and Nigel Roach of the St. Bride Printing Library; John Auchard and Sam Schoenbaum of the University of Maryland's English Department, and Rolf Hubbe of that university's Classics Department; George Stuart of the National Geographic Society; Peter W. M. Blayney and Rachel Doggett of the Folger Shakespeare Library; Eva Hanebutt-Benz of the Gutenberg Museum; Carolyn T. Lee of the Mullen Library, Catholic University of America; Ellen Wells and Leslie Overstreet of the Dibner Library, Smithsonian Institution; David McKitterick of Trinity College Library, Cambridge University; Roger Norris of Durham Cathedral Library; A. I. Doyle of Durham University Library; Enid Nixon of Westminster Abbey Library; Christopher de Hamel of Sotheby's; Julie Anne Wilson of the Bodleian Library, Oxford; Michael Vickers of the Ashmolean Museum, Oxford; Fr. Vittorino Meneghin of San Michele in Isola, Venice; Margaret Cook of the Swem Library, William and Mary College; Esther Potter and Freda and Paul Bates of London; Helen Paterson of Harrow-on-the-Hill; Edwina Burness of Cambridge; Brian Spiller and Vivian Salmon of Oxford; Leona Schecter and James McGrath Morris of Washington, D.C.; Paula DiNardo of Milan.

—*Michael Olmert, Washington, D.C.*

The Editors of Smithsonian Books would like to thank the following people and organizations for their assistance in the preparation of this book:

Smithsonian Institution Libraries, and, in particular, Ellen Wells and Leslie Overstreet, Special Collections; John H. Hyltoft, Rare Book Conservation Laboratory; and Central Reference Loan Services; Elizabeth Harris and Stanley Nelson, Division of Graphic Arts, National Museum of American History; Silvio A. Bedini; Elvira Clain-Stefanelli and Lynn Vosloh, National Numismatic Collection, National Museum of American History; Carol Bolon and Laveta Emory, Arthur M. Sackler Gallery and Freer Gallery of Art; Steven van Dyke and David McFadden, Cooper-Hewitt Museum, NY.

Alvaro Alabard, The Embassy of Spain, Washington, D.C.; Benjamin Alterman, Mount Holly, NJ; Sister Mary Ellen Gleason and Virginia Carew, American Bible Society, NY;

Annette Weir, Jessica Allen, and Ita Gross, Art Resource, NY; Christina Barbin, UNESCO, Paris; Gisel Lambert, G. Cohen, Madeleine Barbin, François Dupuigrenet, Monique Cohen, and Marie-Odile Germain, Bibliothèque Nationale, Paris; Ingmar Bjorksten, The Embassy of Sweden, Washington, D.C.; Piergiuseppe Bozzetti, The Embassy of Italy, Washington, D.C.; Stephen Morgan, Chris Rawlings, Naresh Kaul, and colleagues, British Library; Christopher Walker, Michael Boggan, Paul Dove, and colleagues, British Museum; Ed Castle, Chevy Chase, MD; George Breeze and Anna Stanway, Cheltenham Art Gallery & Museums, England; Michael Coe, Yale University, CT; John Y. Cole, Center for the Book, Library of Congress, Washington, D.C.; E. M. Coleman, Pepys Library, Magdalene College, Cambridge, England; Catherine Grosfils, John Ingram, and Sharon Mountain, Colonial Williamsburg Foundation, VA; Margaret C. Cook, College of William and Mary, VA; Suzanne DeMott, Brandywine River Museum, PA; Paul Donoghue, London; Carol Callaway and Nancy Ševčenko, Dumbarton Oaks Research Library and Collections, Washington, D.C.; Elizabeth L. Dudley, ARAMCO, Washington, D.C.; Maria de Jong Ellis, University Museum of Philadelphia, PA; Robert Elwood, Bushwood, MD; John Frank Mowery, Laurie S. Lewis, and Rachel Doggett, The Folger Shakespeare Library, Washington, D.C.; Karen Gillman, *Calligraphy Review;* Tom Graves, London; The Grolier Club, NY; Mark Gulezian, QuickSilver Photographers, Washington, D.C.; Melissa

Henderson, Chadwyck-Healey, Inc., Alexandria, VA; Dr. Brian Hillyard, National Library of Scotland; Roland Hoover, Yale University, New Haven, CT; Alan Jutzi, Thomas V. Lange, Brita Mack, Virginia Renner and Mary Robertson, The Huntington Library, CA; Tom Kren, J. Paul Getty Museum, CA; Sandra Kirshenbaum, *Fine Print;* Carl Kurtz, Kansas City Art Institute; David Kusin, Dallas Museum of Art; Peter Van Wingen, Allen Thrasher, Carol Armbruster, George Atiyen, Lee Avdoyen, Clark Evans, Joan Higbee, Robert Shields, Reed Baker, and Kay Eisinger, Library of Congress, Washington, D.C.; Don Lindgren, Center for the Book Arts, NY; Vita Lund, Gudhjem, Denmark; James McGrath Morris, Arlington, VA; Elisabeth Murray, Sussex, England; Roger Norris, Durham Cathedral, England; Marius A. Péraudeau, Ambert, Auvergne; Phone Reference Services, Montgomery County, MD; Nancy Schmugge, Inge Dupont, and Marilyn Palmeri, Pierpont Morgan Library, NY; Nigel Roach, St. Bride Printing Library, London; Ori Saltes, B'nai B'rith Klutsnick Museum, Washington, D.C.; Bent Skaou, The Embassy of Denmark, Washington, D.C.; Frances Smyth, National Gallery of Art, Washington, D.C.; Jay Dillon and Bronwyn Albrecht, Sotheby's, NY; Marie Stöklund, Nationalmuseet, Copenhagen; Douglas Stone, Dard Hunter Museum, Atlanta, GA; Nancy Strader, Concord, MA; George Stuart, National Geographic Society, Washington, D.C.; Brigitte Tchiry, Fondation Mecenat Science & Art, Strasbourg; Van den Bosch, G, Museum

Plantin-Moretus, Antwerpen; Edwin Wallace and Irene Weller, Victoria & Albert Museum, London; Colline Wakefield, Bodleian Library, Oxford, England; the late Edwin Wolf II, The Library Company, Philadelphia; Mohamed Zakariya, Bethesda, MD; Hermann Zapf, Seiterweg, Germany.

Suppliers: Donna C. Ambrette, Ecological Fibers, Inc.; Paul R. Blossey, Lanman Progressive; Christopher P. Boehmcke, The Press, Inc.; Shawn Brooks, Huffman Press; William J. Carter, Permalin Products Co.; Melton Castro, Meadows & Wiser; Harold Cooper, Cooper Direct Ltd.; Bruce B. Cunningham, Lanman Progressive; William F. Dooley, ICG, Inc.; Stephanie Garber, Westvaco; Barbara Gates, Imperial Paper Box Corporation; Donald S. Herdtfelder, Lanman Progressive; L. Michael Holt, ICG, Inc.; Robert F. Jillson, Holliston; Louis C. Jordan, Westvaco; Peter P. Jurgaitis, Lehigh Press Lithographers; William H. Kelty; John G. King, R. R. Donnelley & Sons Company; William Liddell, Creative Automation Company; Charles R. Mann Associates; Marc Meadows, Meadows & Wiser; Clifford Mears, Jr., R. R. Donnelley & Sons Company; Vicki Messer, Holliston; Robert J. Muma, Allen Envelope Corporation; Joseph D. Pinto, Westvaco; Cecilia Ragusa, Permalin Products Co.; Nancy Spangler, Meadows & Wiser; Ira Sukoff, Imperial Paper Box Corporation; Frank Topper, TempoGraphics, Inc.; Phyllis Unosawa, R. R. Donnelley & Sons Company; Robert Volkert, Calmark, Inc.; Edward G. Watters, The Lehigh Press, Inc.; Robert Wiser, Meadows & Wiser.

INDEX

PICTURE CREDITS

Legend: B *Bottom;* C *Center;* L *Left;*
R *Right;* T *Top.*

The following abbreviations are used to identify the Smithsonian Institution (SI) and other organizations.

NMAH *National Museum of American History;* SIL *Smithsonian Institution Libraries.*

BDL *Bodleian Library, The Masters and Fellows of the University College, Oxford;* BL *British Library;* BM *British Museum;* BN *Bibliothèque Nationale, Paris;* FSL *The Folger Shakespeare Library, Washington, DC;* NGA *National Gallery of Art, Washington, DC;* LC *Library of Congress, Washington, DC;* PML *Pierpont Morgan Library, NY;* SBPL *St. Brides Printing Library, London;* V&A *National Art Library, Victoria & Albert Museum, London.*

Jacket: Rosenwald Collection, NGA.
Inside flap: Ed Castle.

Front Matter: p.1 Tschichold, Jan, *Treasury of Alphabets and Lettering,* 1985, Omega Books Ltd., Hertfordshire, England. Translated by Wolf von Eckardt © Otto Maier Verlag, Ravensburg, Germany; 4 V&A; 5 Cotton MS. Nero D.IV, f.210v, BL; 6T, 6C McLean, Ruari, *The Thames and Hudson Manual of Typography,* 1980, Thames and Hudson Ltd., London; 6B Duns, Joannes, *Quaestiones Quodlibetales,* Venice, 1481. SIL, Mark Gulezian/QuickSilver; 7T, 7C McLean, Ruari, *The Thames and Hudson Manual of Typography,* 1980, Thames and Hudson Ltd., London; 7B The Bettmann Archive, NY.

Introduction: p.8 Bayerische Staatsbibliothek, Munich, Germany; 10 Courtesy of British Province of the Society of Jesus, photo BL; 11 MS. Univ. Coll. #165, p.118. Bede, *Life of St. Cuthbert,* BDL; 12 PML MS.399, f.6v; 13 MS. A.135, Royal Library, Stockholm; 14 SIL, photo Ed Castle; 15 LC. 16–17 Scala/Art Resource, NY.

Prologue: p.18 © NTV, Tokyo; 19 Add. MS. 47673, f.71v, BL; 20 The Wallace Collection, (detail) London; 21 Or. MS. 848, f.2r, BL; 22 MS. 1857, f.14r, Österreichische Nationalbibliothek, Vienna; 23 Courtauld Institute Galleries, Lee Collection, London; 24–25 Michael Holford, England; 25 M2092, FSL.

Scrolls and Scribes: p.26 Scala/Art Resource, NY; 27 SIL, photo Mark Gulezian/QuickSilver; 28T Nationalmuseet, Copenhagen, photo Grunnel Janssen, Denmark; 28B BM; 29 Riksantikvarieämbetet och Statens Historiska Museer, photo Bengt A.

Lundberg, Stockholm; 30 The University Museum, University of Pennsylvania, photo John Henry Haynes; 31T Louvre, Réunion des Musées Nationaux, Paris, D82E1462, AO13300; 31B Michael Holford, England; 32,33T BM; 33BL Institut Ramses, Paris; 33BR BN; 34 Akademische Druck-u. Verlagsanstalt Grasz-Austria; 35T The Art Museum, Princeton University. Museum purchase, gift of the Hans and Dorothy Widenmann Fund; 35B Justin Kerr, NY; 36 Gemäldegalerie Staatliche Museen Preussischer Kulturbesitz, Berlin, photo Jörg P. Anders; 37L Israel Museum, Jerusalem, The Shrine of the Book, D. Samuel and Jeane H. Gottesman Center for Biblical Manuscripts; 37R GEOPIC™, Earth Satellite Corporation, MD; 38L BN; 38R Museo Archeologie di Villa Giulia Rome, Bompiani, Milano, photo Baguzzi; 39 Art Resource, NY; 40 Vat. Lat. 3867, f.3v, Bibliotheca Apostolica Vaticana, Rome; 41 Museo Nazionale, Naples, Scala/Art Resource, NY.

The Greatest Story Ever Told: p.42 MS. Am.1, f.Vr, Biblioteca Medicea-Laurenziana, Italy; 44T National Numismatic Collection, NMAH, photo Ed Castle; 44B CT 5261, V&A; 45 Library of the Jewish Theological Seminary of America, NY; 46 Werner Braun, Jerusalem; 47T Culver Pictures, NY; 47B Add. MS.43725, f.260, BL; 48 C35i114(T.p.) BL; 49 C. Dagli Orti, France.

People of the Book: p.50 1963–4–20,01, BM; 51 Courtesy Mohamed Zakariya; 52L Roland & Sabrina Michaud, Paris; 53 Goodrum, Charles A., *Treasures of the Library of Congress,* 1980, photo Jonathan Wallen, courtesy Harry N. Abrams, Inc., NY;

Museum & Library, Philadelphia, PA; 136 LC; 137 The White House Historical Association, DC; 138T The Mark Twain project, The Bancroft Library, University of California; 138B Sotheby's, NY; 139 The State Historical Society of Missouri, Columbia.

"Yes, We Have Now Bananas!": p.140 NMAH/Division of Graphic Arts/SI, photo Ed Castle; 141 LC; 142 Colonial Williamsburg Foundation, photo by Kevin Burke; 143 SBPL; 144 NMAH/Division of Graphic Arts/SI, photo Ed Castle; 145L SIL, photo Mark Gulezian/QuickSilver; 145R SBPL; 146T NMAH/SI, neg.18501-B; 146B NMAH/SI, neg.32060-A; 147T Elaine Sulle/The Image Bank, NY; 147B Quark, Inc., CO; 148 LC; 149 Typefaces assembled by Robert Wiser, Meadows & Wiser; Typography: Composition Systems Incorporated; 150T LC; 150B Massin, *Letter and Image,* 1970, Paris, photo Mark Gulezian/QuickSilver; 151 LC; 152 SBPL; 153 Airport series: "Platter", 1974 by Robert Rauschenberg, NGA.

Morison, Zapf, and Gill: p.154 Hermann Zapf, Seitersweg, Germany; 156 Typefaces assembled by Robert Wiser, Meadows & Wiser; Typography: Composition Systems Incorporated; 157L SIL, photo Mark Gulezian/QuickSilver; 157T SBPL; 157B LC; 158 The Newberry Library, IL; 159T SBPL; 159B, 160 Typefaces assembled by Robert Wiser, Meadows & Wiser; Typography: Composition Systems Incorporated; 160–161 Richard Howard, Marblehead, MA.

The Bookmaker's Craft: p.162 Musée Bonnat, Bayonne, France, photo SBPL #2312; 163 SIL, photo Mark Gulezian/QuickSilver; 164 *Rare books catalogue,* 1991, Charles B. Wood III, Inc., SIL, photo Ed Castle; 165 SIL, photo Ed Castle; 166 Museum Plantin-Moretus, SIGN. MPM: TK 391, Antwerpen, Belgium; 167 Museum Plantin-Moretus, SIGN. MPMB 65 (I), Antwerpen, Belgium; 168 Museum Plantin-Moretus, SIGN. R.45.4(v), Antwerpen, Belgium; 169 Museum Plantin-Moretus, Antwerpen, Belgium; 170 Peter Morse Collection, Honolulu 671.1539; 171 BN; 172, 173 Musée Historique du Papier, Moulin Richard de Bas, Ambert, Auvergne, France; 174 The Dard Hunter Paper Museum at the Institute of Paper, Science & Technology, Atlanta; 175 Lithograph by P. Bineteau after Carl Schulin. Musée Carnavalet, Paris, photo by Jean-Loup Charmet; 176 The Bettmann Archive, NY; 177 Koenig & Bauer AG, Würzburg, Germany.

To Print or Not to Print?: p.179 FSL; 180T Arch G.e.31., BDL; 180B FSL; 181 v.a. 92, octo X, FSL; 182–183 FSL; 183B MS.842, University Library, Utrecht, The Netherlands, photo Mark Gulezian/QuickSilver; 184 FSL; 185T Kemp, William, *Kemps Nine Daies Vvonder,* 1600, printed by E.A. for Nicholas Ling, London, FSL; 185B The Henry E. Huntington Library and Art Gallery, CA; 186L FSL; 186R Joan Marcus, Shakespeare Theatre at the Folger, Washington, DC; 187 FSL.

By Its Cover: p.189 *New Testament* (Greek and Latin), Tiguri, 1559. The Pepys Library, Magdalene College, Cambridge, England; 190 From: Taubert, Sigfried, *Bibliopola,* 1966, Dr. Ernst Hauswedell & Co., Hamburg, Germany, photo Mark Gulezian/QuickSilver; 191T Nathan Benn/Woodfin Camp, Inc., Washington, DC; 191C Fred Ward/Black Star, NY; 191B C. James Gleason, VA; 192T V&A; 192B Henry Groskinsky, NY; 193 PML M.1; 194 Philip Smith, Chippenham Wiltshire, England; 195 Benjamin & Deborah Alterman, Mount Holly, NJ. 196–197 SIL, photo by Ed Castle.

"The Infinite Library, Timeless and Incorruptible": p.198 Michael Freeman, London; 199 SBPL; 200, 201 The Henry E. Huntington Library & Art Gallery, CA; 202 BM; 203 From: Taubert, Sigfried, *Bibliopola,* 1966, Dr. Ernst Hauswedell & Co., Hamburg, Germany, photo Mark Gulezian/QuickSilver; 204 BM; 205T Illustration by Robert Ingpen (detail). From: *Encyclopedia of Mysterious Places,* by Robert Ingpen and Philip Wilkinson, published by Dragon's World Ltd., London, and Viking Studio Books, NY 1990; 205B Snøhetta, Oslo; 206 Biblioteca Apostolica Vaticana/Scala/Art Resource, NY; 207 Biblioteca Apostolica Vaticana, Rome; 208 The Illustrated London News Picture Library, London; 209B Colin St. John Wilson & Partners, London; 209T BM; 210 LC; 211T James S. Douglass/Woodfin Camp, Inc.; 211B Michael Freeman, London; 212 SIL, photo Charles H. Phillips; 213T Cooper-Hewitt Museum/SI, NY; 213B National Museum of American Art/SI.

Heralds of Science: pp.215–223 SIL, photos Mark Gulezian/QuickSilver.

The Best of the Past: p.225 Hulton-Deutsch Collection, London; 226 Cheltenham Art Gallery & Museums, England; 227 William Morris Gallery, London; 228 PML 77381; 229 PML 9660 M; 230L Cheltenham Art Gallery & Museums, England; 230R SBPL; 231 PML 7946 M; 232 Cheltenham Art

Gallery & Museums, England; 233TL V&A; 233BL Cheltenham Art Gallery & Museums; 233R PML 5555 M+.

A Picture's Worth . . . .: p.234 SIL, Mark Gulezian/QuickSilver; 235 *Alphabet of Death,* NGA; 236L "Holy Family with Three Hares", Art Museum, Princeton University, given in memory of Erwin Panofsky by his friends, colleagues, and students; 236R "Holy Family with Three Hares", Art Museum, Princeton University, gift of Alexander P. Morgan; 237 NGA; 238 LC; 239 NGA; 240, 241L Colonial Williamsburg Foundation; 241R SIL, Mark Gulezian/QuickSilver; 241B NGA; 242L LC; 242R BM; 243 NGA; 244 V&A; 245T LC; 245C Bewick, Thomas, *History of British Birds,* Vol. 1, Natural History Museum, London; 245B Bewick, Thomas, *General History of Quadrupeds,* LC; 246TL Philadelphia Museum of Art, gift of Muriel and Philip Berman; 246BL LC; 246R, 247 NGA; 248 Grandville, J.J., *Scènes de la vie privée et publique des Animaux,* LC; 249 Grandville, J.J., *Un Autre Monde,* LC; 250 From the Collection of the New Britain Museum of American Art, CT, Harriet Russell Stanley Fund, photo by Michael Agee; 251 Brandywine River Museum, Chadds Ford, PA; 252L NMAA/SI; 252R Glaser, Milton, *Graphic Design,* 1973, Overlook Press, Inc., Woodstock, NY, photo Mark Gulezian/QuickSilver; 253 Courtesy of the Rockwell Kent Legacies, NY.

Mother Goose and Company: p.254 Potter, Beatrix, *The Tale of Peter Rabbit,* © Frederick Warne & Co., 1902, 1987; 256 FSL; 257 Kitchen, Bert, *Animal Alphabet,* 1984, The Lutterworth Press, Cambridge, England, 1984, Dial Books for Young Readers,

a division of Penguin Books USA, Inc.; 258 Allingham, William, *In Fairyland,* illustrations by Richard Doyle. Longmans, Green, Reader & Dyer, London, 1870, LC; 259 Arthur Rackham Memorial Collection, University of Louisville Library; 260L The Mansell Collection, London; 260R Oxford University Press; 261 Line illustration by E. H. Shepard © 1926 by E. P. Dutton & Co., Inc., © renewed © 1956 by A. A. Milne. Colouring © 1974 by E. H. Shepard and Methuen Children's Books Ltd., London; 262–263 Sendak, Maurice, *Where the Wild Things Are,* © 1963, photograph from The Rosenbach Museum & Library, Philadelphia; 264 Van Allsburg, Chris, *Just a Dream,* © 1990. Reprinted by permission of Houghton Mifflin Company, all rights reserved; 265 *Oh, The Places You'll Go!,* by Dr. Seuss. © 1990 by Theodor Geisel & Audrey S. Geisel. Trustees under Trust agreement, August 27, 1984.

Every Word for Everyman: p.266 NGA, Rosenwald Collection; 267 *Caslon Old Face,* issued by H.W. Caslon & Co., 1924, London, NMAH; 268 Littlejohn, David, *Dr. Johnson & Noah Webster, Two Men and Their Dictionaries,* 1971, Book Club of California, San Francisco, photo Mark Gulezian/QuickSilver; 269L The Beinecke, Rare Book & MS. Library, Yale University; 269R National Portrait Gallery/SI, James Herring (artist), Gift of Mrs. William A. Ellis; 270 BN; 271T Louvre, Réunion des Musées Nationaux, Paris; 271BL,BR, SIL, photo Mark Gulezian/QuickSilver; 272L Johnson Birthplace Museum, Lichfield, England; 272R Johnson Birthplace Museum, photo Rackhams of Lichfield, England; 273 "Samuel Johnson" by Sir Joshua Reynolds,

collection of Loren & Frances Rothschild, CA; 274 Houghton Library, Harvard University; 275 National Galleries of Scotland, photo Antonia Reeve; 276 Elizabeth Murray, England; 277 SIL; 278 Elizabeth Murray, England; 279 Elizabeth Murray, England, photo Mark Gulezian/QuickSilver.

The Book Business: p. 281 "St. Martins in the Fields" by Georg Scharf, the Elder, BM; 282L From: Taubert, Sigfried, *Bibliopola,* 1966, Dr. Ernst Hauswedell & Co., Hamburg, Germany, photo by Mark Gulezian/QuickSilver; 282R Hermann Zapf, Seitersweg, Germany; 283 Paul Van Riel/Robert Harding Picture Library, London; 284–285 BDL; 285R Sotheby's, NY; 286 Bella C. Landauer Collection, New-York Historical Society; 287T The Bettmann Archive, NY; 287B Ronny Jaques/Photo Researchers, NY.

Old Leaves, New Lives: p.288 SIL, Mark Gulezian/QuickSilver; 290 Mark Gulezian/QuickSilver; 291 BL; 292L The Pepys Library, Magdalene College, Cambridge, England; 292R, 293 BDL; 294L OPPS/SI, #86–12661, Horticulture Branch, SIL; 294R OPPS/SI, #89–21868, Warshaw Collection, Archives Center; 294B OPPS/SI, #91–11800, Warshaw Collection, Archives Center; 295 OPPS/SI, #91–11799, Warshaw Collection, Archives Center. 296–297 Ed Castle.

Last Words: p.298 Rosamond Purcell, Medford, MA; 299 LC; 300 Jean-Loup Charmet, Paris; 301 The Bettmann Archive, NY; 302 SIL, Mark Gulezian/QuickSilver; 303 NMAA/SI; 304, 305, 306 LC; 307 From the Estate of André Kertész.

T he *Smithsonian Book of Books* was designed and typeset by Robert Wiser, of Meadows & Wiser, Washington, D.C. Mr. Wiser also created the display typeface *Capitalis,* patterning it after the stone-cut letters on the ancient Trajan Column in Rome. Digital-type composition, page layout, and type design were originated on an Apple Macintosh II computer, utilizing Quark XPress, Adobe Illustrator, and Aldus Fontographer software.

The text of *The Smithsonian Book of Books* was set in Monotype Bembo, a classic-revival typeface first produced for metal typecasting by the Monotype Corporation, under the supervision of Stanley Morison, in 1929. In 1990 the Monotype Corporation adapted the version of Bembo used in this book for electronic publishing applications and for output directly to film on a Linotronic L-300 PostScript language imagesetter. Lanman Progressive, Washington, D.C., provided picture separation, type output, and film preparation.

Four-color web printing and Smythe-sewn binding were done at R. R. Donnelley & Sons Company, Willard, OH, on Westvaco 80# Sterling Web Gloss. The regular-edition binding includes ICG Kennett cloth, Ecological Fibers Rainbow Antique endsheets, and jackets printed four-color sheetfed at Lehigh Press Lithographers, Pennsauken, NJ. The deluxe-edition slipcase was manufactured at Imperial Paper Box Corporation, Brooklyn, NY, and was covered in Holliston Natural Sailcloth with an onlay printed at Lehigh Press Lithographers. The book is bound with Permalin Bonded Leather and Holliston Natural Sailcloth, with a hand-inserted ribbon marker and bookplate. The marbleized endsheets are reproduced from a handmade paper sample in the collection of Robert Wiser and printed sheetfed by R. R. Donnelley on 100# Sterling Litho Gloss from Westvaco.